Who's Controlling You?

Who Are You Controlling?

Who's Controlling You?

Who Are You Controlling?

Strategies for Change

Carol Rogne

Outskirts Press, Inc.
Denver, Colorado

Outskirts Press, Inc.
http://www.outskirtspress.com

ISBN: 978-1-4327-6396-1

Outskirts Press and the "OP" logo are trademarks belonging to Outskirts Press, Inc.

PRINTED IN THE UNITED STATES OF AMERICA

Acknowledgments

I am blessed with family, friends, and professional colleagues who have encouraged me to write about emotional and mental control, and I am grateful for all of the clients who trusted me to walk with them in their recovery journeys. This book is dedicated to Vivian Smith, my friend and colleague. Together, through our learning and processing, we came to understand the ways of control and how we could empower ourselves as well as our clients. I miss you, Vivian, but the maple tree we planted in loving memories of times that we spent together is thriving. We know that your spirit is flourishing as well.

May we all reach a place in our lives where no one is controlling us and we are controlling no one. This is the freedom that was set forth by our forefathers:

> We hold these truths to be self-evident, that all men are created equal, that they are endowed by their Creator with certain inalienable Rights, that among these rights are Life, Liberty and the pursuit of Happiness.
> —United States Declaration of Independence.

Table of Contents

Introduction

There are some situations one simply cannot be neutral about because when you are neutral you are an accomplice. — Christiane Amanpour, international correspondent

Emotional and mental control is interpersonal violence, which causes emotional pain that is often experienced for years. Most dysfunctional relationships involve power being used to control another person, which results in high levels of tension, stress, and anger. Often, one's first response when being controlled is blaming oneself. However, when we are empowered, we can confront emotional and mental control and change behaviors that help to keep the control pattern active.

This book is focused on the type of power that is used to emotionally and mentally control others but is not physically or sexually abusive. Despite the frequency with which control infects relationships, there are relatively few books written on the emotional devastation that is created by emotional and mentally controlling behaviors. Knowing through professional and personal experience the process of controlling and enabling and what transpires in these dysfunctional relationships, I offer strategies for surrendering control, empowering strategies for those who are recipients of control, and a process to restore relationships. These recovery and empowering processes have been effective for many clients and control workshop participants. Controllers can change emotionally abusive controlling behaviors. If we are the recipients of control, we can learn ways to confront the control rather than accepting and enabling the control, which negatively affects us and our children. As couples, we can balance power structures, improve communication, and work together to reduce conflict. We can invest energies in ourselves to become healthier partners and parents who consistently provide an emotionally safe, supportive, and loving environment for our children.

Early on in my therapy practice, I knew I would not serve my clients well if I were a referee, listening to one person reporting on what the other person was doing wrong. I believed there was an underlying dynamic, which was soon clearly identified as control, as I worked with individuals and couples. By intently observing and listening to clients for over three decades, certain patterns routinely surface. Had any other therapist or any individual seriously interested in control dynamics, been sitting in my therapist chair or facilitating control workshops, he or she would have observed the same similarities. Those who struggle with emotional and mental control share characteristic thoughts, feelings, attitudes, descriptions of experiences, and behaviors. Controllers also have characteristic attitudes and are similar in the way they think, feel, describe their experiences, and behave. There are always individual differences in human behaviors, but this does not negate observable, pervasive behavioral patterns.

My approach as a therapist is to use the most useful, uncomplicated, and understandable methods of problem-solving, healing, and empowerment. Professionally, I am known as a person who cuts to the chase and deals with reality in a straight-forward, compassionate way. Through my years as a therapist and educator I have always believed that I am not qualified to counsel or teach others unless I have worked through my own emotionally painful experiences, acknowledged my share of responsibility, forgiven, made amends, let go of past emotional hurts, and learned from difficult challenges.

Though there are many differences between people who control and those who are controlled, our underlying needs are similar. Nearly all of us want to be in healthy relationships with spouses, parents, children, friends, and colleagues. To accomplish this goal we must first have a loving and respectful relationship with ourselves. Healthy relationships require healthy participants. Empowerment, which involves moving out of denial, growing in awareness, and learning strategies to improve our life, is not only important for ourselves but for our children as well. As we grow in awareness and empower ourselves, we will stand up and confront power that is emotionally and mentally abusive, because, as Martin Luther King stated, "Our lives begin to end the day we become silent about things that matter."

Chapter 1

The Many Forms of Power

I am not interested in power for power's sake, but I'm interested in power that is moral, that is right, and that is good. —Martin Luther King, Jr.

Power is the ability to influence others and can be used to empower others by teaching, supporting, encouraging, or providing necessary resources. In contrast, power can be used to physically, economically, mentally, and emotionally harm others. Though silent and unseen, the positive or negative use of power affects all of us throughout our lives. Power operates within personal relationships, work systems, groups of people, and between countries. When power, based on a real or perceived superior intellect, social position, physical strength, knowledge, weapons, or wealth, is used to oppress others for self-serving benefits, the power is used abusively.

Throughout this book, there are diagrams of power structures that have been helpful to individuals, couples, and workshop participants to illustrate the various types of power, and the dynamics of control between more powerful and less powerful people and groups.

Power Structures

Equal power structure

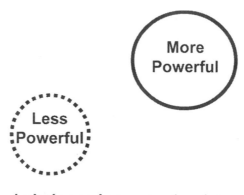

Imbalanced power structure.

This diagram shows an equal power structure and an imbalanced, asymmetrical, one-up, one-down power structure. When there is an equal power structure, each person or group is treated as having equal value and power. An imbalanced, asymmetrical power structure is legitimate when based on the level of responsibility, such as that of employer and employee. This same power structure can be abusive when the power is used to control a person who should be viewed as an equal, as in a primary relationship or when power is used to oppress less powerful groups of people.

Personal power used positively to empower others

When we are aware of our *personal power,* we know our strengths, skills, beliefs, and values, and activate them to achieve goals. We are able to manage our emotions, behaviors, finances, time, and are responsible for ourselves and our children. When we have personal power, self-esteem is higher and our thinking is more positive. We invest our energies into meaningful priorities, rather than being consumed by the need to control others or enable controlling behaviors. We can increase our personal power through education, having positive experiences that expand our vision, and by learning from adverse life experiences that challenge our skills and resiliency. It is personal power that brings a sense of grounding, purpose, and meaning to our lives and prompts us to use our power to empower others.

More Powerful Person Empowers Others

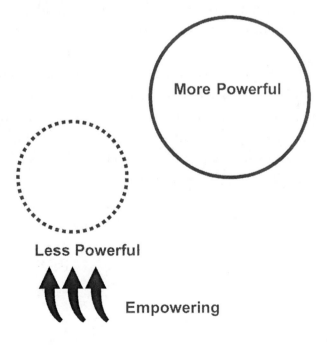

The heroes of history and the heroes of today use their personal power in ways that empower others even when they are faced with criticism and resistance. This use of power involves teaching, supporting, negotiating, and advocating for the safety, dignity, freedom, and well-being of all persons. People have lost their lives because they confronted the injustices that controlling, powerful persons were inflicting on others. But many of these heroes, who had the courage to stand up against injustice, continue to influence us long after their lives have ended.

Becoming fully functioning in our own lives and in our parenting role is the first challenge and responsibility regarding our personal power. Other positive ways of using personal power are: parents empowering their children; teachers educating; policemen working to keep our communities safe; physicians and nurses caring for sick and injured people; and people confronting controlling behaviors in efforts to create more peaceful and productive relationships. We may be able to use our power to walk the path of the activist, the humanitarian, the visionary, and the peacemaker. We can be ordinary persons, doing the extraordinary by using our power in positive ways. Our freedom and the power to make our own choices comes with the challenge to be accountable for our personal power, whether it be minimal or whether we have achieved, earned, or inherited a high level of power that can be used to empower others. Using our power and resources to create peace within ourselves and within our families is necessary before we will experience peace in our world.

Achieved, legitimate, and temporary power

Power Based on Responsibility

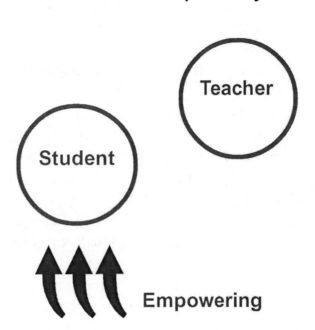

Achieved power is gained through accomplishments, such as level of education; particular areas of expertise; having a broad range of knowledge and life experiences; exceptional verbal abilities; skills in persuading others; and a reputation for being honest, dependable, and competent. Our achieved power may also be a gateway to being selected by even more powerful groups, such as prestigious law firms, health care facilities, or institutions of higher learning. Most people with achieved power are committed to using their power in healthy ways. They teach and mentor others. When they are in a position to make decisions that affect other persons, they use honesty, integrity, and wisdom. Examples of achieved power differences, based on knowledge and experience, are patient and doctor, client and therapist, and student and teacher. The power difference may not be emphasized in efforts to create a power structure that resembles a team type of relationship where each person is responsible for doing his or her part in efforts to become healthier or expand knowledge and skills.

Legitimate power is determined by the degree of *responsibility*. Legitimate power is the power of a supervisor over a staff. The supervisor has control of resources, provides rewards or reprimands, and is the person who is notified when there are problems. People with legitimate power usually have more information than others because they are involved in making executive decisions that affect the lives of other people.

Temporary power is power used to help others until they can function on their own. An example is parenting. The power difference between parent and child is natural, based on age, knowledge, experience, and responsibility. Parents' adult power is used to protect, teach, and empower their children by facilitating the accomplishment of developmental tasks, fostering self-esteem and encouraging their children to accept responsibility commensurate with their age. When a child is consistently nurtured and empowered, many parenting functions naturally diminish in the child's late teen years or early twenties. Young adults will have been given the freedom to make decisions and to make their own mistakes. They will have gained wisdom from the consequences of their poor choices. Optimally, when children are of the age to leave home, they are prepared to move on and parents are willing to let go. This is not always a smooth transition if parents are overly controlling.

Problems arise when parents do not recognize the responsibilities of their legitimate parental power, or their parental power is continued rather than viewed as temporary and is long-term, oppressive and controlling, even when their children are adults.

Other examples of temporary power are: mentoring interns and consulting in organizations. Knowledge, expertise, and skills are shared, which empowers others.

Rather than being used to empower others, achieved, legitimate, and temporary power may be abused. We are all aware of powerful people, including politicians, athletes, and clergy who have taken advantage of their legitimate power and are abusive to others for self-serving purposes.

Attributed power

Power is Attributed to Another

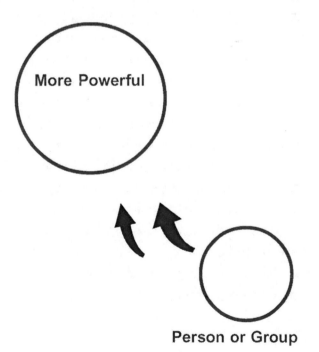

Attributed power is power that is given to others. In our culture we often assign power to persons who are male and are of the majority race. We may also attribute power to persons who have high intelligence, special talents, wealth, and are attractive. People who have inherited a powerful name or reputation from their parents may be viewed as having more power than others. We view these people as superior, which causes an imbalance in the power structure. In personal relationships this imbalance will eventually cause communication and other relationship difficulties.

Attributed power situations are common in societal groups, work settings, and marriages. Being assigned power by others may be beneficial, but can also be a negative experience. In organizations, the people who attribute power to a certain person may collude with each other against that person who then becomes a target for criticism. When people are placed in positions of power without realizing what is happening, confusion and self-doubt are created. When gifted people become aware of this dynamic, they often submerge their strengths, enthusiasm, talents, and skills in order to emotionally protect themselves and be accepted by others.

In personal relationships one partner may view the other as a "parent" and take less responsibility for performing the normal activities associated with being an adult partner. Or, a partner may be controlling and *take* a superior position to the other. When one spouse is put in a one-up position or takes a one-up position, an imbalanced relationship is created, which sets the stage for high levels of stress and tension and places a relationship at risk.

In contrast to attributing power *to* a person or group, there are minority and disadvantaged groups of people who are attributed *less* power by dominant groups and as a result, are not treated as equals.

Collaboration power

Persons of Equal Power Working Together

Collaboration power is the power generated by relationships among knowledgeable, competent, and capable people. Social networking is used to exchange information and cooperatively move projects and careers forward. People form collaborative groups for the purpose of achieving many types of goals, including pooling knowledge for developing and improving technology, upgrading corporate procedures, making neighborhoods safe, and providing educational programs. Collaboration involves sharing creative ideas, cooperating, and implementing plans. Participants are viewed as equal and having equal power.

The opposite of using collaborative power to empower others is using group power to create powerful and controlling groups, such as gangs or terrorist groups which are oppressive and abusive in their plans and actions.

Emotional and mental control

Controller Takes a Superior Power Position

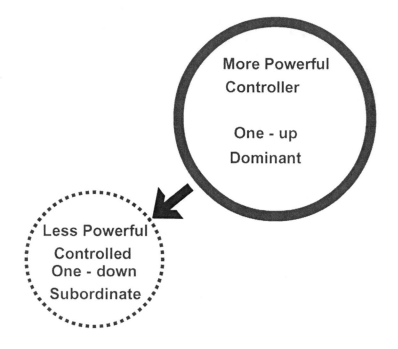

An imbalanced, asymmetrical relationship is created when power is used to emotionally and mentally control others. *Less powerful persons* actually have less power or give away their power in what should be an equal relationship. *More powerful persons* actually have more power or take more power in what should be an equal relationship. Dominant persons who use their power to control others have no intention of changing the power structure because they are receiving benefits from subordinate people. This diagram of power differences describes personal relationships as well as groups within and between countries. The main method of control is the one-up, one-down maneuver, which takes many different forms of overt and passive ways of controlling others.

The one-up and one-down control maneuver

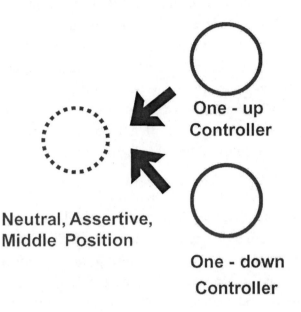

One - up
Controller

Neutral, Assertive,
Middle Position

One - down
Controller

This diagram illustrates the positions of one-up, one-down and the neutral position. There are only *two power positions: up or down* when one uses a competitive, dichotomous, either-or way of thinking. Taking a one-up position is sometimes called *capping.* Being critical, taking over conversations, or ordering, directing, and commanding are ways of taking a *one-up* position. Sometimes one-up comments are about trivial things, for example, "You eat weird." But more often, controllers establish a one-up, superior position by more serious personal attacks such as, "You can't think your way out of a paper bag!" or, "You wouldn't last a day without me!" or, "It's always better to do it myself because you always mess things up!"

In contrast, a controller might take a *one-down* position, especially *when a one-up position is not successful* at getting compliance. This is posturing as being helpless or victimized and using guilt or other one-down strategies to control another person. An example of a one-down statement is, "You have time for everyone else, but not for me." The unspoken message is that the person being manipulated is unkind and inconsiderate. Or, "I can't possibly pay you because I have so many other bills." The unspoken message is that the other person is insensitive because they expect to be paid by someone who is financially overburdened. By taking a one-down position, the other person will often agree or comply because they feel obligated or guilty. When this happens the controller *re-claims the one-up position.*

While controllers continue their one-up, one-down tactics, they overlook the fact that there is a neutral, middle, assertive position, which is increasingly being understood and utilized by people who refuse to be manipulated and is neither a one-up nor a one-down position. When someone holds firm in a neutral position, rather than being manipulated by a one-up or by a one-down statement, controllers are often unsure of what to do, because their control maneuvers are not working.

The following is a one-up, one-down scenario:

Controller A: "You are over-reacting!" (This is a one-up statement to establish a superior, one-up position).

Person B: "I am not over-reacting. Your behavior is abusive." (This is an assertive statement. Person B is not manipulated into a one-down position.)

Controller A: "Abusive! What is that supposed to mean?" (Another one-up statement. The unspoken message is that Person B is exaggerating and way off base.)

Person B: "I am not over-reacting. Your behavior is abusive." (Person B is taking an assertive position and repeating what was previously said.)

Controller A: "Well, I guess I must be a really bad person!" (This is a one-down statement, meant to manipulate Person B to retract the statement. If the person retracts, Person A resumes the one-up position.)

Person B: "Your behavior is abusive." (Person B does not retract the statement.)

The outcome of this communication is that the controller did not succeed in putting Person B in a one-down position. Person B did not give away his/her power and was not manipulated by Person A. More examples of one-up, one-down manipulative maneuvers are presented throughout the following chapters. It is the main method of emotionally and mentally controlling others.

Chapter 2

Emotional and Mental Control
IS Interpersonal Violence

It has always been a mystery to me how men can feel
themselves honored by the humiliation of their fel-
low beings. —Mohandas Gandhi

Despite how controllers stay in denial and distort the truth, emotional and mental abuse is *interpersonal violence* because it is an assault on the emotional and mental health of the recipients. The harm
that is caused by emotional and mental control is like a broken leg
that does not heal, causing everyday pain and hindering movement
and life itself.

Controlling persons use their power to create fear or guilt so that
less powerful persons will be subservient and compliant. They feel
that if they don't control, others will control them. As a result of
thinking in this way, the power of another person or group of people
is often seen as a threat. More powerful people, to maintain their
power, describe less powerful persons with pejorative labels regarding race, sex, class, nationality, or religion, and view these biased
descriptions as truth. In controllers' minds, others are inferior, which
they believe justifies their controlling behaviors.

Our social problems have roots in power used in dysfunctional ways from verbal put-downs and other emotional and mentally abusive behaviors to extremely abusive acts that threaten or destroy life. We live in a civilized society, but there are countless numbers of people who struggle with emotional and mental abuse every day. When control is a dynamic in personal relationships, there are high levels of tension, stress, and emotional pain, which create a vulnerability to divorce, addiction, and physical disease.

Education and early intervention may be successful in changing the following *emotional and mentally abusive behaviors*:

- ✓ Bullying and sexual harassment
- ✓ Put-downs and teasing
- ✓ Blaming others
- ✓ Ridicule and embarrassing others
- ✓ Unjust criticisms
- ✓ Lying and spreading rumors

These are abusive behaviors that are possible precursors to more extreme forms of abuse. Positive change and growth starts with recognizing that these behaviors are interpersonally violent. Many schools are taking a position of zero tolerance for bully behaviors and have both prevention and early intervention programs and procedures. Self-advocacy and confrontation skills are taught to all students regarding bullying and sexual harassment. There are consequences for harassment behaviors including expulsion or police intervention. Our schools are reflections of our society. Our society would have less abuse of all types if the *reverse* was true and society was a reflection of our schools. There would be zero tolerance for emotional, mental, and physical violence. There would be preventative education and serious consequences for infractions.

Controlling and bullying behaviors can lead to extreme forms of interpersonal violence. If we are experiencing extremely abusive controlling behaviors, we need to access professional assistance from law enforcement and legal agencies. We also need to use community resources, such as rape and abuse agencies, safe shelter centers, churches and synagogues, or any other organizations in our community that provide assistance so that we can stay safe and also keep our children safe. In our society we have these support systems available in many but not all areas.

Extreme abuse requiring protective assistance:

- *Physical abuse* involves physically harming another by physical actions with or without a weapon, such as slapping, punching, kicking, biting, beating, spanking, or shaking.
- *Sexual abuse* involves forcing another person to perform sexual acts or allow sexual touching. Sexual abuse of children is treating children, who are powerless to resist, as sexual objects or possessions to be used for sexual gratification. This causes emotional and mental damage that profoundly affects victims and is illegal.
- *Expressions of rage, both verbally and physically* involve throwing objects, kicking or punching walls and doors, or making threats to destroy property. These are violent behaviors that are emotionally damaging to others.
- *Threats* may be made in an effort to dominate and hurt a spouse and/or children on an emotional, sexual, or physical level. This includes threats to kidnap children; to commit suicide; or to make false, distorted, and self-serving reports to welfare agencies or social services.
- *Harassment* involves making lewd comments or gestures and/or insinuations of harm. Sexual harassment involves

making sexual remarks or acting in ways that create disgust, emotional discomfort, and fear.

- *Extreme verbal abuse* involves destructive criticisms, name-calling, and false accusations, usually combined with threatening body language, which creates fear in others.
- *Using children* is threatening to harm a child, using a child as a messenger of false or threatening information to the spouse, or being uncompromising and demanding in regard to visitation schedules with the intention of harassing.
- *Intimidation* involves creating fear through angry and abusive language, threatening body gestures, a loud voice, invasion of another's privacy, or threats of abandonment regarding a spouse or children.
- *Isolation* means preventing or restricting the freedom of a spouse or significant others to do, see, go, or talk to whomever they might want. There may be pressure to spend free time with the controller rather than having any other outside activities.
- *Humiliation* involves verbally assaulting another and/or forcing another person to do humiliating acts.
- *Economic abuse* involves making a spouse beg for money to spend for legitimate family needs, confiscating a spouse's money, or keeping a spouse from getting a job or returning to school.
- *Coercion* is the restraint or domination of another person by force or threats, or emotionally blackmailing another person by creating fear.
- *Creating unsafe conditions* involves high-risk behaviors, such as driving recklessly; driving under the influence of alcohol or drugs with other adults and/or children; lifting children in the air and threatening to drop them; or engaging in risky behavior while children are watching.

> **Regarding extreme abuse:**
>
> - **We cannot stop physically and sexually abusive behaviors by ourselves. We need law enforcement and legal assistance, safe shelters, and social service agencies for support if we are to keep ourselves and our children safe.**

Emotional and mental interpersonal violence: growing in awareness

Emotional and mental control within relationships adversely affects people that we claim to love, sabotages healthy communication and problem solving processes, and slowly destroys emotional bonding and intimacy. Very often, neither the controller nor the person controlled realizes that power used to control others is corroding the relationship. Emotional and mental abuse can be overt and recognizable, but often is subtle, manipulative, and difficult to describe. When we are controlled, we often struggle for too long and experience chronic emotional and mental pain. Educational classes on how to identify control and handle controlling people were never provided in our formal education, so most of us have not learned about power used to emotionally and mentally control others, though we may be experiencing it every day.

The first step is raising our awareness and recognizing the harmfulness of emotional and mental control. Though it may be difficult to believe, we are often unaware of how we are controlling or how we are enabling the control, though it is often evident to others. In contrast, there are controllers who deliberately control and they are acting in full awareness. Whether the controlling behaviors are intentional or unintentional, they are behaviors that are disrespectful, abusive, and interpersonally violent.

Emotional and mental abuse is often minimized by powerful people who use their power to control others. Their response is often, "What's the big deal?" Smokers minimize the dangers of smoking and controllers follow the same pattern. Based on the harmfulness and prevalence of emotional and mental control, *control is a big deal* because it creates stress and anger in adult relationships and negatively affects children as well. We cannot stay in denial and think that emotional and mental abuse happens to other people when it is happening in our own homes.

We have increased our awareness individually and collectively on other human issues. In the past, we may have viewed not only smoking, but littering as normal behaviors. We now realize that these behaviors are harmful to ourselves and to the environment. As a result, smoking and littering have been considerably reduced. Individual awareness has expanded to a societal awareness. Though we are growing in awareness about emotional and mental abuse, it is still too prevalent in personal relationships, organizations and societal groups.

We are socialized in ways in which more powerful persons are given silent permission to control others and less powerful persons are expected to comply and enable the controlling behaviors. Though enabling behaviors help to keep the controlling behaviors active, this does not mean there is equal responsibility and fault when compared to dysfunctional, abusive, controlling behaviors. If blame is placed on the recipient of control for enabling, it is unfair and re-victimizing because they are trying to prevent or minimize conflict and protect themselves and their children from hearing repeated heated arguments or sarcastic and angry accusations and remarks. However, enabling actions serve to contribute to the pattern of control. A spouse enabling an alcoholic partner is an example. Both contribute to the dysfunction, but the alcoholic elicits coping responses from others, such as enabling the behavior. Controlling behaviors are abusive and therefore controllers need to acknowledge and accept responsibility for the harm they inflict on others.

When we are emotionally or mentally controlled, our emotional pain can be devastating but it is not helpful to view ourselves as victims. Emotional and mental abuse can often be positively impacted by intervention through therapy, books, or other educational opportunities. Rather than stay in pain for years, we can learn strategies to empower ourselves and confront, rather than enable the controlling behaviors. With self-awareness, education, skill-building, and a willingness to grow, we, as individuals can recover. We can be an active part in breaking the cycle of control. In this way, we can create a better life for ourselves and our children.

We live in a society where many of our basic needs are met. Many of us are educated and can make our own choices, unlike the millions of people who are made powerless by poverty, disaster, or abusive dictatorships. We can *choose* to stop controlling behaviors that sabotage our relationships. We can *choose* to learn the many ways that we enable controlling behaviors and make changes in our enabling and passive behaviors. We can *choose* to start a recovery process for our addictions and enhance our mental, emotional, physical, and spiritual life. We can *choose* to leave abusive relationships and find help in doing so. Not only can we make our own choices, but most of us have the resources to support our positive choices by accessing whatever supportive services are needed, such as counseling, workshops or retreats. We can *choose* to honor the blessing of being able to *choose* by being responsible and making the healthiest choices possible. Since we have the privilege of choice, we are especially responsible to empower ourselves, our children, and people whom we meet on our path of life who are also experiencing emotional and mental abusive control.

Key premises

1. Emotional and mental control is interpersonal violence. The control addressed in this book is *emotional and mental control* rather than physical, sexual, or extreme abuse, which needs law enforcement intervention.
2. Through education, intervention, and empowerment, positive changes are possible for individuals and relationships that are struggling with emotional and mental control.
3. We are often unaware of how we control or how we enable the control. In contrast, there are controllers who deliberately inflict emotional harm on others.
4. Controllers and recipients of control have different degrees of responsibility and fault. Controlling behaviors are harmful to others. Enabling behaviors are attempts to pacify the controller and prevent conflict, but result in fueling, rather than reducing controlling behaviors.
5. Being controlled is emotionally devastating. However, it is not helpful to view ourselves as victims. We can learn strategies to empower ourselves and reclaim our life.
6. We have personal power when we can exit a relationship, job, or other toxic situations. Optimally, as young men and women, our future goals will include securing a good education and developing skills or talents that generate financial resources. We will then have more options for ourselves and our children. We can carry this message to the next generation as a way to stop the high prevalence of emotional and mental abuse.

7. This book describes attitudes, ways of thinking and behavioral patterns that describe persons who use their power to control and of persons who are controlled. There are exceptions to these descriptions because of individual differences, but exceptions do not negate pervasive, observable patterns.

Chapter 3

Emotional and Mental Controlling Behaviors

An error does not become truth by reason of multiplied propagation, nor does truth become error because nobody sees it.—Mohandas Gandhi

The controllers in our lives can be:

✓ Spouses, dating partners, friends, children
✓ Parents, siblings, in-laws, neighbors, colleagues
✓ Dominant groups in society
✓ Oppressive government, economic, religious, and political systems
✓ Addictions and addictive behaviors

...ional and mentally controlling behaviors lie on a continuum:

1	2	3
The controlling behaviors are often communicated through criticism, demeaning statements and sarcasm; are intermittent and often related to certain on-going relationship issues.	The controlling behaviors are frequent, anger-based, critical and sarcastic, with unpredictable causes, and with unpredictable levels of intensity.	The controlling behaviors are pervasive and noxious, creating emotional fear in adults and children. There is an underlying threat that the control may escalate into physical abuse.

The emotional harm done to others is on a continuum as well:

1	2	3
The emotional harm causes irritation, frustration, disappointment and diminished self-esteem.	The emotional harm causes frequent stress, anger, and tension. There is compliance to prevent conflict, as well as enabling and accommodating.	The emotional harm is severe, abusive and debilitating. One sacrifices beliefs, values and is hindered from developing one's life.

As the continuum on this chart indicates, the degree of control differs and the amount of emotional damage created by the control varies as well, but all control is interpersonally violent. Controllers use many control tactics, which are all versions of the one-up, one-down method of control. Controllers are both male and female, but our society gives permission for males to be dominant and discourages the same for females. Some controllers are highly successful and some struggle every day. They have different educational levels and different levels of intelligence. They can be of any race or religion. Controllers can be polite and very caring, especially in the early stages of relationships. They can also be mean, moody, and critical of others to get what they want. The common perception that emotional abusers are low-class, ignorant, and macho is an inaccurate description of many emotional and mental controllers who could be a neighbor, the Little League coach, or a customer-service employee.

Research confirms that people who use their power to control others act more selfishly, impulsively, and aggressively. They have low self-esteem, are often insecure, are self-consumed, and have difficulty taking others' perspectives. Controllers are more likely to interrupt others, fail to make eye contact with the speaker, use sarcastic and hostile humor toward others and often lack skills in handling their stress, anger, and disappointments. The most common forms of controlling behaviors are anger causing fear in others (the one-up position), and projecting guilt toward others (the one-down position) in an effort to get compliance. Emotional and mental controllers have distorted attitudes, ways of thinking and behaviors that justify and excuse their emotional and mentally controlling behaviors.

There are a number of reasons why controlling behaviors are not immediately recognized by people who are emotionally and mentally controlled:

✓ Controlling behaviors can be subtle and manipulative.

✓ Controlling behaviors are so prevalent that they are often viewed as normal.

✓ Recipients of control often blame themselves for relationship problems.

✓ It is difficult to think clearly when being badgered with criticisms and other controlling tactics. Energies are spent emotionally dodging arrows rather than stepping back, assessing the situation, and developing proactive strategies for coping or dealing with the control.

✓ Often, controlled persons come to believe that they are doing everything wrong and are incapable of making the right decisions. It is easy to think that one is powerless and has no options.

✓ When experiencing depression and hopelessness, we have little energy to make healthy changes.

✓ We love someone who we thought was right for us and to acknowledge that a controller is emotionally harming us is an assault on our beliefs.

✓ During courtship we may not have experienced being controlled. Controlling behaviors often escalate as the relationship progresses.

✓ Because we usually like and trust people, it takes time to realize that controllers do not have our best interests in mind. Rather, they have *their* best interests in mind.

✓ We may not share our experiences of being controlled with other people because we don't want to complain about the person we love. We may think that it is bad-mouthing when we decide to talk about the emotional and mentally abusive behaviors we are experiencing. We often feel guilty about sharing what goes on in our relationship because we think we need to keep the family secrets. However, this only serves to protect the controller's dysfunctional behaviors.

Several people have shared their experiences regarding emotional and mental control. We may be experiencing many of the same controlling behaviors directed toward us. Here is an interview that provides insight about living with a controller:

An interview:

Interviewer: Today we are interviewing people, asking the question, "Who's Controlling You?"

How would you respond to this question?

Answer: My husband used to control me.

Interviewer: What was communicated to you by your controller?

Answer: Don't think your thoughts; don't express your feelings; and don't complain. Be compliant and meet all of my needs.

Interviewer: Did you really know these were the expectations?

Answer: Yes, without a doubt.

Interviewer: Were these expectations ever spoken directly?

Answer: No, not directly but in sarcastic ways.

Interviewer: Did you realize that these were unrealistic and unhealthy expectations?

Answer: No. For a long time, I thought the problems were my fault.

Interviewer: How long did it take to become aware of these dysfunctional expectations?

Answer: Over twenty years.

Interviewer: How would you describe yourself?

Answer: Mother of three children, an intelligent, well-educated director of medical records.

Overt control

Controller Strives for One-Up Position

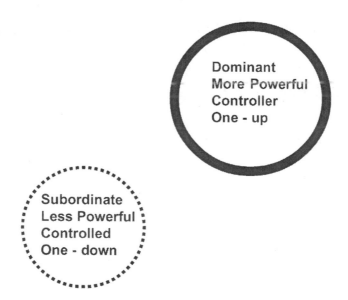

Overt emotional and mentally controlling behaviors are usually directly spoken and are often accompanied with emotional undertones such as anger or sarcasm. The method of control is taking a one-up, superior position to others. This is often accomplished by putting others down and communicating that they are inadequate and inferior. Controllers are likely to control more in personal relationships than with colleagues or friends, but there are exceptions.

1. Control by aggressive expressions of anger: The aggressive expression of anger is one of the most commonly used forms of controlling others. People comply and do not confront the controlling behaviors because they are fearful of the controller's anger.

- Becky shares her experience of being controlled by anger:

  My husband was angry a lot of the time because I was not living up to his expectations of being a perfect wife, which meant that I was always supposed to be available and put his needs first, before mine or the kids. Besides angry words, his body language clearly expressed anger or disappointment. I often wondered how he could be so mean and then go to bed and sleep. It seemed like he was getting some sick pleasure when I was emotionally beat down and crying. The distance between us increased. Besides feeling guilty for not living up to his expectations, I felt guilty for not wanting to be with him. I wanted to leave the marriage but I wasn't sure I could make it on my own with the kids. One time, when I was really serious about leaving and he knew it, he started being nicer. Now I think he is trying to keep his anger inside but I'm afraid he'll explode one of these days, so it's hard for me to want to be close to him. I used to think that everything was my fault. But now I know that it isn't always my problem.

2. Control by acting superior: This is done by putting others down and taking a superior position. Statements are made, such as, "You always get things mixed up!" or, "You just don't have a clue!"

■   Claudia shares her experience:

> With the help of my therapist, I grew in my understanding that controllers take a superior, one-up position by putting the other person down. That was a revelation to me because that was what I was experiencing, but never could explain. I started listening more closely and really hearing when he was one-upping me. He always thought he did things right and I did things wrong. If the kids made noise while he was watching TV, I was at fault for not making them be quiet. If I happened to be watching an interesting show on TV and he came in the room and wasn't interested, he simply changed the channel and I felt like a non-person and that he must be better than I am. There was never any compromising. As a result, I stopped watching any TV.
>
> He didn't like it when I felt good and was excited about something, so I started to act like I felt badly when I was really feeling good. I didn't show my excitement if I was excited. I didn't share my ideas and feelings either. I tried not to focus on my controller. I started believing in myself. I realized that much of my pain was rooted in codependency and I was continually internalizing criticisms. I sacrificed my own self and my values in the process. When I started detaching, I felt better, but the relationship became even more distant. I feel better, but now I have to decide what I am going to do with my life.

3. Control by using sarcastic humor: This popular controlling communication involves comments such as, "If you're leaving, don't let the door hit you on the backside on your way out!" or "Why didn't you call . . . did you lose your fingers or don't you know how to push the buttons?" or, if a partner chooses not to be sexual, "You are as cold as ice! There must be something wrong with you!" If one confronts these remarks, the controller often says, "Can't you take a joke?' This implies that if you are offended there is something wrong with you, so therefore you are inferior in some way. The controller takes a one-up position once again.

- Cindy shares about sarcasm:

> My controller used sarcasm to express anger, such as, 'Oh, you finally got the garage cleaned. What took you so long?' or 'The kids are just like their mother,' implying that there was something wrong with all of us. If I confronted the sarcastic remarks, I was met with, 'Can't you take a joke?' or, 'You always overreact.' My controller thought it was humorous when telling people about how poor I was when he met me and that he rescued me. The story was very twisted and exaggerated, but made him look good.

> I have decided that sarcastic humor is a coward's way of expressing anger because the anger is not expressed directly and appropriately. With this realization, I once asked him, 'Let's talk about what you are *really* angry about.' He had no response. Usually, when he was confronted, he would be silent and walk away. But as far as sarcastic humor, I've been there, heard that, done that and won't put up with any more of it.

4. Control by invading others' personal boundaries: The separateness and individuality of another person is not acknowledged or respected by controllers who infringe on the personal boundaries of others. Controllers impose their needs, wants, and opinions on others and don't hear or respond respectfully to the word "no."

- Sue talks about boundaries not being respected by her controller:

> It felt like I was not a separate person from him. I felt owned and totally surrounded by him. I thought that meant he loved me. But it didn't feel like love. My own interests and ideas were ridiculed. My time was not important. His needs were to be top priority. He thought he knew my likes and dislikes, but he really didn't. He consistently took credit for my accomplishments by saying that I couldn't have done it without him although I did. I did not protect my boundaries, which meant I continued letting him tell me who I should be and what I should do. The decisions were made by him and his ideas were always supposed to be applauded. According to him, he was a saint, because he put up with me, who was inadequate in so many ways. It was years before I came to realize that as an individual, I had my own likes and dislikes and had a right to be my own person. I started protecting my boundaries, started to reclaim my feelings and started appreciating my ability to think.

5. Control by blaming others: Controllers like to believe that all of their problems are the fault of other persons. They seldom understand how they contribute to their own pain, bad luck, or their loss of family and friends. Shifting the blame to others is a way of avoiding responsibility and is often successful because others will accept the blame and believe that they are at fault.

- Megan shares her experience with her controller's blaming:

> With problems, the first step for the controller I was

married to was blaming me or the kids. If anything broke down, it was because I did something wrong, rather than a routine maintenance issue. I started ignoring his blaming statements when I realized that blaming someone was his consistent pattern. Sometimes, I found humor in his need to blame and in my mind would say, 'Here we go again!'

6. Control by maintaining one knows what is right: Controllers think that they are right and anybody that questions or confronts the controller is wrong, stupid, or incompetent. They overtly or covertly communicate that the imbalance in relationship power is *right* and is how relationships should function. Controllers' spoken or unspoken words are, "I need to correct you!" However, the other person is never allowed to decline the offer. Another tactic is patronizing and giving advice with a haughty attitude of superiority.

Controllers also think that people should have the *same priorities* because they think they are right about priorities and get upset when others have different views as to what is important and less important.

- Ellen shares her experience:

  What were perceived as the right answers were always *his* answers. My controller thought that he was always right and everybody else was wrong. Because I was just as sick, I thought that I wasn't capable of thinking straight so I went along with him. The more I observed my controller's behavior, the more I started to realize that we had a different understanding of what was right and wrong. At first this was only a hunch, but it kept playing out the same. I think that what is wrong is harmful to others or wrong in a moral sense. The way he thinks about what is right and wrong is that what is *right is what is convenient* and *what is wrong is inconvenient.* It was wrong when the kids were playing inside when he wanted to watch TV. It was wrong when family life and schedules interfered with his leisure time. Anything that inconvenienced him was deemed as either wrong or unnecessary. This different way of thinking was a major discovery for me. Once I saw through this self-serving way of thinking, I could more easily dismiss it and not take it seriously.

▪   Kelly talks about her priorities being different from those of her husband:

His priorities for me were that I work, be sexually available, keep the house clean and last, be the primary caretaker of our children. My priority list was different. My top priority was my children, then work, then keeping the house clean and bills paid, and last, be sexually available because I had difficulty being sexual when there was no emotional intimacy between us. He often told me I had my priorities all wrong.

7. Control by diminishing the self-esteem of others: Attacking what persons say, do, or their personhoods, diminishes self-esteem and self-confidence. If self-esteem is diminished, the recipient of control is less able to confront or leave a controller. Controllers will sometimes preface their conversations by such statements as, "Don't take this personally, but . . ." or, "I'll be honest with you . . ." and then say something that is very demeaning and often untruthful. If the recipient is offended because the statement *was* personal, he or she is accused of being too sensitive or inadequate in some way.

▪   Debbie talks about her mother:

My mother was always criticizing. Since grade school, she made me feel like I couldn't do anything right. I can't ever remember having self-esteem or thinking I was capable of anything. Teen-age years were a real battle between us and I couldn't wait to graduate, get out of the house and be far away. Nothing much has changed over the years. She is still harping on me, despite the fact that I am doing well. I live far away from my mother because I don't want my children to go through what I went through with her. I don't know what I ever did to be treated so badly and I don't know how my dad put up with her. Sometimes, when I was crying, he would say to me, 'That's just the way your mother is,' like I was supposed to just accept it.

8. Control by not apologizing: Apologizing requires surrendering a one-up position and taking a one-down, humble position, which controllers are often unwilling to do. Controlling people also have a distorted reality in their minds that tells them that there is no reason to apologize, even if they have been verbally abusive.

- Sue talks about her mate never apologizing:

   There were never any apologies because he claimed that it was always my fault. Therefore, he thought there was no need to apologize. He said and did things that emotionally hurt me, but I was the one who apologized so we could get connected again and break the silence. If he gave in at all, he had a silent signal. He made the bed the next morning before he left the house. No kidding, this is what he did. That was his apology and the issue was supposed to just disappear.

9. Control by directing a partner to stop associating with family, friends, coworkers or a support group: Controllers often criticize anyone connected to the recipient of control or make guilt statements when spouses choose to be with other people. Often, controllers insist that the relationship with them should be top priority, despite the fact that their behaviors provide no motivation for a spouse to be with them.

- Ellen shares her experience:

> He was very critical of my family so we didn't have much contact with them. But he expected full participation with his family who he thought were perfect and wonderful. I once went to a family member to discuss how he was so critical of our kids and when he found out, there was a major war. I saw my family on special occasions, such as graduations but did not spend any other time with them. I kept in contact with friends but he never liked my friends. He called them crazy and that they were putting ideas into my head, so I shouldn't call them or talk to them. I asked my friends if this was happening to them and they said 'sometimes,' but in my relationship, it was often.
>
> Now I am learning what control is all about. I realize that when I went to a family member out of desperation and frustration, I was not keeping the family secrets and this enraged him. I am no longer willing to protect his abusive actions, which only serves to fuel the dysfunction. I now realize the importance of my family of origin and how we all got lost to each other in our marriages. Regarding my friendships, I know that my friendships helped me to tolerate my marriage. My friends filled the emotional void that I felt in my marriage. I slowly lowered my expectations on my spouse regarding wanting an emotional connection. I finally came to realize connecting emotionally would only happen if there were some kind of miracle.

10. Control through exciting a conflict, thus preventing further

negotiation or discussion of the matter: This controlling maneuver is a way to avoid dealing with challenging or painful issues.

- Shari relates how her partner exits conflicts, which stops communication:

> Many times, my controlling partner walked out, slammed the door, took off in his truck and returned whenever he felt like returning. Then we would have silence for three or four days which used to bother me, but later became a welcome break from the relationship. There was never a time when a problem was really solved. The problem and the conversations about the problem went underground, and would re-surface but again, nothing would change. When we argued and he had said a lot of hurtful things, he wanted to forget about it. I finally realized that he wanted to move on as quickly as possible because his behaviors had been abusive and he didn't want to acknowledge that. When I tried to talk about the things that were happening in our relationship, I was told to stop dwelling on the past. That was good for him, but didn't work for me because I was hurt and confused and needed to talk it out so it wouldn't happen over and over again. Nothing was solved because he would usually leave. I suppose he thought he was punishing me by leaving in a huff.

11. Control by expressed or unspoken expectations: Controllers' expectations regarding activities, need for help, or need for attention and affection are seldom expressed directly, but in round-about and subtle ways. If controllers' expectations are not met, they do not believe that it is because their expectations are unreasonable. Rather, controllers believe it is because of the controlled person's inadequacies, faults, or lack of compliance in not meeting what is viewed by the controller as reasonable expectations.

- Sue talks about the unrealistic expectations of her controller:

The bottom-line expectations in my marriage were, 'Don't think your thoughts and don't express your feelings, so don't be you. Rather, be compliant, don't create hassles and be grateful for being connected to me.' There were also the daily expectations of adjusting to his work schedule because his work was of utmost importance. I knew that my work was viewed as insignificant by him. So I would tend to the children, do the housework and then, if there was time and energy, do my work that I had taken home, which he disliked seeing me do and usually had some sarcastic comment to make. His expectations were also expressed by making comments about household tasks, such as 'it isn't done yet? Why not?' Or, a sarcastic remark, such as 'What's that smell?' which was a way of criticizing my cooking, but I was also supposed to have his meal ready the moment he came home.

At this point in my life, I actually had four jobs: my paying job, the primary caretaker for the family, all of the housework and bill-paying. My women friends were experiencing the same kind of life style. By staying busy, I didn't really think about any other way of being a wife. I loved being a mother, but his priority was that I work. I followed his priority rather than my own. I was pleasing him as far as working every day for long hours, but my mother-role was shrinking, causing me a lot of distress.

I finally realized that I did not need to respond to unreasonable expectations, so I phased out of meeting those expectations one by one, thinking that if I changed slowly and quietly, he wouldn't notice. He is pretty predictable and I was pretty much right. He didn't seem to notice and if he did think that things were changing, he didn't say anything. Now I am more centered on myself, with an inner focus, rather than being focused on him. I am not sacrificing myself by trying to be who he wants me to be, whatever that is; I'm not sure. It may not look from the outside that I have made changes, but on the inside, I am very different in a good way.

12. Control by having an attitude of entitlement: Controllers often think that they are entitled to others' services, love, and attention. There is often an attitude that one *possesses* a spouse or child. Some controllers, claiming they are entitled because of parental rights, will demand visitation rights no matter how fearful and unhappy their children are when they have to be with them. The most serious outcome of a sense of entitlement is the sexual abuse of children.

- Gracie explains how it is living with a person who feels entitled:

    He believed that he was entitled to being the center of attention, so we couldn't be talking on the phone to friends or family or there would be snide comments. Increasingly, I felt that my 'doing' was all-important, rather than who I really was. When I was ill, he would get angry, which was confusing to me, but I suppose I wasn't able to serve him. My controller felt entitled to my services and I felt like a servant a lot of the time. Being sexual was viewed as the solution to any relationship problem and I thought it was my duty. The only time he said the words, 'I love you,' was when he was satisfied sexually. This never felt like love to me. But it was a lot easier to be sexual with him, than to put up with his moodiness and sarcasm the next several days. I still remember the morning when I was taking a shower that it occurred to me that I did not have to be sexual if I did not want to be because I had a right to make my own decisions about my body. It took years for this realization to enter my mind and this was a revelation for me! My choice in this area resulted in being called weird, frigid, and other derogatory names. I finally left my controller. I am grateful every day that I no longer have to live like that. Now, living without criticism and his attitude of entitlement feels like emancipation.

13. Control by lying, exaggerating, or distorting information: Controllers frequently lie, exaggerate, distort information or are dishonest in order to win an argument, be superior, or be the center of attention. Remarks are made such as "You never get home on time!" or, "I always have to work and you stay in bed all day and do nothing," or, "The only reason you have to work overtime is because you are screwing around during work hours!" The words "never" and "always" are clues to untruthful or exaggerated statements. Besides taking a superior stance, these communications are used to protect or defend the controller or to make another person feel guilty. These tactics create a lot of unnecessary confusion and drama in a relationship and nothing is accomplished.

- Ted describes his experience about dishonesty in his marriage:

> There was no end to her exaggerating or distorting information to win an argument and be superior. With this motivation, she used any tactic. It got to the point where I could not trust what she was saying. When I realized this, I stopped thinking I was crazy, that I was to blame, that I was the only problem and that there was something wrong with me. It didn't change the manipulative tactics she used. But it changed my reactions, when I had the awareness and

understanding of the ways she controlled.

14. Control by discounting and minimizing: There are many ways that controllers use this approach. Sometimes they trivialize what the other person is saying, conveying that it isn't important and not worth listening to. Controllers minimize and reject others' grievances as inconsequential. There are dismissive communications that shut down communication, such as "You are making a mountain out of a mole-hill" or "You shouldn't feel like that." Another version of minimizing is when controllers deny *their* abusive behavior, saying it was no big deal or that it was provoked by another person, so their behavior was justified.

Controllers may negate confrontations by saying, "it was the *way* you confronted." Because the confrontation was not spoken in a sweet and nice way, the whole conversation is rejected. Regardless of how a confrontation is presented, it is likely to be discounted or not heard.

- Mark relates how he was discounted:

  Very often I was discounted and minimized, but I did not have an awareness of what was happening. When I would confront issues in our marriage, she would say, 'Oh, poor baby, you think you have it so bad.' She would turn my words back against me which discouraged me from complaining again, until it got so bad that I couldn't hold it in any longer. Then, because of the backlog of anger, I was at times a little too loud and forceful, and then I was viewed as out-of-control. My loud voice gave her the ticket to discount everything that I said. I came to the conclusion that sharing anything was futile and emotionally unsafe. My work was also discounted because it was not a high-paying position according to her standards. Her dream was a beautiful home in the wealthy part of town, which we could not afford on my accountant's salary.

When I learned about discounting and minimizing, they were the exact words for what I had been experiencing. Hearing those words was so powerful that I decided to learn more words to describe my feelings. Though I started with only a small number of feeling words, I learned to express my emotions. When I was told, 'You shouldn't feel that way.' I said, 'These are my feelings and you can't change them.' It took a long time to acknowledge my feelings, because I thought I wasn't supposed to have feelings.

15. Control by taking a statement to extremes: This is a defensive and manipulating way of controlling. When asked, "Why didn't you pick up Johnny on time?" the defensive response may be, "I can't do anything right! You think I'm a terrible parent" (one-down, feel sorry for me statement). This manipulative statement is meant to elicit the response of, "No, of course you aren't a terrible parent!" When controllers take a defensive and manipulative approach, they often move it to an absurd extreme so that the other person will retract the statement. When this happens, the controller retrieves the one-up position. Too often, the one-up, one-down maneuver works, so the manipulative behavior continues.

16. Control by keeping the "Relationship Rule Book": Controllers make the rules and enforce them whenever, however, and wherever they can. They believe that they know what is best for other persons. Rules are changed when it is beneficial to the controller. They set standards for others and apply them at will, often raising the original standards for the recipient of control so that true success can never be achieved. Controlling parents may convey to a child that they are never quite good enough when they look at the child's report card or when they play sports. When the child really does excel, the expectations go up as well, so true success is never experienced.

- Shari talks about the relationship rule book:

    I did not realize that a lot of rules came along with my wedding vows, but they did, some spoken and some unspoken. The relationship rule book in my marriage was designed by the controller. The rules were, 'I am superior, you are inferior, and you are to be subservient and compliant. You need to please me, but I don't have to please you. I am important but you are not important. I can scold, interrupt and have expectations of you, but you cannot scold, interrupt or have expectations of me. You are to make all the emotional investments in the relationship because that is your responsibility, not mine. You are to dress, act, think, and feel in ways that please me. You need to appreciate me but I don't need to appreciate you. I am independent.' I tried hard to go by these unreasonable rules until I realized the unfairness and that it was all about control. I feel terrible when he points out one small error and negates the whole project that I have been working on and he does this often.

17. Control by withholding information: If one has more information than others, it can be withheld from a spouse, colleagues, employees, or children. Being terminated from a job without any prior notice, or discovering that bills aren't being paid or there have been major withdrawals from a retirement account, are a few of the ways that controllers withhold information causing shock to others, when they become aware. Children are very disappointed when plans they were anticipating are unexpectedly changed and no reasons are offered. Controllers also withhold emotional information such as refusing to give others the satisfaction of knowing that they care.

18. Control by delegating the power and later, taking it back: Controllers may delegate a task or plan and later criticize the other person's efforts. An example of this is when a spouse is given permission by the controller to do a remodeling project. Having completed the arrangements and the remodeling is about to start, the controller is critical of the efforts and may even decide to change all the plans. All of the time and work is wasted.

19. Control by non-approval: This critical approach conveys the message, "Regardless of what you do, I know you'll mess it up some way."

- Ted shares his experience with non-approval:

    I felt that there wasn't anything that I did that met my wife's approval. She would get huffy and treated me with what I felt was disdain. With some professional help, I finally decided to live up to my own expectations and give up my need for her approval, which I finally realized I would never receive. The fact that I had a right to live by my own standards and not hers was a major, life-changing revelation for me. When I ignored her silence and moodiness and went about my life using my own rules, I was amazed that a bolt of lightning didn't strike me down. Rather, I felt better.

20. Control by distorting reality: Controllers distort reality in ways that are self-serving and self-protective. An example of this is when sexual abuse perpetrators say that the child wanted to be sexual with them so therefore, the perpetrator was simply responding. Controllers often believe their own perceptions even though they are totally false. This is the way they excuse their abusive behaviors.

- Cindy relates how her partner distorted reality:

My controller created his own reality and thought that he was superior and that life should be all about him. If it wasn't all about him, he had ways to make it all about him. His reality was that none of us could function without him and that the kids and I created hassles, when actually *he* created the hassles. What he was doing was important and valuable, while everything that everyone else was doing was unimportant. He called people stubborn when they didn't agree or do exactly as they were told. He twisted the story to make it sound like he was right and superior to everyone else.

I had other friends that were having the same experiences and we helped each other sort through what was happening. I started to realize that my controller's reality was a self-designed reality so that he was always right. He never wanted to learn anything about relationships and didn't like it when I would read articles or books about marriage. After many years, I decided I couldn't deal with his control, dishonesty and never working on the relationship, so I am still married but we live in different houses. I tell my friends, 'I picked up my marbles and am going to play with people who make more sense.' There are no behavior changes on his part to this day so I am glad I made the decision to separate. Now the people that I am involved with don't spin their own reality in order to be one-up on other people.

21. Control by threatening abandonment or betrayal: Threats are made about leaving a partner stranded financially, taking the children with them, or saying that they are going to find a new relationship because of needs not being met.

- Greg shares his experience of a controlling relationship:

  My wife was quick to say that she was going to get a

divorce, that I would be sorry and that I'd never see the kids. It took me years to figure out how she controlled me even though I am intelligent, well-educated, healthy and active. We are still together but now I am detached and live a parallel life to her. I still get different kinds of remarks about leaving, but so far, her actions don't follow her words. Some days I wish they would!

22. Control by directing, commanding, and warning: The communication of a controller is not communication that invites negotiation. Rather, it is directive and commanding in both words and body language. Making warning statements are common tactics of controllers, such as, "If you do that, you'll be sorry!" or, "You won't get a penny out of me!"

- Mel shares his experience:

    My wife ordered me around like I was a child. I am usually very up-beat, positive and happy. But when I was around her, I became sullen, had no energy, felt hopeless, and had no desire to talk to her or be with her at all. These feelings would start when I left work and was going home. I felt like two different people.

23. Control by using outside authorities to prove a point or by claiming to be directed by a higher cause: Individuals will make untrue statements to win an argument by saying, "My father says . . ." or, "my sponsor says . . ." or, "the minister/priest/rabbi says . . ." Controllers may have actually received advice, but often distort it to be superior or create guilt in personal relationships. On a wider scale, controllers may claim that they are being directed by a group of other superior people and have knowledge and power to punish transgressors or people with different views and beliefs.

24. Control by not sharing personal feelings in a relationship: Controllers often believe that sharing feelings is being weak. Withholding feelings and not allowing others into their emotional life protects the controller from feeling vulnerable in relationships.

- Shari shares her experience about dating a man who was emotionally closed:

   I think I did all of the emotional work in the relationship because he never shared how he felt about me. It seemed like our relationship was not important to him. I felt like he would infrequently throw me a few emotional crumbs, much like giving treats to a pet dog. I had to magnify these crumbs so that I could believe I was actually in a relationship. I waited for some statement of caring and it never happened. I finally decided that I didn't want to be in a relationship where I was a beggar waiting for emotional connections. This was very demeaning to me and I knew I didn't deserve such treatment. The only time I saw his true emotions expressed was when I told him that I wanted to break up with him. But even then, his emotional response was very shallow given the fact that we had dated for over two years. The feelings that he did express felt like he would miss the things I *did for him*, rather than missing me. He didn't take any responsibility and thinks that I am the bad person who did him wrong because I left.

25. Control by rarely affirming or saying "Thank you": Controllers rarely affirm others or express appreciation. One of the reasons for their hesitancy is that affirming places them in a one-down position. Another reason for not affirming is that relationships may become more emotionally intimate, which may be uncomfortable for controllers.

▪ Rocky shares his experience:

> There are no positive and affirming words about people, especially our immediate family. It doesn't matter how hard I try to please or how hard the kids try to please. I can't remember her ever being appreciative. My children are more courteous than she is!
>
> I think she thinks she is entitled to everything so doesn't have to say 'thank you' or other words of appreciation. I started working for a female boss who respected me and I was amazed at the difference between how I was treated by her compared to how I was treated by my wife. I started realizing how controlling my wife is and that her behaviors are just plain rude.

26. Control by withdrawing love: Though a controller may really care about the people they are controlling, they may withdraw love and be emotionally distant. Sometimes this is their way of punishing the recipient of control who may not be meeting the controller's needs or living up to the controller's expectations.

▪ Ted shares his experience about love being withdrawn:

> I am not sure whether she had any real love to withdraw. When she was upset with me or our children, she would punish us by treating us like we were non-persons and invisible. Nothing I ever said made a difference. Being sexual with her was disturbing to me because we had no emotional connection and as a result I felt that she was just using me. When she didn't come home as a way to punish me, our family was happy because when she was gone from the house, we worked, played, enjoyed each other and had fun together. I love the life and experiences that I have with my children, but I didn't expect so many problems in my marriage. I am

trying to work on believing that I am not the unlovable screw-up that she thinks I am. My self-esteem has diminished, but I think I am getting better. I used to think she was perfect and that I was inferior to her.

27. Control by justifying one's behaviors by pointing out the mistakes of others: This is a defensive tactic to minimize the controller's questionable behaviors, by pointing out another person's faults. This takes the focus off of the controller. This is similar to alcoholics who often talk about others' excessive drinking rather than acknowledging their own problem, or, they excuse themselves by saying that "everyone else is doing it."

28. Control by judging, criticizing, and verbally attacking others: Judging and criticizing others are ways of taking a superior and dominant position. Controllers verbally attack others when they have negative feelings about themselves, which is an underlying cause for many types of bullying behaviors.

▪ Cindy shares her experience of how her partner criticized:

He would frequently judge and criticize others and set himself up as faultless and perfect. Our children would come with some incident and say, 'Don't tell Dad!' because they were afraid of their dad's anger, criticisms or lectures. I felt stuck in the middle because I knew that their dad should know, but that the incident would be blown way out of proportion if I were to tell him. So I just took care of things without saying anything to my controller. Once in a while the truth would come out and there would be a huge argument, but he never understood why we didn't share every situation with him. I eventually realized that controllers have personality characteristics that create emotional and psychological damage to the person or persons they control. I also realized that if he put others down, he temporarily felt superior, just like any bully. Because of his constant criticism, I increasingly did not want to be with him. When I was coming home from work or taking the children to practice or lessons, my energies and mood changed when I drove in the driveway. I called it my driveway sickness, and it was a mood-altering experience because my mood hit bottom immediately.

One day a painter was coming to paint and I had moved the furniture out of his way and he said to me, 'Good job!' I heard those words echo in my mind all day. I hadn't ever heard those words from my spouse. That was sort of a wake-up call—how someone I didn't even know would compliment me about a little thing, but it was like a song that was playing in my head, over and over again. How pitiful was that! I must have been starving for a compliment.

I grew strong inside while dealing with my emotional pain. If there had been one ounce of growth on his part, I could have managed to stay, I think ... but maybe not, since too much water had gone under the bridge and I would not have been able to trust his changes to last more than two or three days because that was his pattern.

29. Control by communicating crazy-making messages: This type of one-up message communicates, "If you do it one way, you will be wrong. And, if you do it the other way, you will also be wrong." Actually, if you do it *any* way, you will be wrong. And if you don't do it, you'll be wrong. Persons who encounter frequent crazy-making messages begin to believe they are crazy and the conclusion is, "There is something wrong with me."

- Greg shares his experience with crazy-making messages:

I was totally baffled about her crazy-making messages. It is pretty confusing because you never win. It is a heads-I-win-tails-you-lose set up. My controller wanted me home when she was home, but did nothing but watch TV when I was home. Her crazy-making silent communication was 'I want you home, but I won't interact with you.' Many times she said, 'You need to make a high income, but you can't travel because you need to be home.'

When she would tell me to do something, there was the implied message that I would screw it up. With no awareness of what crazy-making messages were, I was pretty confused. It's nothing that you talk about at the gym and I don't have any men friends that would want to listen. But I finally did realize that I did not have to respond to crazy-making messages, where I was condemned and criticized if I did one thing or the opposite thing. When I gained the awareness, I said, 'Your logic is not logical' and she was totally silent.

30. Control by speaking *for* other persons who are viewed as unable to speak for themselves: This display of power is used by dominant persons and is a total disregard for the feelings, thoughts, beliefs and values of others. Dominant people often make decisions for the subordinate people, thinking that they know what is best for them.

- Cindy shares her experience:

  My controller thought that he knew how I was thinking, feeling and what I liked. And he never hesitated to provide his opinion on how I *should* think, feel or what I *should* like. He was usually wrong when he told me how I was thinking, feeling, or what I was doing. Sometimes he would tell me that I was chasing around with someone else, and I learned to respond by saying, 'If you want to believe that, I can't change your mind. But I don't know why you want to think that because it just makes you angry!' It took me a long time to be able to stand up for myself.

31. Control by making promises about the future: A parent may say to a child, "Someday, I'll take you to the baseball game, Teddy," or to a spouse, "When things slow down at work, we'll go to counseling," or the promise of, "I'll stop drinking after the holidays," or to an adult child, **"Why complain about all the work you do or your low salary? You're going to get this company when I'm dead!"** Such promises are empty words that end up in broken promises or are ways of manipulating others.

32. Control by projecting onto others: Projecting is accusing the other person of whatever the controller is actually doing. A spouse may accuse the other of overspending when the reality is that the accuser is stretching the credit card to the limits.

- Jayson shares his experience:

  I was often accused of what she was doing, as I later found out. She would say, 'You are out-of-control with your life.' I would think, 'So what's out of control?' I did nearly the same thing every day, working, exercising, coaching my son's football team and coming home. Nothing was out of control, unless something broke, like the washing machine or lawn mower to upset the routine. I was often accused of spending too much money, but she didn't say this directly. She would say, 'Where is all the money going?' She would insinuate that I was a big spender or that I was stashing money away. Actually, it was my controller that was out of control. She was spending excessive amounts of money and was out of control with her life because she was so disorganized.

33. Control by saying one thing but doing something else: This control tactic involves actions that are not congruent with spoken words. This is dishonest, deceiving and disrespectful, and demonstrates a lack of integrity.

34. Controlling by giving gifts that carry a self-serving message: Giving gifts to children or adults with a hidden agenda, pacifying the person whom the controller has hurt, or convincing a person to be in a relationship with the controller, is an upgraded version of perpetrators luring children into their cars by offering them candy or an interesting toy. It is also a way of having others believe in the goodness of the controller.

- Susanne talks about the gifts she was given:

  > Receiving gifts seems like a nice gesture, but I felt that it was all about manipulation and control. Gifts felt like they had a hook and that there should be a pay-back to the controller, such as being more compliant and more responsive to his expectations. So, because of these feelings, I would get angry at the gifts, but I kept the anger inside of me. Sometimes it was expensive jewelry that he insisted that I wear to a party. There were gifts of lingerie and when he wasn't pleased with me, I would be given roses that were droopy and dying. Most of his gifts sent some kind of message.

35. Control by frequent fault-finding: An insecure controller points out others' faults, as determined by the all-knowing controller: "You're hair is too long"; "That shirt doesn't look good on you"; "That outfit makes you look fat"; or, "You have strange friends."

- Cindy relates her experience of constant fault-finding:

Constant fault-finding drove me crazy. Every meal there would be criticizing the kids for something. And it wasn't only the kids. I could clean all day and he would come home and wipe his finger on the top of a door casing and if it was dusty, he would discredit all of the cleaning I had done. When I was doing errands, I was 'chasing'; when he was doing errands, he was accomplishing great things. I was always accountable to him, but he was never accountable to me and I used to say that he was like the Internal Revenue Service, creating fear, making rules and never appreciating the taxpayers.

I once asked him to treat me as nice as he treats the waitress in a restaurant, which is a pretty sad statement. I was emotionally scared of him. I told him that, but he thought that was stupid because he had never physically hurt me. The only way I could explain it was that when he came home, I never knew his mood and I would get emotionally tense and frightened.

I sometimes would think, 'If I am so bad, why doesn't he leave me?' Then it got to the point where I didn't like myself when I was with him because I had anger, resentments, and negative thoughts. Finally, my awareness led to the realization that I shouldn't have to work so hard for what should be normal actions in a relationship, such as respect and mutual caring. I had a right to be respected and was respected by my employer, colleagues and friends, but not in my primary relationship. I know now that there was no way my love and caring could sustain or grow with a controller, but he expected me to love him unconditionally even though it never was returned. I didn't want to spend a lot of time with a person that was always harassing and criticizing me. People don't do that if they love someone. The time came when I had to leave. I had tried everything. I gave him what I thought were the best years of my life and wasn't going to give him more of my precious days. Later, I discovered that the best years of my life were after I left my marriage. I'm doing the same thing as I always did as far as living life, but no one is constantly finding fault in what I do. I am glad those years are behind me.

36. Control by put-downs and name-calling: These are demeaning statements that belittle, criticize and convey disapproval of a person, in order to be one-up and superior. "You're no good, you're incompetent and you'll never make it without me." Communications carry the theme of "you are inadequate." Sometimes, the phrases become more offensive. "You are crazy"; "You are sick and need to go see a shrink!"; "You are psycho!" These verbal attacks are difficult to ignore and are a form of interpersonal verbal violence.

- Claudia shares her experience of put-downs by her partner:

    There were repeated put-downs, wiping out my self-confidence. I was told that I was too fat, but he was the one that was out-of-control with his weight. That was the kind of logic he had! He questioned what I would wear with, 'Are you wearing *that*?' It was a gradual chipping away at my self-confidence and self-esteem. I was declared to be 'the only reason our relationship didn't work.' I used to think I was like Avis Rent-a-car, wearing a sign on my forehead, 'I try harder.' I always tried to make things work, so I had to figure out how to go around, under, or over the top of him to prevent conflict. I can't say I was all that successful.

    The put-downs did not stop with me. He did the same to our kids, my family, and friends. That should have given me a clue that being critical was his control problem and not my issue. One night, after an evening of criticisms, he was coming on to me, being all lovey-dovey and I said, 'You want to be sexual with me after you have emotionally thrown me under a bus? Are you crazy?' I couldn't believe I said it, but after so many years it just came out of my mouth.

I learned that control is because of feeling inadequate and insecure, but he looked really strong and powerful. He had me believing that I couldn't do anything right. I had to work through the anger that built up inside of me from all of the put-downs.

37. Control by spreading false information about situations or people: If controllers are invested in winning at any cost, they are not above using false information to accomplish their goals, which is dishonest and abusive.

38. Control by taking over the conversation: When someone is sharing, controllers often take over the conversation telling another story, or saying that their problem is far worse than the other person's problem. Someone says, "I didn't feel well yesterday," and the controller is likely to say something like, "I was really sick and couldn't even get out of bed, but finally struggled to get to the doctor, but the doctor didn't help. And I remember when I was a kid, the same thing would always happen." Taking over the conversation is rude and disrespectful.

- Sharon talks about how her partner takes over the conversation:

   It didn't matter what I was talking about, he would take over the conversation. I could be talking about a problem I was having at work, and he would start going on endlessly about either why I was having problems, or how his problems were much worse than mine. The kids could be talking about how cold it was to walk three blocks to school and he would take over and exaggerate how far he walked to school, even when there was a blizzard. He always had the worst headache, the worst flu or the worst pain in his shoulder. No one compared to his suffering or to the sacrifices that he made for everyone. After a while, 'Good morning' or 'Hi!' and plans about the kids was the extent of our conversations. If I shared anything else, the conversation was taken over, or I was told how to think and feel. So I reacted in a sane and logical way and emotionally and verbally shut down.

39. Control by diverting the conversation or changing the topic: Circling a topic without addressing the main point or changing the subject all together are ways of avoiding or sidetracking uncomfortable conversations in a relationship, leaving no possibility for resolution. As a result, the conflicts get stuffed away, stockpiled, and may at some time resurface with a vengeance. When one tries to hold a conversation with a controller who is skillful in diverting the conversation, it is like taking conversational detours.

- Ted explains how his controller would divert the topic:

    If the conversation was even slightly uncomfortable for my wife, she would divert or change the topic to something entirely different. I wasn't aware this was happening for a very long time. I would just follow the conversation and wonder how we got to where we finally ended up. There are no longer any important topics between us and I hear her doing the same thing with our grown daughters.

40. Control by insisting and badgering: Controllers use this tactic to get their own way with others. Badgering and relentlessly pushing often results in the other person finally giving in, out of frustration and exhaustion. It is similar to children's temper tantrums, where a parent gives in to put an end to the screaming. Unfortunately, children learn that tantrums work to get what they want and in a similar way, adults continue to push and badger if the behavior works in getting their way.

- Terry shares what happened regarding his controller's insisting and badgering:

> Her tactic was to push and badger me until I finally gave in because I got so frustrated. She is absolutely relentless and fixated if she wants something. Now I recognize that badgering is controlling and giving in isn't always the best thing to do.

41. Control by attributing another person's actions to ulterior motives: Examples of this control maneuver are, "You're just starting a fight because you like to argue," or, "You cleaned the house—are you having someone special come over when I'm not here?" or, to get more compliance from a spouse, "You aren't trying to make this relationship work because you don't care enough." These statements are scolding and shaming and are ways of manipulating to get compliance.

42. Control by interrogating: From a desire to control, rather than sincere concern, many questions are asked in an intimidating way, such as, "Where are you? Who are you with? What time are you coming home? What is taking you so long? How much money are you spending this time?"

- Sue shares her experience:

I was shocked and confused at what happened after my wedding. As the saying goes, the honeymoon was over and this was very true for me. My husband became increasingly critical and controlling. I was questioned often about what I was doing, like why I took so long at the grocery store, why I went to visit my mother in the hospital, why I cut my hair, and why I wasn't home at some exact time. At first, I did not recognize all of the questioning as control. I had no experience with control because my family of origin did not control me. They trusted me to do what I was supposed to do. They had no reason to question me because I was a good student, took responsibility, and made good choices.

During courting days, there weren't any questions or criticisms. I thought we had love and friendship. I entered marriage with a good sense of self-esteem and it was systematically diminished because I often felt that I could do nothing right. I was successful in what I was doing in my job and had other friendships that worked, but my marriage was a different story. It did not feel like a good relationship to me because of all the questions that sent a message that I was doing everything wrong.

43. Control by sabotaging another's efforts or plans: Some controllers interrupt schedules of their spouse, demand attention so that the spouse has less time for their commitments or purposefully sabotage a partner's plans, activities, success, and friendships.

44. Control by being defensive: This maneuver is used so that the other person will back off and stop confronting the controller's abusive behaviors. Controllers also deflect confrontations by accusing the confronting person of choosing a bad time to talk.

According to controllers, there is never a good time to confront them. If their partners confront them in the morning, they will be accused with statements such as, "What's the matter with you? You have ruined my whole day!" If a controller is confronted in the evening, they may say, "Can't you see I'm tired and just want to relax? I shouldn't have to put up with your complaining!" How about the week-ends? No. "There is something wrong with you because you are spoiling my whole week-end! You always start an argument at the worst time!" Expressions of hurt feelings or having different opinions is often called "creating a fight" so nice people will become silent and the controller is successful in stopping unpleasant communications.

45. Excluding or treating a person as a non-person: A type of bully behavior involves excluding people who should actually be included in a group. In personal relationships, examples of these types of behaviors are: not introducing a spouse to others; turning off the TV when someone else is watching; asking for an opinion and then dismissing it; and purposefully ignoring someone when they enter a room. The unspoken message is, "I am superior and I'm not going to acknowledge or bother with you."

- Melinda shares her experience:

> When we would be with his business partners or other people he knew, he did not introduce me, so I had to introduce myself. I wondered what those people thought about his rude behavior. But there were many ways that he communicated that I was not important and sometimes I felt invisible, like a nonperson except for when he wanted something.

46. Controlling by creating drama: Unnecessary hassles, confusion, chaos, and emergencies are created, especially if the controller is active in an addiction, which is upsetting to a spouse, friends, relatives, and children.

47. Controlling by making things excessively and unnecessarily complicated: When things get very complicated, in words, in length, or in convoluted statements, many people become discouraged in their attempts to understand. They may give up and surrender their power to the more powerful persons or groups of persons. This is the experience of many people regarding insurance policies, legal documents, religious doctrines, legislative bills, credit card policies, Internal Revenue policies and procedures, and medical charges. Because of not completely understanding, they agree to what the more powerful persons are saying and writing, despite the fact that what is being done may be detrimental to them.

48. Controlling others because we are losing control in our own lives: Because we are not managing or being accountable for our life, we may escalate our controlling of others. Losing control in our own lives may be caused by our own unhealthy choices or being in an addictive process. We can also lose control over parts of our life when we experience a debilitating illness, lose a job or have a financial crisis. If we lose control over parts of our lives, we may control whatever or whoever we are able, which is likely to be family members.

Passive control

Controller Poses as Weak But is More Powerful

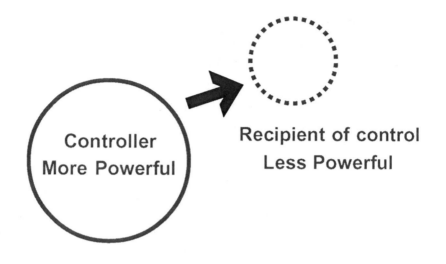

Controller
More Powerful

Recipient of control
Less Powerful

Passive controlling behaviors involve taking a one-down position to achieve a one-up power position. These behaviors can be difficult to recognize because their methods are subtle, deceptive, indirect, dishonest, and manipulative. Appearing to be weak, passive controllers are actually powerful because people will respond to them out of obligation and guilt, rather than choice.

1. Control by creating guilt: This popular way of passively controlling others is taking a one-down position to achieve a one-up position to get requests met. This method employs various messages, such as, "You should be ashamed of yourself," or "If you really loved me, you would …" or, "If you were nicer to me, I wouldn't…" or, "You are working late because you don't want to be with me." Guilt makers will act incompetent, stressed, and overwhelmed as a way of manipulating others to do things for them. People respond out of obligation rather than choice, thinking, "I should, or I better do…" Guilt messages are often accompanied by a pained look, tears, withdrawal, or silence. If there is hesitation or refusal, they insinuate that the person whom they are manipulating is selfish, unkind, and uncaring.

- Greg shares his experience of how he lived with guilt:

   My controller had her ways to get me to submit to her wishes by putting a guilt-trip on me. If I didn't do certain things, I would feel guilty so it was easier to do them. This could involve things like remodeling a room that didn't need it or spending a week with her relatives who drank a lot, which bothered me. I have learned that if I take on the guilt, it is a choice I make. So most of the time, I am no longer a guilt taker. Interestingly enough, I think my wife respects me more for confronting when she tries to make me feel guilty. So my getting clearer has helped us both and our relationship is better.

2. Control by being a martyr and sacrificing self for others: Sacrificing oneself is done in efforts to be loved, but when people don't respond as the passive controller would like them to respond, they are viewed as being unkind and ungrateful. Martyrs perceive their sacrificing as virtuous, but they are usually not reciprocated in ways they would like.

- Ted shares his experience:

   My father thought he was the only one that made any sacrifices for our family. He was the martyr and we were all ungrateful for everything he did. He felt that the only reason he was valued was the money he provided to the family. But in reality, that was the only thing he gave to the family since emotionally, he shared nothing.

3. Control by pouting, being moody, and sulking: These immature behaviors communicate "Feel sorry for me," or, "You aren't doing what you should be doing for me." This behavior is often a response to not getting one's way. Sometimes the pouting and moodiness is disguised as joking, but the joking is not perceived as humorous by the other person.

4. Control by being dependent, weak, hopeless, and helpless: This is a "I'll-fall-apart-without-you," one-down approach, and is a way that dependent people passively control others. What they fail to realize is that if they do win by getting their way and their demands are met, the other person's actions are usually driven by a feeling of obligation rather than free choice. Dependent persons often ignore the emotional undertones of compliance and don't consider how they place others in an obligatory position. The facade of weakness also makes people hesitate to bring up conflictive issues. Sensitive and nice people don't confront people who are fragile, overworked, and stressed out. In couple relationships a good guy–bad guy dynamic is created, by the passive controller communicating, "I'm too kind and caring to discipline the children or handle unpleasant situations, so *you* do it," or, "You tell the neighbors to keep their dog out of our yard!"

5. Control by taking the victim role: When we take a victim role our one-down message is, "I am a victim and everyone, including life, which is unfair takes advantage of me and I am helpless to do anything about it." Victims project an attitude of being at the mercy of everybody and being mistreated. Yes, there are true victims. But there are also people who take this role in an effort to manipulate people to take care of them. They usurp others' energies, rather than generating their own. They look for a rescuer rather than taking responsibility for themselves. However, people who take a victim role often sabotage efforts to rescue them by rejecting any suggestions for changing the situation.

- Jackson shares his experience:

    My wife thinks she is always the victim, always has it so bad and if anything is going to go wrong it will happen to her. This is absolutely exhausting to me. I am almost convinced that she thinks it is saintly to be a victim because she acts like she is superior to everyone else. I used to feel sorry for her, but now I am just irritated at her negativity. I don't like to spend time with her and want to be someplace—anyplace where she is not around.

6. Control by being extremely kind and understanding: "I'm so nice, kind, and understanding that you couldn't possibly be upset or leave me." It is difficult to confront these people, knowing that we would be viewed as insensitive, selfish, and unkind.

7. Control by being unknown, aloof, cool, distant, mysterious, and formal: This is a behavior pattern that is a way of intriguing others and challenging them to get closer. They silently communicate, "Come closer but don't come closer." The other person is expected to do the emotional work of the relationship. When the other person becomes unwilling to do the emotional investments for both persons, realizing that it is a one-way relationship, the relationship becomes distant.

8. Control by acting deeply hurt: Acting deeply hurt, as a one-down manipulation is different from the times we experience real feelings of hurt. When there is a pattern of acting deeply hurt, people will often be consoling because they feel obligated. Sometimes, out of frustration with this passive manipulation, the controlled person becomes irritated and impatient. They are then viewed by the passive controller as cruel and uncaring.

- Ed shares his experience of his mother:

> Every time I decide not to visit her, she acts crushed and I feel guilty. She thinks that on my vacation days and holidays, I should be with her and a lot of the times I do go visit. She usually has a long list of things she wants me to do around the house even though she has Dad doing whatever she can't do. Sometimes it is easier for me to go visit her, rather than dealing with the guilt that I know I would have if I didn't go. I am always torn. I know I should be a good son, but I have a life of my own which she doesn't seem to care about. Our conversations are all about her. Yikes. She drives me crazy.

9. Control by having unrealistic expectations, spoken or unspoken: Expectations are imposed on partners, friends, parents and/or children and are often expressed with "shoulds". "You should always be here when I need you," or, "You should always want to be with me."

10. Control by expecting the worst and focusing on the negative: This way of thinking can create the exact opposite of what we really want. An example is, "I know you are going to leave me," or, "Everyone will desert me when I need them the most." Unfortunately, this constant barrage of negative statements increases the probability that persons who fear abandonment *will* experience being left and will be alone. Rejection is an experience that is always unpleasant, but behaving in ways that invite rejection or obsessing on the possibility of a relationship failure often creates the very experience that one wants to avoid. Seldom does the controlling person see, understand, or take responsibility for the self-created abandonment.

11. Control by putting another on a pedestal, eliminating the possibility for mutuality: By putting someone on a pedestal, a personal relationship loses balance and equality. Rather than experiencing trust and sharing with ease, there is disappointment and struggle in the relationship. Conversations become guarded and increasingly superficial. There are also misinterpretations and misunderstandings resulting from mind-reading, which further fragments the relationship.

12. Control by feeling one way but saying we feel another way: This is being emotionally dishonest. It is saying, "No, I'm not hurt," when in fact we are hurt, or "I'm not angry!" when our body language makes it obvious that we are angry. When children see a parent crying and ask what is wrong, they may receive a dishonest response of, "Nothing." This emotional dishonesty and incongruity between what is being said and body language is confusing to children because they begin to doubt what they see and mistrust their own perceptions. We don't have to offer details with children, but we can be honest in a general way and give them some assurance that we will be okay and they will be okay as well. In family or close relationships, we may think it is virtuous to say that there is nothing wrong when we are upset or crying but it is not virtuous. It is being dishonest.

13. Control by saying what people want to hear: Saying what we know people want to hear is being manipulative and deceitful. We may do this to be accepted, loved, to avoid confrontation or to get what we want.

14. Control by *not* hearing or selectively hearing: Some people listen only to what they want to hear. Or, they act as if they *are* hearing, but in reality, they are not really hearing. Controllers often ignore the warnings, pleas or wishes of others. They self-protect by not hearing communication that may be unpleasant. In this way, they avoid dealing with reality and continue to think that there are no problems in the relationship. If a controller does not hear what is being said, efforts to problem-solve are futile. When pushed to the limit, the person who is being controlled communicates frustration and anger. When a partner decides to leave, controllers often act shocked because they have not heard any of the previous conversations regarding the deteriorating relationship. They will try to place the blame on the partners and accuse the other of being unkind, uncaring, or unreasonable.

- Ted shares his experience of how his controller did not listen:

  Talking to her was literally, like talking to a brick wall. By not hearing, she did not take responsibility and it was frustrating. I started to realize that there was no hope for change if she won't listen. I finally gave up talking, became silent and went about my own life, which involved being a father, taking care of the finances and being a draftsman for my company. I didn't have time or energy to be talking to someone who was choosing to not hear. We are still together, but live separate lives. Some days it's OK, and some days I am miserable. I would like to hear and be heard. I would like to speak and be spoken to. I would like to care and be cared for. This is exactly what we had in our early relationship. But something happened and now we are just in a holding pattern.

15. Control by being silent and isolating: These behaviors send messages such as, "You're inadequate and I'm angry at you,"

"You've displeased me," or, "I'll ignore or avoid you and will not communicate." There is a refusal to talk, so problems aren't solved. However, the person really doesn't want us to leave and is usually more dependent on us than they care to admit. These behaviors are also common behaviors *as a response* to being controlled and are honest, normal and legitimate self-protective actions, rather than being manipulative behavior.

16. Control by igniting jealousy: This tactic might be expressed, "If you don't care for me or meet my needs and expectations, then I'll find someone, or *have* someone, who does!"

17. Control by denying or making excuses for the controlling, abusive behavior: Controllers often deny their abusive behaviors and refuse to admit that they've done anything wrong. They lie to themselves as well as to others. Common excuses made by controllers for their inappropriate behaviors are: "I am under so much stress and that's why I lashed out at you," or, "I can't help it because I have a bad temper," or, "I just had a little too much to drink."

18. Control by agreeing, then complaining: An example of this is, "Yes, I suppose I will go to the baseball game with you," and after the game is over, there is the comment, "Baseball is so boring—I've always hated baseball games." Passive, dishonest compliance ends up in aggressive, negative, and complaining statements, which is confusing to a partner.

19. Control by creating conflict among people: Passive controllers may create dissension among others when trying to control family members or colleagues in a work setting. These are "under-the-table" covert tactics that may involve bad-mouthing, distorting communications through exaggeration, omitting certain information, or spreading false rumors. Sometimes one parent will align with a child against the other parent to win an argument, keep a secret, or do something that they know would be opposed by the other parent.

■ Sheldon shares his experience:

> In our family, if you aren't at a family function, which is always expected of you, you can be sure that you are the topic of conversation and it won't be good. As the drinking proceeds, the conversations become more derogatory and siblings take sides and start attacking each other. If you would ask them, they would say that it is just the way the family is and has always been. It starts out with a little bit of hassling, exaggerating stories of people's mistakes or obnoxious personality traits and just keeps going. People go to bed and start the same routine the next day. If someone doesn't come home for Christmas, their gift gets left under the tree and is wrapped in black paper. And it isn't a joke!

20. Control by being overly sympathetic: Trite solutions are accompanied by pained facial expressions and sweet voice tones.

■ Deanna talks about her friend:

> My friend always gave me advice in her sweet voice, but it was always a quick fix like saying that she knew I'd get through whatever I was going through. I can't explain it, but it felt so phony, like getting a pat on the head and being dismissed. I can still see her pained look that was supposed to make me believe that she was so sensitive and caring. It took me a long time to recognize the insincerity, because I wanted to trust my friend, but eventually I didn't want to spend any time with her.

22. Control by pleading innocence and being wrongly accused: When a controller is confronted about controlling behaviors, they may take a one-down position and self-protect by claiming innocence and respond with "I don't know what you are talking about!" When controllers play innocent, it often makes the recipient of control feel uncomfortable for having reported or confronted the abusive behavior, which is exactly what controllers want, so that they can continue the same behaviors toward others. When acting like the *wrongly accused*, the controller gets others to back off, stop confronting, and in some situations, retract or apologize for their statements.

Reactive control

Original Controller is Being Controlled

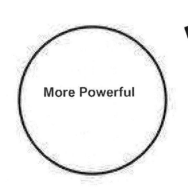

Less Powerful

More Powerful

Reactive Controller

Reactive control is a reaction to being controlled and involves taking a one-up power position. It is a getting even, I'll-get-you-back type of control, following the universal law of, "To every action there is an equal and opposite reaction." Adolescents frequently rebel against controlling parents. This is the risk controllers take when they are emotionally and mentally controlling their children. Like any type of control, we may not be aware of our reactive behaviors or our behaviors may be conscious and deliberate. The person who is reactively controlling uses many of the same control tactics that they have experienced and learned from controllers.

Sometimes, reactive behaviors become a self-fulfilling prophecy. If children are constantly told by a parent that they are inadequate and will never amount to anything, children may begin acting according to what the controller has told them. One outcome is that the controller may end up supporting them when they become adults because they cannot manage their life by themselves.

1. Rebelling: Children or adolescents often respond to excessive control by rebelling in a variety of ways: angry episodes, threatening to run away, being non-communicative, under-functioning in school or home, abusing alcohol or chemicals, destroying property, failing to come home when expected, self-mutilating to lessen emotional pain or gain parental attention, or completely ignoring or going against family rules. When young adolescents have car accidents, destroy property, skip school often, or behave in ways that involve police, the controller parent is responsible to take care of the problem and pay for any financial costs. This is upsetting to the controller, which is often the exact purpose of reactive behaviors. Controllers rarely understand how rebelling behaviors of young adults are often responses that are brought on by the controlling behaviors of parents.

When the rebelling adolescent reaches adulthood, there may be remorse and blaming the self for the controlling behaviors that were done *in response* to dysfunctional controlling parents. It is healthy to take responsibility for our harmful behaviors, but we also need to understand the causes for our reactive behaviors. Reactive behaviors do not stem from being innately evil or inadequate. Rather, they are reactions to abusive control.

- Steve describes his experience:

> For years, I felt guilty for punching out my dad. I should have never done that, but he kept criticizing, badgering and making me feel lousy about myself. One day the argument got heated and I just had enough and lost control. I hit my dad and left. I don't ever want to talk to him again. But I suppose I should.

2. Being dishonest with the controller and withholding information: Being dishonest with a controller is a way to escape arguments and unpleasant encounters.

- Shari explains:

> I was dishonest or would leave some things out about what I was doing although I wasn't doing anything to be dishonest about! I would do this because I didn't want to get him angry. However, this didn't always work. He would be angry over some little thing anyway. I still withhold information as far as what I am doing or where I am going or who I am with, because he tries to micro-manage me and I can't stand it. My controller twists things around so even if I have done nothing wrong, I have done something wrong according to him.

3. Starting arguments with the controller to get the controller upset: When controllers frustrate people, badger them, and try to get some kind of reaction from them, they may receive the same behaviors in return. There is a sense of power in getting the controller on the defensive and making the controller upset and angry. The dynamics between a controller and a reactive controller often involve each person knowing how to agitate the other person. Both the controller and the reactive controller behave in ways that are disrespectful, harmful, and diminishing of the other person.

4. Destroying the controller's property: The controller's property can be used and not returned, broken, destroyed, or left out in the rain. This is a way of getting back at the controller.

5. Not hearing the controller: Adults learn to ignore the negativity of a controller and often roll their eyes (to themselves), as the controller goes on at length about what everyone else is doing wrong. Some children tune out controllers who are constantly preaching, moralizing and pointing out mistakes.

6. Becoming dependent on the controller: Adult children who do not launch themselves and become independent may return home and become dependent on the controller because they are using chemicals, are without a job, or are emotionally disabled and cannot function as an adult.

- Harold, a father, shares his story:

    I had a controlling father and I raised my kids the same way. They didn't get by with anything and I made all of their decisions. I wanted them to be afraid of me because I thought that is how fathers were supposed to be. Their mother left when the youngest kid left for the first time. She never came back. None of my kids amounted to much, just like I always figured. Four out of six of my grown-up kids are now in my home. They can't support themselves. I don't want this and they are all driving me nuts because they are so helpless. They are drinking and drugging and only two are working, but their jobs aren't good enough to pay their own way. A couple of them say they are depressed and I think that's just a cop-out. I wonder how this happened to me. I feel like I am a hostage to my own kids. I don't have the heart to tell these adult kids to leave because I'm not sure that they could make it on their own.

7. Emotionally closing down and not communicating: This is a way to have another person work hard to get us to communicate with them, and is passively controlling. In contrast, emotionally closing down is a way to self-protect oneself from a controller who may become angry or distort what is said.

Under-functioning controlling behaviors

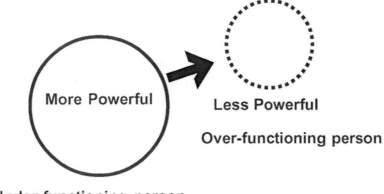

More Powerful

Less Powerful

Over-functioning person

Under-functioning person

Under-functioning is taking a one-down position, which creates imbalance in a relationship. *Legitimate* adult under-functioning may be due to a serious illness or a disability. Or, under-functioning happens when someone is involved in an addiction. Under-functioning can also be due to a mental health issue that takes the form of a personality disorder. Under-functioning may be a learned behavior that has been effective in getting others to do whatever we are not doing and in this sense it is controlling. Because the behavior has rewards, it continues, much to the consternation of people around them.

Typical under-functioning behaviors are:

- Being inert, rather than functioning in a normal, adult responsible way
- Constantly asking for help or delegating the work to others
- Claiming to forget what was said, what was planned, appointments, deadlines, and commitments
- Failing to keep a job
- Procrastinating and having minimal task-completion
- Refusing to fully participate in decision-making
- Being self-involved, rather than contributing to a relationship
- Demanding love, but not acting in loving ways
- Having more power because other people have to make adjustments, such as doing our work, but appearing to be powerless

The under-responsible adult often forms an imbalanced relationship with an over-responsible person who accommodates and enables by over-functioning. It is a relationship that eventually falters or fails, due to anger, frustration, and exhaustion that is bound to be experienced by the over-functioning person. Under-functioning persons often act like children, depending on their spouse who is viewed and treated as a "parent" to help them with routine tasks and decisions in life. Over-functioning spouses often provide most of the family income, do more than their share of household chores, and make sure the children make it to their activities. There are situations when over-functioning is unavoidable, such as bill paying which, if the over-functioning person did not do it, the bills would not be paid on time.

Under-functioning controllers are passive and uninvolved when there are situations that need to be addressed. They seem to let life just happen *to* them. They are not proactive; nor are they reactive. Partners of under-functioning spouses will make statements such as, "They act like a child; they act helpless and can't do anything by themselves; they act like they are entitled to having someone else do everything," or, "They are so frustrating that I'd like to put some dynamite in their chairs to get them moving!" Decisions are left to the over-functioning partner who is then often accused of being controlling in the relationship. Over-functioning persons become extremely frustrated because they are carrying more than their fair share of the load in many areas of the relationship.

The over-functioning person may confront in efforts to change the relationship dynamics but is seldom successful, which is similar to other types of controllers' resistance to changing behaviors. When the over-functioning person becomes angry because of being on overload, which is certain to happen, the over-functioning person is ignored and not heard, the promises begin, or some short-lived efforts are made to pacify the over-functioning person. The under-functioning person often creates a full-blown "nag" for a partner, which is a result of the continual frustration of living with someone who is under-responsible in too many areas of living. Rather than taking their adult responsibility, they will use typical controlling behaviors such as blaming others and making excuses. Restoring healthy functioning in this type of relationship involves balancing the power structures so that the under-functioning person steps up and takes more responsibility, while the over-functioning person modifies the over-functioning behaviors. However, the pattern of the under-functioning person usually plays out the same in marriage therapy, reading about improving relationships or attending relationship classes. The under-functioner does not activate or fully participate and there is no change in behaviors that would be beneficial to both the under-functioner and his/her relationship.

- Kim shares her experience:

> I became a nagging wife to Joe because he was so irresponsible. Nothing would ever get done if I didn't remind him. He forgets to pick up the kids from school and the kids panic. He spends money irresponsibly, while I am trying to spend within our budget. Once he took over the checkbook rather than me, and within two months, we were getting late charges on bills and the bank was calling about bad checks. But on the outside, he acts kind and caring and everybody loves him. They think he is the nicest guy that would do anything for anybody. But at home, he is a nothing … like he just doesn't care or just doesn't get it. I have lost all respect for him. I am angry and frustrated.

Over-functioning persons take a position of strength, take the lead, do more than their share, make the decisions and get the job done which leads to eventual emotional and physical burn-out. If the dysfunction persists, the over-functioning person may start having thoughts of leaving. However, this is a very difficult decision when there are children involved. Under-responsible spouses can be very nurturing parents because, as spouses describe, "They are like kids, themselves." Other family members may not understand why the over-functioning person is leaving such a nice person or such a good parent, not realizing the frustrations within the relationship.

Elicited control

If people are not functioning age-appropriately or are making bad choices, they elicit control from others. This may involve more rules, consequences, and limited or banned activities. Many parents have stricter rules for children in recent times because of increasingly unsafe environments. In addition, there are more harmful choices available for adolescents who are naive and vulnerable. Though children may resist what they perceive to be over-supervision by controlling parents, it has become increasingly necessary. An example of elicited control which is brought on by irresponsible behavior, is removing computer privileges when an adolescent has failing grades in school. Because of not being responsible, a parent takes restrictive action, which may be viewed as overly controlling by the adolescent.

To review:

1. Emotional and mental control is interpersonal violence. The control addressed in this book is *emotional and mental control* rather than physical, sexual, or extreme abuse, which needs law enforcement intervention.
2. Through education, intervention, and empowerment, positive changes are possible for individuals and relationships that are struggling with emotional and mental control.
3. We are often unaware of how we control or how we enable the control. In contrast, there are controllers who deliberately inflict emotional harm on others.
4. Controllers and recipients of control have different degrees

of responsibility and fault. Controlling behaviors are harmful to others. Enabling behaviors are attempts to pacify the controller and prevent conflict, but result in fueling, rather than reducing controlling behaviors.

5. Being controlled is emotionally devastating. However, it is not helpful to view ourselves as victims. We can learn strategies to empower ourselves and reclaim our life.

6. We have personal power when we can exit a relationship, job, or other toxic situations. Optimally, as young men and women, our future goals will include securing a good education and developing skills or talents that generate financial resources. We will then have more options for ourselves and our children. We can carry this message to the next generation as a way to stop the high prevalence of emotional and mental abuse.

7. This book describes attitudes, ways of thinking and behavioral patterns that describe persons who use their power to control and of persons who are controlled. There are exceptions to these descriptions because of individual differences, but exceptions do not negate pervasive, observable patterns.

Chapter 4

How Controlling Behaviors Are Enabled

The most common way people give up their power is
by thinking they don't have any. —Alice Walker

We often enable controlling behaviors as a way to be loved,
prevent conflict, and/or to protect ourselves and our children.
Enabling stems from good intentions, but results in fueling the
controlling behaviors. We comply with a controller's requests because we don't want to be viewed as someone who creates hassles,
or is mean, selfish, and uncaring. However, enabling is helping
the controller to be successful in their controlling behaviors. It is
like buying alcohol for the alcoholic, calling their workplace to
report their illness when it is actually a hangover, and cleaning up
their messes. Our enabling allows the controller to avoid the consequences of dysfunctional and abusive actions. When we enable,
we allow, accommodate, adjust, comply, protect, sacrifice preferences and dreams, and pretend that everything is fine when everything is not fine.

When the word "enable" is used in this book, it includes all of
the following behaviors:

- **Allowing is enabling**:
  - ✓ Being silent when we are experiencing controlling behaviors
  - ✓ Being silent when our children are routinely verbally attacked and unjustly criticized
  - ✓ Failing to recognize that permitting is promoting the controlling behaviors
  - ✓ Going along to get along

- **Accommodating is enabling:**
  - ✓ Changing plans to do what a spouse was supposed to do
  - ✓ Lowering valid expectations regarding the relationship
  - ✓ Accepting a relationship where there is no meaningful communication
  - ✓ Trying to meet the controller's numerous expectations
  - ✓ Not being honest to prevent conflict
  - ✓ Being frugal to compensate for the controller's spending
  - ✓ Agreeing and aligning with a controller's decisions, even if we know they are wrong
  - ✓ Going to another place to get away from the controller
  - ✓ Doing the jobs, errands, and details that are necessary for family life without help
  - ✓ Moving personal items to make room for the controller's items
  - ✓ Internalizing the controller's guilt statements
  - ✓ Doing things for controllers that they should be doing for themselves
  - ✓ Failing to set limits on what is acceptable and what is not acceptable
  - ✓ Contending with the controller's inflated ego

- **Adjusting is enabling:**
  - ✓ Trying to be, do, think, feel and behave according to what the controller wants
  - ✓ Changing personal preferences and interests to match the controller's preferences and interests
  - ✓ Praising the controller's positive behaviors that should be expected in relationships, such as saying, "Thank you for being nice to me."
  - ✓ Being compliant, passive, and not standing up for what we believe
  - ✓ Laughing at inappropriate humor that is offensive to us
  - ✓ Letting the controller take over conversations
  - ✓ Not telling the controller about the children's problems in order to prevent conflict

- **Complying is enabling:**
  - ✓ Doing everything that the controller wants to do to pacify her/him
  - ✓ Being compliant to prevent, avoid, or stop a hassle
  - ✓ Trying to do things perfectly to avoid the controller's criticism and anger
  - ✓ Saying yes when we really want to say no
  - ✓ Teaching children to be compliant, even if requests are unreasonable
  - ✓ Cleaning up the controller's messes
  - ✓ Agreeing to participate in disliked or uninteresting activities

- **Protecting is enabling:**
  - ✓ Keeping the family problems within the relationship
  - ✓ Taking on the responsibility of keeping children quiet so the controller doesn't get upset

     ✓ Not talking about anything controversial
     ✓ Hiding emotional pain that is created by being controlled
     ✓ Not upsetting or irritating the controller
     ✓ Minimizing the emotional damage that is being created
     ✓ Confronting the controlling behavior but then retracting what is said
     ✓ Not confronting dysfunctional behaviors
     ✓ Making excuses to oneself, children or others, for the controller's inappropriate behaviors

- **Sacrificing preferences and dreams is enabling:**
     ✓ Placing more importance on the controller's preferences and dreams than our own
     ✓ Putting efforts and energies into the controller's interests and goals
     ✓ Not actualizing our life regarding our work or personal development

- **Pretending that everything is fine when everything is not fine is enabling:**
     ✓ Crying but insisting that nothing is wrong
     ✓ Pretending to be okay when in emotional pain
     ✓ Saying that we are not angry when we are angry
     ✓ "Psyching up" to be nice, pleasing, and tolerant of ego, self-serving, and controlling behaviors

Enabling dysfunctional or controlling behaviors may have begun in childhood. These were our best efforts to prevent angry or disapproving responses from parents, to be accepted and loved, or sometimes, to survive. When we were children, enabling played out in different ways. Some of us tried to be the perfect child to please parents and are now trying to please a partner. Some of us became an overly self-sufficient child and we are now over-functioning in a relationship. Being good or being invisible were strategies for some of us and now we are trying to do everything right and not bother anyone. We may still be keeping family secrets which are now in our own family. Giving up our old ways of handling life is difficult, because we have lived with our self-designed and unique ways of enabling for a long time. Part of our personal empowerment will be identifying the ways that we allow, enable and give our power away, when we are experiencing being controlled.

Women are socialized to be nurturers, which is a role most women enjoy. However, they enable when they are doing things for people that they should be doing for themselves. When caretakers modify their caretaking, they are likely to be called selfish which is a way controllers manipulate to maintain their benefits. Enablers, whether female or male, have to be confident and deflect this common accusation so they are not persuaded to return to their enabling patterns.

- Claire talks about accommodating and adjusting:

> I slowly began to see how I was enabling by changing my thinking, my schedule and my values to try to make my relationship work. But I never was successful at making the relationship better, despite how hard I tried. Nothing that I did prevented him from putting me down. With the help of books and counseling, I finally realized that I don't have to make excuses for him, change my values and beliefs, stop seeing my friends and family and all of the other things I did trying to please him. I can hardly believe how busy I was thinking about how to make our relationship work while he could care less. Well, at least I no longer think that I'm in charge of fixing our relationship and always making things

easy for him. That is real growth for me!

- Shari describes her experience:

> I love all kinds of vegetables, and when Ed and I were dating, I would cook a lot of different vegetables and he seemed to enjoy the variety. Then we got married and after a year, we are only eating peas and corn because that's the only vegetables he'll eat. So I go along with this so we don't get into a ridiculous argument. And that is exactly what has happened in all the other parts of our marriage. Our communication and sex life is emotionless and boring. He is more focused on the TV than our relationship. I think that the TV never asks anything of him so that is easy for him. Everything has dwindled down to boring, just like peas and corn. I can't believe how different these days are from the days when we were courting!

- Clarice shares her thoughts:

> My controller drives me crazy with his control, but then I also look at his positive side like his work. He works on an excavating crew and sometimes the work is very dangerous. And he volunteers at the fire department and doesn't hesitate to be on a rescue team when there is a fire. So I put up with his demands, thinking that I wouldn't want to be doing a lot of things he does at his work and in his spare time. I am willing to go along with what he wants and know his likes and dislikes.

Twelve Step Al-Anon Groups are helpful in learning to stop enabling emotional and mentally controlling behaviors. Many people attend Al-Anon, even if their controlling spouse is not using alcohol or drugs because controlling behaviors are much the same as behaviors involved in addictions.

Besides being socialized to enable controlling behaviors, women are more likely to enable when they believe that they do not have the option to *exit* a relationship. Usually, the key issues regarding a divorce decision are a) safety, b) the effects on children, and c) financial resources. This brings to the forefront the importance of directing efforts into becoming self-sustaining from young adulthood. Financial resources provide options in life, including leaving a toxic relationship or job. We are less likely to enable or remain in an emotionally and mentally abusive relationship if we can financially afford to leave. With sufficient financial resources we can also make the divorce transition less traumatic for children. We may be able to keep them in their same school and activities, provide learning opportunities and not have to work two jobs, as many single parents have to do to support the family. There is less stress when there is not every-day financial pressure, which children are sure to feel. In contrast, there are people who are controlled to the point of deciding that regardless of what happens to them financially, they leave, believing that they will survive in some way or another. When we are this desperate, the leaving process can be very traumatic for every member of the family.

To review:
1. Emotional and mental control is interpersonal violence. The control addressed in this book is *emotional and mental control* rather than physical, sexual, or extreme abuse, which needs law enforcement intervention.
2. Through education, intervention, and empowerment, positive changes are possible for individuals and relationships that are struggling with emotional and mental control.
3. We are often unaware of how we control or how we enable the control. In contrast, there are controllers who deliberately

inflict emotional harm on others.

4. Controllers and recipients of control have different degrees of responsibility and fault. Controlling behaviors are harmful to others. Enabling behaviors are attempts to pacify the controller and prevent conflict, but result in fueling, rather than reducing controlling behaviors.

5. Being controlled is emotionally devastating. However, it is not helpful to view ourselves as victims. We can learn strategies to empower ourselves and reclaim our life.

6. We have personal power when we can exit a relationship, job, or other toxic situations. Optimally, as young men and women, our future goals will include securing a good education and developing skills or talents that generate financial resources. We will then have more options for ourselves and our children. We can carry this message to the next generation as a way to stop the high prevalence of emotional and mental abuse.

7. This book describes attitudes, ways of thinking and behavioral patterns that describe persons who use their power to control and of persons who are controlled. There are exceptions to these descriptions because of individual differences, but exceptions do not negate pervasive, observable patterns.

Chapter 5

Major Reasons Why We Control and Enable Controlling Behaviors

Every man must decide whether he will walk in the light of creative altruism or in the darkness of destructive selfishness.—Martin Luther King, Jr.

There are major influences that form similar patterns for why we control others and why we enable controlling behaviors. We are unique and complex individuals, having different reasons for our behaviors. The following are major factors that influence the reasons for controlling or enabling behaviors.

1. Cultural socialization involves learning the attitudes, values, and behaviors of our culture that are seldom in our conscious awareness. We are socialized differently as males and females. Though cultural socialization promotes positive values, such as basic pro-social behaviors, it also promotes attitudes and behaviors that are oppressive to people. Although our society is moving toward equality for all, there are still differences in power between dominant and subordinate persons and groups. These power differences create misunderstandings and conflict, which range from negative put-downs to oppressive and abusive actions toward others.

2. Painful childhood experiences: childhood physical, sexual, emotional, and mental abuse or neglect; and/or traumatic loss of a significant person or persons are other major causes for controlling and enabling controlling behaviors. Most people enter adulthood with some degree of emotional wounding from family of origin dysfunction or from experiencing a traumatic loss. When we, as children were made powerless by physical, sexual, emotional or mental abuse, we may repeat the pattern and become an abusive adult controller. Or, we may remain in the feelings of powerlessness and as adults, continue the pattern of enabling controlling behaviors, in efforts to be loved, to prevent conflict and to protect our children.

3. Personal insecurity and low self-esteem are reasons for using power to control others and why we allow people to control us. Personal insecurity and low self-esteem involve beliefs that we do not have adequate abilities to face life situations, maintain a relationship, or be successful. These feelings are buried so deeply within us that they may not be in our conscious awareness. Personal insecurity and low self-esteem are often a result of living in a dysfunctional family of origin, where we were told that we were inadequate and received many guilt and shame messages. Insecurity is revealed when controllers demand to know what their partner is doing, saying, thinking, and feeling. Controllers are critical of others because they are critical of themselves and compensate by making others feel inferior. Controllers are like bullies who feel inadequate or are troubled but act powerful.

4. Codependency contributes to controlling or enabling behaviors. Codependent relationships are "A-frame" relationships, and if one side of the A-frame falls, the other person topples over as well. We try to orchestrate each other's life at the expense of keeping our own life in order. In our codependency, we emotionally wrap ourselves around another person, think we are indispensable, and at times act like martyrs. Or, there may be high levels of controlling criticism, anger and sarcasm in our relationship. We are socialized to be codependent from many sources, including movies and popular songs suggesting that we will have one true love, that we cannot live without each other, and that we will live happily for the rest of our lives. Codependent relationships are so prevalent in our culture that we think they are normal. People say, only partly in jest, "A bad relationship is better than no relationship at all," or, "I am nothing without a relationship!" With these kinds of attitudes we are not likely to be in healthy, mutually satisfying relationships that will sustain over time.

5. Addictions are controllers in our lives: When a substance or activity has control over us, rather than our being in control of our intake, or the amount of time in self-absorbed, meaningless and harmful activities, we are in an addictive process. We have problems in one or more areas of our life that are directly related to our addiction. Both controllers and persons being controlled are vulnerable to addictions. A controller in an addictive process may become even more controlling and a controlled person may be more willing to allow and enable the emotionally abusive behaviors.

6. Biologically based gender differences: At the cellular level, there are differences between males and females. There are also differences in brain structures. There are even different interests when we are infants. Male infants are more interested in objects than people. Female infants respond more readily to the human voice than do male infants. Dominance is fueled by testosterone in men, and males are typically more aggressive than females. Whereas men excel in spatial relationships, women excel in verbal ability and have a keen awareness of emotions and the way that emotions are communicated. Some people believe that the primary reason for a dominant and subordinate society structure is socialization, while others will claim that inequality in power between males and females is based on biological differences.

7. Mental illness and mental disabilities, whether genetic, inherited or environmentally induced, are factors in why people control or are controlled.

8. Other factors, unique to the person may contribute toward using personal power to control others or enable controlling behaviors.

These factors, to varying degrees, explain why control dynamics are so common in relationships. Our biological gender differences, disabilities, and mental illness are reasons that are beyond the scope of this book. The factors addressed are the following:

- ✓ **Cultural socialization**
- ✓ **Painful childhood experiences**
  - ○ Childhood trauma created by physical, sexual, mental and emotional abuse and neglect; and/ or traumatic loss of a significant person or persons
- ✓ **Personal insecurity and low self-esteem**
- ✓ **Codependency**
- ✓ **Addictions**

Cultural socialization

In our formal education, academic subjects were taught to us directly unlike the socialization process, which is covert and subtle in nature. Cultural socialization affects all of us to various degrees and is what we learn from parents, teachers, clergy, friends, and the many types of media regarding behaviors, attitudes, values, and power structures. Our social conditioning is a part of our learning that is usually unknown to us, unless we make conscious efforts to explore what we have been taught. We may erroneously think that our socialization is quite harmless, but among the positive aspects of socialization there are negative and false notions that create problems in our life and in our relationships. As our awareness grows, we will view socialization as a powerful influence that sets the stage for a high rate of controlling and enabling behaviors, which is a cycle that underlies many relationship problems.

Though we are making progress toward a more egalitarian social structure, we are far from achieving what the United States Declaration of Independence sets forth: "We hold these truths to be self-evident, that all men are created equal, that they are endowed by their Creator with certain inalienable Rights, that among these rights are Life, Liberty and the pursuit of Happiness." There are power structures comprised of dominant people with more power and subordinate people with less power. The dominant group is more powerful in defining a culture's attitudes, values, priorities, activities, and behaviors. The dominant group believes that controlling actions are justified and there is opposition to all persons having equal status (Miller, 1987). Controllers minimize the significance of power differences so that the existing inequalities remain as they are, and the unfairness is not confronted. The history behind the Civil Rights Act attests to the fact that changing power structures is very difficult and sometimes requires exceptional acts of courage and bravery to the point of risking and losing one's life.

Dominant and Subordinated Groups

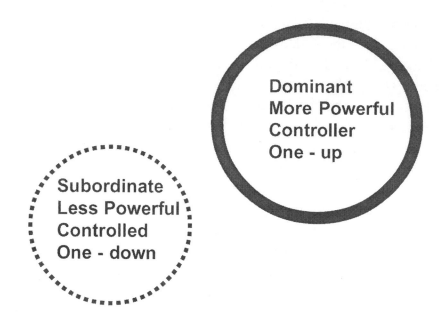

More powerful persons think that they know what is best for the subordinate groups, believing that they have special qualities that subordinates do not have. If subordinate people confront the unequal power structure or resist the dominants' controlling behaviors, they are labeled as trouble-makers, or given other negative and pejorative labels. Dominants often have higher salaries and status, than do subordinate persons. To the extent that subordinate people or groups are willing to conform to the standards and expectations of more powerful persons, they are considered to be well adjusted. This requires them to be submissive, compliant, and dependent, which are behaviors that are contrary to all definitions of positive mental health. A tragic outcome of a dominant and subordinate society structure is that some less powerful persons or groups actually *become* the disparaging descriptors that are promoted by the dominant group.

It is not uncommon that when women demonstrate their personal power, the outcome is criticism from men and often from other women who view their leadership behaviors as aggressive. This discourages the use of personal power in a direct way. As a result, women often use their power indirectly to get around, under, or over men in order to proceed with a project. In administrative positions, where there can be difficult decisions regarding people's lives, such as work lay-offs and termination of employment, women walk a fine line between acting decisively and still being responsive to the expectation that they be emotionally warm and nurturing.

A marriage relationship is often a reflection of society's groups, comprised of a dominant and a subordinate person. When we understand our behaviors in the context of society's power structures, it does not excuse controlling behaviors. However, it provides a reason why controlling and enabling behaviors are so common in personal relationships. Men are given more societal permission to control, and women are expected to be compliant and enable the controlling behaviors. This pattern may be reversed and the female is the person with the controlling behaviors. Whenever there is an imbalanced power structure, there is anger, distance, dishonesty, stress, and distance within the relationship.

Because we often do not realize the corroding effects of control and enabling, many relationships have on-going stress and tension, which children are bound to sense. We may terminate our relationships prematurely, not fully understanding that a major source of conflict within the relationship is control and that relationship recovery is indeed, possible. When both partners are interested in learning and growing, dysfunctional patterns can be changed and the relationship can become more functional and vital. Children benefit as well, when their parents discover ways to solve relationship problems and keep the family intact rather than separate or divorce.

As we grow in awareness, we can recognize negative aspects of our social conditioning and can reject faulty premises. Many of us can create our own ways of relating and living, rather than behaving as a dominant or a subordinate person. We recognize that these cultural directives are not life fostering and set us up for relationship misunderstandings, which spill over into the lives of our children. We can surrender our control if we are controlling others and learn ways to confront emotional and mental abuse, rather than enabling it. We can be our own person, functioning in ways that make moral and ethical sense to us.

- Melody shares her experience of how socialization affected her marriage:

> In my own awareness and growth process, I started out by blaming myself for the problems in my marriage. I was convinced that there was something wrong with me. Then I moved from blaming myself to blaming *him* for our problems. The third phase was concluding that we were both involved. He was controlling and I was enabling the control. We were both set up for relationship problems because of our socialization. We had both taken our marriage vows with good intentions, but when we had difficulties we had no skills to resolve conflicts. The process of understanding control was slow for me. Now I know that neither one of us were mean-spirited. We simply did what we were told based on what we learned from our parents and our culture. We were both set up to have personal and relationship problems and possible failure.

Some people say that societal divisions seem to be disappearing. Others say that there have been changes, but there has been no *real* change. Though the lines may be blurring between the dominant group and the subordinate group, we still do not have equality for all within our society and within our relationships. What we do know is that not all powerful people use their power to control others. There are many powerful and influential members of the dominant group who use their power to advocate for the rights, respect, and dignity of all persons. They use their power to empower others.

The dominant and subordinate power structure is part of our socialization, which influences all of us. Rather than viewing the problem as coming from a partner who is intentionally harming us emotionally and mentally, or that we enable the control because we are inferior and weak, we can view our behaviors within the context of our socialization. However, this does not justify or excuse controlling behaviors. We also know that there are some controllers who deliberately and routinely emotionally and mentally abuse others, which alerts us that more is going on within the person than socialization.

Reflecting: An important part of an empowering process is erasing, removing, and discarding that which is false, negative, and detrimental.

What have I learned from my culture that is false and needs to be discarded?

What unhealthy behaviors are directly related to my cultural conditioning?

My current plan:

Gender differences in communication

Women and men, from the time they are born are treated differently, are talked to differently, and talk differently as a result. Adults learn their ways of communicating as children and there are basic gender differences, which is the research of Dr. Tannen, a professor of linguistics (1990). By listening to how men and women speak, she identified many differences between male and female communication.

When there is a discussion of gender differences in communication, despite the fact that these differences were identified by extensive research, many people become upset and defensive. Men feel attacked and women protect the behaviors of men. In almost the same breath, women acknowledge that the way that men communicate has been confusing, irritating, and hurtful. Men are also puzzled at times when talking to their female partners.

Dr. Tannen's research indicates that most men strive to be independent, whereas most women view relationships as equal and affiliation is important. Men's communication is often competitive with the motivation to be one-up and superior, which creates asymmetrical relationships. When one is directed to, and given permission to be one-up, it will naturally necessitate learning how to achieve and stay in a superior position to others. This is another version of the dominant and subordinate power structures in our society, but is based on linguistic research, rather than psychological and sociological studies.

There are differences between males and females, and there are differences within genders. Not all men are competitive and not all women relate out of a cooperative, egalitarian paradigm. Both males and females may act differently in their work roles than they do in their primary relationships that involve emotional and physical interactions.

Competitive and Cooperative Communication

Competitive, unequal power structure.

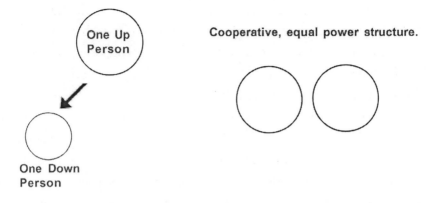

Cooperative, equal power structure.

Socialization begins in early childhood. Boys tend to compete and concentrate on being a winner, and sometimes honesty is sacrificed in the process. They race to be the first in the lunch line, compete in their games, push and shove when getting on the bus, and are sometimes quite physical in their attempts to be first, the best, or the leader. Sometimes they compete to be the class clown or the most disruptive student. They often make excuses when confronted, in efforts to protect themselves from consequences and to maintain a status position.

The center of a girl's social life is having friends which involves being nice and helping each other. Girls' games are usually not competitive, as they often play "let's pretend," "family," or play cooperatively on the playground. When games are played, everyone usually gets a turn. Kindergarten students are learning to key-in their lunch numbers and one girl said to the other, who is struggling with the task, "I'll help you practice punching in your lunch number." In the same situation, boys' communication is more aggressive, such as "Hurry up!" or "Don't be so slow."

Many adult men use a competitive approach, which requires knowing ways to be superior and maintain a one-up status. They strive to be independent in their relationships as their partners attempt to create more closeness. Activities take a high priority with males. Men prefer side-to-side relationships and listen to women less frequently than women listen to men. For some men, listening places them in a subordinate role, according to their perceptions.

Most women are interested in connection and want emotional intimacy. Cooperation with others and affiliation are important. Being superior or winning is usually not a concern in relationships. Women create symmetrical relationships, viewing others as having equal status. Relationships are more important than activities and they prefer face-to-face, close relationships. When there is distance in a relationship, they are uncomfortable and often direct efforts into restoring the connection. When women listen to men, they expect that men will reciprocate and listen in return, but often they are disappointed. Females are often not skilled in the competitive paradigm of men, so find themselves in the one-down position often, which at first is quite perplexing for them. If females use a competitive approach, they are often called aggressive. When less powerful persons increase their awareness, and the one-up, one-down paradigm is understood, skills can be developed to dismantle the power of the one-up, one-down approach.

- Melanie shares her experience:

> I realized that we had different ideas as to what relationship meant. I thought that relationship was being close and being best friends. My priority was relationship and his seemed to be about money. Now I realize that money gave him power and allowed him to fill the male role of being

a good provider. We are both good people but because we communicated differently, we experienced many difficulties within our relationship. He criticized, put me down, and was often sarcastic. He would ridicule my feelings, so I shared feelings with my female friends. We became a relationship of few words. We said 'Hi, good-bye' and the necessary information about the kids.

Neither the male paradigm nor the female paradigm is all right or all wrong. The down side of the competitive model is that it does not work well in personal relationships. It also explains why men who use this model, often hesitate and even refuse to ask for help, admit they are wrong, apologize, or share their true feelings because they perceive these behaviors as placing them in a one-down position. It also carries an expectation of men to be right and convince others that they are right in order to maintain the one-up position. With these types of expectations, it is no wonder that men at times, feel insecure.

For women, trying to maintain a one-up approach seems like a sure way to exhaustion. Most women cannot fathom being in a competitive paradigm that requires them to always be right and win, and think in terms of the either-or option of being one-up or one-down. Asking for information doesn't put women in an inferior position, nor does making amends. Affirming others is not self-diminishing in the women's way of thinking and communicating. In fact, it builds relationships, which is an important aspect of women's lives.

If our ways of communicating work well with same-sex friends, we have no reason to believe that communication would be different in an opposite-sex relationship, but that is what we often experience. First, there may be power and gender differences. Second, more conflicts arise in marriage relationships because there is an emotional and physical connection, there is a considerable amount of time spent together, and what one partner does often affects the other.

Gender differences in communication are influenced by socialization. When experiencing communication difficulties, we often blame our partner, conclude that he/she is being intentionally unkind and wonder if there is any love in the relationship. It is more helpful to recognize that there are differences in communication styles between the genders, rather than think our partners are at fault. However, there are some controlling people who intentionally communicate in ways that are hurtful to their partners and other family members, way beyond the influence of gender differences in communication.

Reflecting:

How have I experienced confusing communication because of gender differences?

How is my controlling, or enabling the control, related to gender differences?

My current challenge:

Cultural socialization regarding stereotypes

Our social conditioning promotes stereotypes, which are a set of directives as to what males and females should think and feel and how each gender is to behave. Stereotypes are not truth, but are presented as truth in advertisements, movies, songs, and other media.

Though we may not be aware of the socialization process and how it affects our lives, we are very aware of what is it to behave like a male or behave like a female. Acting in stereotypical ways results in social approval while acting in ways that are contrary to stereotypical directives, often results in being criticized. Males are expected to be dominant and are given societal permission to control, whereas women are expected to be passive, subservient and enable the control.

A sampling of male stereotypes:
- ➤ Be strong and productive.
- ➤ Be good at problem-solving and base your decisions on logical thought.
- ➤ Don't be emotional and if you have feelings, don't express them.
- ➤ Crying is not okay.
- ➤ Be independent and dominant in relationships.
- ➤ Be aggressive, powerful and conquer.
- ➤ Your opinions are important and are correct.
- ➤ Never walk away from competition.
- ➤ Be bold, brave and in control.
- ➤ Fix things that don't work.
- ➤ Make things happen.

A sampling of female stereotypes:

- ✓ Be nurturing and care-taking of others.
- ✓ Make adjustments and be accommodating.
- ✓ Be weak, adaptable, passive, compliant, selfless, nice, passive, and attractive.
- ✓ Please others.
- ✓ Your decisions and opinions are inferior because they are

based on feelings and intuition.

✓ Don't rock the boat, don't feel important, and don't complain or criticize.

✓ Don't be so emotional.

✓ Don't be angry.

✓ Don't talk about anything sad or too deep.

✓ Don't challenge others' viewpoints or behaviors.

✓ Don't be too intelligent or competent.

Stereotyping is categorizing individuals and does not account for individual differences. Men like some of their stereotypes and there are stereotypical directives to women that are welcomed, such as nurturing others, unless their nurturing is taken for granted. However, there are young boys who are labeled and teased if they do not conform to masculine behaviors, and there are young women acting less intelligent than they are in efforts to be accepted by their male and female peers. Women say they are attracted to men who show feelings, but at times they become uncomfortable when males express deep feelings and cry. Men often say they want to couple with a strong, intelligent woman, yet they may feel intimidated and insecure by these same qualities.

As we grow in our awareness, we move beyond functioning within stereotypical expectations because we come to realize that stereotypes are only constructs which are not based in truth. Many of us, in our society, can make the choice to reject predetermined descriptions and patterns of behavior that do not fit us or that we know are unhealthy.

The dangers in cultural socialization

1. Violent acts are extreme outcomes of a one-up, one-down, competitive paradigm. Physical and sexual abuse, hate crimes, bullying and harassment arc rcsults of the competitive paradigm taken to an extreme, which requires being superior, winning and being one-up. Rather than using power to be superior and over-power others who are less powerful, our current social problems are in need of an egalitarian approach, where honesty, diplomacy, and negotiation are valued and used for achieving respect, cooperation and peace among people.

2. A cooperative, egalitarian power structure does not fit into a one-up, one-down power structure. However, having only two power positions is not reality. The *neutral, assertive position,* which is neither one-up or one-down is *unrecognized* when viewing life through a competitive paradigm of one-up and one-down. People are learning to hold this neutral, assertive position when a controller takes a one-up or one-down position. When the middle position is recognized and accepted, controllers discover that *not* being one-up does not automatically *place them in an inferior*, one-down position. They may even realize that an egalitarian structure is just as valid as a competitive view. Both views are effective when used in the appropriate situation. What is often not always recognized is that for any family, community or society to exist, there must be a degree of cooperation.

3. Viewing society as having dominant and subordinate groups ushers in a permission to use power to control others. Having the most influence in a society, more powerful persons often use their power to control and justify their emotional abuse of less powerful persons. Subordinates are expected to support the behaviors of the dominants. Most white males have the skills of staying in the one-up position, but are also *given* the one-up position by females because of the way women have been socialized. Imbalanced power structures create a "we–they" mentality, with "we" being superior, and "they" being inferior, which separates people.

4. Imbalanced power structures result in communication breakdowns. Anger, distance, dishonesty, fear, and mistrust are generated within an imbalanced relationship. Communication becomes ineffective. Stress and tension progressively erode the relationship. Though many people have good intentions, negotiating differences is almost impossible when there is an imbalance in power structures. However, the break-down of communication will often be attributed to the other person's meanness, stubbornness, or lack of caring.

5. Aspects of our socialization are oppressive. Men are socialized with expectations that they need to be right, know everything, never show feelings, and be in competition with others. Women are socialized into believing that men's ways are superior and that women's priorities and ways of relating have less value. *Both* genders are oppressed if they follow and adhere to societal expectations. Men's growth will involve acknowledging the cooperative paradigm, seeing its value and realizing that the competitive paradigm is oppressive to them, even though it is sanctioned and encouraged by society. Women's growth will involve realizing that they are not always wrong or inferior and that a cooperative way of approaching life, with a value on affiliation is as valuable as the competitive power structure.

6. Being competitive creates a one-up and one-down, hierarchical power structure which causes conflicts in personal relationships. A competitive approach does have an important role in our society. We buy computers at competitive prices and computer costs have decreased over the years. We have made great strides in communication and electronic technology. We love watching or participating in competitive sports. But a competitive approach in personal relationships sets up a power structure of superior and inferior. This unequal power structure causes strife and sabotages personal relationships.

7. Dominant people and groups that use their power to control others, *undervalue, discount, and discredit* people who value affiliation, cooperation, and an egalitarian power structure. The differences in communication between genders can be surmounted with greater knowledge and understanding. The *real problem* is that being dominant in a competitive mental paradigm *requires* devaluing the egalitarian, cooperative style of communicating.

8. If one is dominant and using control over others, compliance is often mistakenly viewed as cooperation. Subordinates are compliant, often out of fear of consequences. Very often, dominants put a verbal spin on compliance and call it *cooperation, when it is actually forced compliance.* This is not true cooperation, which is more likely to happen in an egalitarian power structure.

9. A competitive way of thinking breeds personal insecurity and low self-esteem because it requires being superior, right, and in control. These criteria are impossible to meet on a consistent basis, unless one is being dishonest, blaming others, bluffing, or designing one's own reality. Furthermore, when using a one-up, one-down way of thinking, the empowerment of subordinate persons is viewed as *coming up*, which many dominant persons view as being put in a *one-down* position, since a *middle* position is not recognized. As females and minorities gain more power and visibility in our culture, many powerful persons are threatened because their socialized mental viewpoint is that if they are not superior, they are one-down, subordinate, inferior and powerless. When dominant persons think in this dichotomous way, they will view empowering others as depleting their power or that what others receive will mean less for them. This way of thinking becomes problematic in primary relationships, among groups of people and between countries. The fallacy in this thinking is failing to recognize that the motivation behind empowerment is to achieve *equal* status, and not a superior status. There are exceptions to this when oppressed groups intentionally overturn dominants and dictators who are abusing less powerful people. When we think that the empowerment of others will result in losing privileges and status, it is likely that we will feel insecure, angry, and be resistant to any change in power structures.

10. Because both genders are usually unaware of how they were socialized, the pattern of control and enabling continues to be active. If we do not recognize what we are doing and why we are doing it, the existing power structures are unlikely to change. Persons who use their power to control others will continue their control, often thinking that they are doing nothing wrong. The recipients of control will continue to enable the controlling.

11. Both powerful and less powerful people sacrifice honesty. Powerful people, who use their power to be superior, sacrifice honesty to win and be one-up. Less powerful people are not honest in efforts to pacify controllers and prevent conflict. Being dishonest compromises both controllers and enablers and is contrary to spiritual principles.

12. We lose our authentic self when we accept, think, believe, and behave out of cultural directives. If we promote unequal power structures in relationships, follow gender stereotypes, and adhere rigidly to male and female ways of communicating, we will not achieve personal growth to higher levels of thinking or embrace who we really are, emotionally, mentally, and spiritually. Rather than increasingly becoming self-actualized persons, our personal growth and our relationships are put at-risk. In addition, we become messengers to the next generation, passing on false information, which is oppressing to both genders.

13. We cannot experience wholeness if we function out of social conditioning. Dominant people are socialized out of their feelings, because they are taught that feelings are a sign of weakness. Subordinate people often nurture others at the expense of themselves and are criticized for expressing their feelings. Neither males nor females experience wholeness if cultural directives are followed. Our wholeness requires deleting false information, integrating the best qualities in both genders, and being responsible, authentic, proactive, and evolving human beings. Rather than thinking in terms of separate genders, we can integrate the best of both genders and reach a new level of awareness and wholeness.

Some solutions to toxic socialization

1. We can realize that socialization directives are only constructs and can be rejected. If we have the awareness of socialization and its outcomes and have the freedom and personal power to make our own choices, we can reject the harmful aspects of socialization. We are not going to be struck dead if we reject the negative and life-diminishing directives that we learned from our culture. We can choose to be neither dominant nor subordinate, function in both a cooperative and competitive paradigm depending on the situation, and reject stereotypes that inaccurately describe us. They are only constructs, blueprints, theories, or designs that are set forth as truth, but are not truth. We are not bound to them. Many of us in our society can be who we really are, based on our core principles and values.

2. We can use both competitive and cooperative paradigms for different situations. Rather than thinking that we have to use one or the other paradigm, we can *use both paradigms* and use a competitive approach or a cooperative approach, depending on the situation. Men may have jobs where competition is valued and come home, switch to a cooperative model and be emotionally close as they work and play with their families. Women are more likely to be working cooperatively all day at work and can use their same approach with family. We can competitively play a tennis game, walk off the court and change to a cooperative mode when we are with our families, colleagues and friends. There are many people who are flexible and use both approaches effectively and automatically. It is as easy as behaving differently when we are at a religious service or when we are at a football game.

3. Rejecting life-diminishing cultural conditioning is empowering. Controllers can learn that their personal relationships can be transformed if they surrender their controlling behaviors and cooperatively work together. Both controllers and enablers can grow in awareness, reject life diminishing directives and create a sane, safe and supportive way of life for themselves and for their children.

4. Though both the competitive and cooperative paradigms have value, the female paradigm values affiliation and sharing emotions. On our death bed, we will not be comforted by our possessions. We will not experience peace of mind by thinking about how often we were able to win and/or be superior over others. Rather, we will want to be with the people that we love and who love us in return. This will require embracing the female paradigm and integrating emotional closeness and healthy communication into our lives.

Changes are happening

On an individual level, our emotional liberation and freedom means freeing ourselves from any categories that hinder mental, emotional and spiritual growth. Men are learning to explore and express their feelings and are rejecting the competitive way of thinking. They are working with their partners as equals and are more invested in their families. There are more men in the park playing with their children, more fathers standing at school doors waiting for their young children to be dismissed from school, talking to each other, their wives, and their children. They are laughing and obviously enjoying themselves. They hug their children when they see them. Some of them join with other parents and coach children's sports and car-pool to activities and lessons. These men have escaped the tyranny of cultural directives. They are learning, embracing, and joining women in a cooperative approach that is necessary for healthy family and relationship functioning.

Increasingly, less powerful people, who are often women and minorities, are overcoming societal expectations that encourage passivity and compliance and are developing their full potential. More people are refusing to view themselves as subordinates and take pride in working in human service occupations, taking leadership positions and confronting society's inequities. They are realizing that their enabling helps to sustain the cycle of control, rather than change it. Their expectations are that their partners will actively participate in relationships and in parenting. All of these changes, by both men and women, are beneficial to our children who may learn a new way to relate that is far more life-fostering.

Reflecting:

How have I been adversely affected by cultural socialization?

How are my relationships being affected?

What behaviors are life-diminishing and need changing?

My current challenge:

Painful childhood experiences

Childhood physical, sexual, emotional, and mental abuse and neglect, and/or traumatic loss of a significant person or persons are painful childhood experiences that affect us well into our adult years. Family dysfunction is any dynamic in the family that limits the emotional, social, mental, spiritual, or physical development of family members. In a perfect world, children would grow up in families that treated them as worthwhile and valuable. They would be provided learning opportunities, and given support and encouragement. Their positive efforts and achievements would be affirmed. In this type of family, children learn that their feelings and needs are important and can be expressed, rather than hidden. They develop healthy self-esteem, coping skills and resilience. These children are likely to form healthy relationships in adulthood. In contrast, there are people who emotionally struggle as adults because of the ongoing dysfunction they experienced in their family of origins.

Many books have been written about family dysfunction and many persons could write their own book about how it was, what happened, and how it is now. The dysfunction in our family of origin, combined with socialization and other factors, often set us up to be controllers or recipients of control. This book is limited to looking at typical *responses* to family dysfunction.

We are all different in the degree of the dysfunction experienced in our childhoods. Some of us have experienced minimal family dysfunction, while others have had abusive experiences that are emotionally as painful as physically walking through fire. One or both parents may have been in an active addiction process. Our parents may have been divorced, our daily routines were chaotic and unpredictable, and we may have felt emotionally torn between our parents. Some parents provide for their children's physical needs, but neglect their emotional needs. Some of us had controlling parents, who we could never please. If we had parents who were verbally and mentally abusive, we may have been severely criticized for our behaviors, simple mistakes, appearance, or personality characteristics. If we had parents who were physically and/or sexually abusive or were unpredictable in their moods and behaviors, we may have lived in fear every day and cannot remember ever feeling physically or emotionally safe. For some of us, it takes a good share of our adulthood to recover from the dysfunction we experienced as children.

Many of us brought abandonment experiences into our adult lives. Parents emotionally abandon children by being emotionally closed, unsupportive, working long hours—often out of necessity— or were absent because they were involved in an addiction. As a result, we are like unfinished products, looking for someone to complete us, but when we discover this person, we are often too dependent, too controlling, or we cling to our negative outlook on life which infects our daily relationship interactions. Our mate grows tired of our dysfunctional behaviors, leaves and once again, we are alone. The search resumes finding someone who will give us attention and fill the emptiness inside. It rarely occurs to us that no one else can do this for us. This is an emotional challenge that we have to do for ourselves.

Dysfunction affects all family members and involves control in some form. Rather than take the risk of confronting, family members will enable behaviors that are negative and controlling in efforts to not upset the controller and prevent conflicts. As children, we adjusted to family dysfunction, kept the family secrets and either knew there was something wrong in our families or came to believe that our life was *normal*. Working through family of origin issues involves looking at our experiences, not in a blaming and accusing way, but with objectivity. We were a child like all children who needed love and nurturing, which we may not have received.

We may have experienced emotional and mental abuse outside our families, such as being tormented by a bully, or teased about a disability, our difficulty in learning, being overweight, or being the slowest runner in physical education class. Echoes of these experiences may be heard in our adult life and affect our current experiences and relationships.

Our emotional healing is unique to each one of us, but there are some important steps in a healing process. First, we need to move through our denial because we tend to minimize the effect that adverse childhood experiences had on us. Second, we may still think that we were at fault in some way, but as children, it was the adults who were totally responsible for any type of abuse or neglect we experienced. Putting the responsibility for the trauma created by parents, adults, or siblings where it belongs, clears out the faulty guilt and shame that we may have carried for years. Third, we cannot use our adult minds to make judgments on our younger self because we could not fix or escape the abuse. Nor could we protect siblings or a parent from the abusive behaviors of a dysfunctional parent. As young children, we had very little power in our dysfunctional families and a majority of our energy may have been used for surviving and keeping ourselves functioning as best as we could.

As children, we unknowingly responded to the dysfunction in our families by creating and using *survival strategies.* To cope and survive, we accommodated and made adjustments to the family dysfunction that we were experiencing, whatever it was and to whatever degree it was. We bring our survival strategies along with us into adulthood, packed away in our emotional and mental suitcase that we don't realize that we are carrying. Then we choose a partner, not realizing that our mate is likely to have his/her survival strategies as well. We have no idea what survival strategies are in *our* suitcase or in *our mate's* suitcase. At this point, we only know that we have good intentions, we are committed to the relationship, and we think that love will solve any problem.

Survival strategies that may lead to adult *controlling* behaviors are:

- Being dishonest
- Acting superior and dominant
- Building emotional walls
- Staying in denial
- Procrastinating
- Rebelling excessively
- Repressing feelings
- Being overly independent
- Becoming ego driven

- Creating drama for attention
- Using or abusing chemicals when available
- Joining a group that participates in unhealthy behaviors

Our survival strategies create personal and relationship problems in adulthood. Our emotional healing involves recognizing and giving up our ineffective survival strategies and learning more life-fostering behaviors because:

➢ Being *dishonest* may have helped us avoid punishment as a child, but creates mistrust in adult relationships.

➢ Being *superior and dominant* ushers in controlling behaviors that are likely to sabotage relationships.

➢ *Emotional walls* isolate us from others and hinder our participation in a close relationship.

➢ *Denial* protects us from unpleasantness but distorts reality.

➢ Being *untruthful* will create mistrust within relationships.

➢ *Procrastinating* will diminish our success and disappoint our partners, employers and colleagues.

➢ *Rebelling* may involve participating in high-risk behaviors.

➢ *Repressing feelings* may create emotional, relationship, and physical problems.

➢ Being *overly independent* will create distance in significant relationships.

➢ Becoming *ego-driven* will lead to controlling others for one's own gain.

➢ *Creating drama* for attention will be exhausting to other people.

➢ *Using or abusing chemicals* or being involved in addictive activities will adversely affect our lives and the lives of people that we love.

➢ *Not giving up our group*, such as spending excessive time with drinking friends, will sabotage family relationships.

Some of our survival strategies were more passive and were our best efforts to cope with family of origin dysfunction.

Survival strategies that may lead to adult *enabling* behaviors:

- Being dishonest
- Being compliant
- Being over-responsible
- Staying in denial
- Over-functioning
- Being overly dependent
- Not trusting self or others
- Self-sabotaging
- Trying to be perfect
- Being silent, withdrawn, and isolating, in efforts to be invisible
- Being overly nice

As adults, our emotional healing involves recognizing and giving up our ineffective survival strategies and learning more life-fostering behaviors because:

➤ Being *dishonest* may have helped us avoid punishment in our childhood, but creates mistrust in adult relationships.

➤ Being *compliant* will result in accepting, enabling, and accommodating controlling behaviors.

➤ Being *over responsible* is taking too much responsibility in relationships, such as trying to stop someone from indulging in their addiction. When we are not successful, we feel incompetent.

➤ *Denial* helps to protect us from unpleasantness but distorts reality.

> ➤ *Over functioning* is often a response to a mate who is under-functioning and leads to high levels of anger, stress, and eventual burn-out.
>
> ➤ *Being overly dependent* will be exhausting to mates, friends, and colleagues.
>
> ➤ *Not trusting oneself or others* may lead to emotionally protecting oneself, even from trustworthy people.
>
> ➤ *Self-sabotaging* will keep us from achieving our goals.
>
> ➤ *Trying to be perfect* may lead to procrastination, self-reprimands, and guilt.
>
> ➤ *Being silent, invisible, withdrawn and self-isolating* may lead to depression, low self-esteem, passivity, and a vulnerability to addictions and physical illness.
>
> ➤ *Being overly nice* encourages internalizing the controllers' criticisms and enabling the controlling by accommodating, adjusting, complying, protecting, sacrificing preferences and dreams, and pretending that everything is fine when everything is not fine.

It is not uncommon to behave in ways that are similar to a dysfunctional parent's behavior, but we seldom recognize this and usually become defensive when someone points out, "Your behaviors are just like your father's," or, "are just like your mother's." Despite our intentions of being the total opposite of a dysfunctional parent, we frequently end up displaying the same behaviors, which may not be in our awareness, but is often evident to others.

One of the outcomes of family dysfunction is mental and emotional abuse of ourselves through our thoughts and inner dialogue. When we become adults and are no longer with our parents, we may continue with the criticisms that are echoes of what our parents told us. Our self-talk may be blaming and shaming, which sabotages our self-esteem and confidence. When we realize the ways that we are disrespectful to ourselves, we can start improving our self-talk so that it is more positive. We can become more kind and nurturing to ourselves in other ways as well.

We may have experienced a traumatic loss in our childhoods, such as the loss of a parent, grandparent, or sibling. Some of us were affected by a natural disaster, a parent's deployment, or a parent's chronic illness. We may also have to grieve the *loss of our childhoods* because the natural playfulness and joy of childhood were stripped away when we were young due to family dysfunction. Whatever our loss, our healing involves actively grieving, which involves the stages of denial, anger, bargaining, depression, and acceptance. All of the emotional stages and feelings are natural to us, but if we ignore or suppress our feelings or abuse chemicals, the healing process of grieving is hindered or arrested.

The first stage of grieving is denial and/or shock, and we may not be fully aware of what has happened. Then we move into the next stage which is anger. This may pose a problem because we may not know how to work effectively with our anger. Many adults think that anger is wrong and evil. It may be easier if we think of being *hurt* rather than feeling angry. We can acknowledge and process hurt feelings easier than acknowledging and processing what we think is the less acceptable feeling of anger. In between the stages of anger and depression, we may bargain with ourselves. This is a stage where we ponder on what we should or could have done, given the situation. The bargaining stage requires clarity of thought so that we don't take on responsibility or guilt that doesn't belong to us. After the bargaining stage, depression is experienced. Eventually, we have some degree of emotional relief by accepting and making some semblance of peace with the loss.

A part of our healing is forgiving those who have harmed us. This requires moving beyond our feelings of hurt, resentments, and anger. It might take a long time before we are able to truly forgive.

We know that we have truly forgiven when we have no negative emotional reaction upon encountering the person or having passing thoughts about the person. There is not a stir of anger or resentment. It is like meeting a stranger that we are able to greet pleasantly.

We are all unique in the depth of our emotional wounds, but we are all in need of emotional and mental healing. Making a commitment to do whatever it takes to recover is respecting and taking care of ourselves. We will know that we are on the right path when we realize that we are learning to love ourselves, are experiencing more peaceful days, and are reaching out to others in love and kindness.

Reflecting:

What emotional pain from childhood is affecting my current behaviors?

What survival strategies am I using?

Are they working for me?

My current challenge:

Personal insecurity and low self-esteem

Personal insecurity, which is usually combined with low self-esteem, is another major reason for using personal power to control others or enable the control. Insecurity and low self-esteem are the feelings of being inadequate or lacking in competency to meet the challenges of life, including forming and sustaining relationships. If we grew up in a dysfunctional family that was abusive and chaotic, we were likely to become anxious and insecure because there was no way to predict what was going to happen to us and members of our family. We may have reacted to the family dysfunction by acting tough, building emotional walls for protection, misbehaving to get attention, and attempting to control whatever we could control. Or we may have taken on the insecurity and low self-esteem of a parent who was a recipient of control, which left us thinking that we had to contend with controlling behaviors to be loved and pacify the controller in efforts to prevent conflict.

Our self-esteem was fostered or diminished in our families of origin. We may have had experiences when we were young, where we concluded that we were not OK, were unworthy, and could do nothing right. We may have tried to earn self-esteem by trying to be perfect, pleasing others, not being a bother to busy parents and being good. We may have been bullied, had difficulty learning, or didn't dress as well as the other students in school. All of these types of experiences are detrimental to our self-esteem. Some children are never encouraged to celebrate their successes or feel good about themselves.

As insecure *controllers* with low self-esteem, we:
- Are selfishly driven to control others to get what we want
- Surround ourselves with possessions to feel more secure
- Demand constant attention from other people
- Are driven by an out-of-control ego
- Are often jealous
- Are vulnerable to addictions or addictive activities
- Steal energy from others
- Act powerful by controlling others
- Take advantage of passive, compliant, and nice people

As insecure *enablers* with low self-esteem we:

- Are passive and compliant
- Go along to get along
- Enable controlling behaviors in attempts to receive love and approval
- Give our energy to a controller at the expense of ourselves
- Are vulnerable to addictions or addictive activities
- Internalize controller's critical statements
- Stay too long in abusive relationships

Inflated egos are attempts to cover up insecurity and low self-esteem

An out-of-control ego may begin with a belief that we are inferior, unworthy, and unimportant. As children, we may have learned this from parents or other adults. This emotional deficit is often covered up by swinging the pendulum to the opposite side and becoming grandiose, self-serving, and controlling. Our inflated ego also promotes dysfunctional ways of thinking, feeling, and behaving. We think that being superior to others is legitimate and important so we justify our controlling behaviors.

Inflated egos display themselves with "all-about-me" statements and actions. They direct us to resist our feelings. By criticizing and discounting others we feel superior. Egos prompt us to avoid difficult emotional situations. When someone triggers our unresolved issues, our ego is reactive and lashes out in angry defensiveness to stop the unsettling conversation. When an unhealthy ego is controlling our lives, we expect others to provide comfort by meeting all of our needs, but we are often unwilling to give what we expect our partners to give to us.

One of the reasons why it is difficult to change ego behaviors is that these behaviors are often successful, so that a partner or spouse *will do* the chores, pay the bills, be sexual, or be compliant to our other requests and expectations which are often unrealistic. However, when the recipients of control start to understand the manipulative control dynamics that are directed by an inflated ego, they will often choose to rebel, become emotionally distant, or leave.

An inflated ego:
- Wants to control and feel superior
- Is fearful and views itself as a victim
- Wants to feel needed and indispensable
- Feels that something can be taken away
- Is prideful, grandiose, arrogant and at times, rude and obnoxious
- Is preoccupied with the self and expects personal desires to be met by others
- Needs constant reassurance
- Usurps others' energies
- Views the self as separate, rather than connected with others
- Feels that one is an exception, so rules and requirements do not apply

A life directed by an unhealthy ego is bound to lead to eventual alienation from others, though we are unaware of these possible consequences. We place hand grenades on our relationship path that we do not see because of our denial. It is only a matter of time before we will experience crisis.

Reflecting:

Does personal insecurity and low self-esteem contribute to my controlling others?

Does personal insecurity and low self-esteem contribute to my enabling controlling behaviors?

What behaviors are life-diminishing and need changing?

My current challenge:

Codependency

We are socialized to be codependent rather than interdependent in our relationships. Our socialization shuffles us into roles that are unequal in power, prestige and value. Below are typical descriptors of subordinate and dominant people. These divisions may be influenced by biological differences as well as societal influences. These descriptors are presented to show how relationships appear to be hand-in-glove fits. Not all of the characteristics are unhealthy, and are embraced by people who function out of their prescribed roles. However, the comparisons in behaviors reveal the many ways that subordinates enable, accommodate, and make adjustments to dominant people who use their power to control others. As a result, relationships become codependent, the power structure is imbalanced and the behaviors of the more powerful group are more highly valued than the behaviors of the less powerful group.

Codependent enablers who take a subordinate role.	Codependent controllers who take a dominant role.
• Are willing to care-take others	• Expect to receive care-taking from others
• Readily empathize with others	• Are less likely to empathize with others
• Are chosen	• Choose
• Focus attention on the relationship and do more of the emotional work in a relationship	• Are less attentive to a relationship and do less emotional work in a relationship
• Are less confident about the relationship, but eventually realize that confronting, detaching, or leaving a relationship is possible	• Are often confident that their partner would never leave them
• Try to be the kind of person that meets the controller's expectations	• Try to influence others so that personal expectations are met
• Are *guilt takers*, accepting the guilt and often acting out of obligation. Their guilt is mostly irrational guilt	• Are *guilt makers*, using guilt to control others to get compliance. Appear to not accept guilt from others, nor do they seem to feel guilty when they emotionally hurt others

• Often underestimate their abilities and overestimate the abilities of their controllers	• Often overestimate their abilities and underestimate the abilities of others.
• Internalize criticism and may not question the validity of the criticism; are less likely to criticize a controller	• Often criticize but become defensive when criticized
• Feel undeserving and are hesitant to ask for help	• Feel entitled to others' services
• Will often surrender personal freedom	• Often take away others' personal freedom
• Allow partners to invade personal boundaries; give away personal energy, and allow personal joy to be stolen	• Invade personal boundaries, usurp energies, and steal the joy from partners
• Are less visible, more passive, and are supportive to others	• Are more visible and aggressive, and expect to be supported
• Are space-makers, taking up little space, often curling arms around the body	• Are space-takers, taking up maximum space, often extending arms out from the body
• Withhold information to avoid criticism and conflict	• Withhold information as a way to maintain power

• Are likely to be less dependent on the controller than is realized	• Are likely to be more dependent on people they are controlling than is realized

Occupations often reflect these descriptors. Many women serve in human service professions and this is their choice and preference. Many men are part of the majority gender that serves in the military defending our country, cleaning up and restoring the environment after natural and man-made disasters, and doing physical labor often in adverse weather conditions. Men work at dangerous heights and in the dark and treacherous depths of the earth. The problem that arises is when the behaviors of one group are deemed to have more value, or the more powerful group oppresses the less powerful group.

Reflecting:

How do subordinate behaviors support the dominants?

How do dominants support the subordinates?

My current challenge:

Addictions

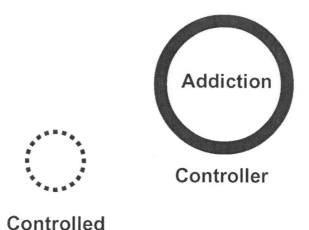

Addiction

Controller

Controlled

Addicted Person

When we are struggling with an addiction, we are the small circle. The big circle represents the addiction, which has the potential to destroy our mental, physical, emotional, and spiritual health. Our addictions or addictive activities are an extreme example of an unbalanced relationship. Instead of being controlled by a person, we are controlled by a chemical or addictive activity.

Addiction can be generally defined as a substance or activity that is creating a problem in one or more areas of our life. The substance or activity has control over us, rather than our being in control over the substance or activity. Our addiction often becomes our "first love" and everything else in life is secondary. Our behaviors are often secretive, and we protect our addiction with lies and defensiveness. We engage in our addiction to escape, fill the emptiness or feel normal. Besides addictions to alcohol and mood-altering drugs, we can be in an addictive process with work, money, sexuality, television, video games, and chat rooms. We can also be addicted in a relationship and wrap ourselves around a person in efforts to fix, control, be taken care of, or have a reason for existing. Being controlled by an addiction can lead to the escalation of our controlling behaviors, as well as making us more compliant and willing to *enable* controlling behaviors. Addictions cause our relationships to become increasingly dysfunctional, and there are high levels of stress and conflict.

The feelings we experience in an addictive process are similar to the feelings of a person who is being emotionally and mentally controlled. We feel powerless, empty inside, and trapped. In moments of truth, we know we are on a self-destructive path that is likely to lead to a crisis.

Reflecting:

Do I struggle with an addiction?

Does my partner struggle with an addiction?

How is addiction affecting my primary relationship?

My current challenge:

To review:

1. Emotional and mental control is interpersonal violence. The

control addressed in this book is *emotional and mental control* rather than physical, sexual, or extreme abuse, which needs law enforcement intervention.

2. Through education, intervention, and empowerment, positive changes are possible for individuals and relationships that are struggling with emotional and mental control.

3. We are often unaware of how we control or how we enable the control. In contrast, there are controllers who deliberately inflict emotional harm on others.

4. Controllers and recipients of control have different degrees of responsibility and fault. Controlling behaviors are harmful to others. Enabling behaviors are attempts to pacify the controller and prevent conflict, but result in fueling, rather than reducing controlling behaviors.

5. Being controlled is emotionally devastating. However, it is not helpful to view ourselves as victims. We can learn strategies to empower ourselves and reclaim our life.

6. We have personal power when we can exit a relationship, job, or other toxic situations. Optimally, as young men and women, our future goals will include securing a good education and developing skills or talents that generate financial resources. We will then have more options for ourselves and our children. We can carry this message to the next generation as a way to stop the high prevalence of emotional and mental abuse.

7. This book describes attitudes, ways of thinking and behavioral patterns that describe persons who use their power to control and of persons who are controlled. There are exceptions to these descriptions because of individual differences, but exceptions do not negate pervasive, observable patterns.

Chapter 6

Common Characteristics of Controllers and Recipients of Control

Freedom is never voluntarily given by the oppressor; it must be demanded by the oppressed. —Martin Luther King, Jr.

There are several differences between more powerful, dominant controllers; and subordinate, less powerful recipients of control. These differences are apparent when listening to communication

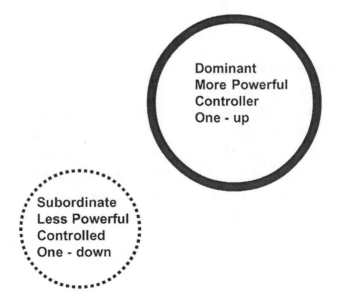

and observing controlling and enabling behaviors. In this diagram, the larger circle represents a person or group of persons with more power; the smaller circle represents a person or group with less power. The larger circle is the dominant, one-up person or group; the smaller circle represents the subordinate, one-down person or group. This creates an asymmetrical, imbalanced relationship. The larger circle, whose perimeter is a thick line, represents a *closed mind*, and emotionally, controllers are usually closed as well. The smaller circle, represented by a dotted line represents an *open mind* and people who are controlled are usually open emotionally, until they learn that it is not emotionally safe to share freely with a controller. The power imbalance illustrated by this diagram involves two adults or groups of adults who should have equal power, according to our Declaration of Independence, but are not treated as equals. The controllers in our lives can be:

- Primary relationships
- Relationships with parents, colleagues and friends
- Dominant groups in society
- Oppressive government, economic, religious, and political systems
- Addictions and addictive behaviors

Listed below are descriptors of controllers and recipients of emotional and mental control. By intently observing and listening to clients for over three decades, certain patterns routinely surface. Had any other therapist—or individual seriously interested in control dynamics—been sitting in my therapist chair or facilitating control workshops, he or she would have observed the same similarities. Those who struggle with emotional and mental control share common thoughts, feelings, attitudes, descriptions of experiences, and behaviors. Controllers also have similar attitudes and have predictable patterns in the way they think, feel, describe their experiences, and behave.

When viewing these descriptors, it is important to consider:

- These descriptors stem from how we are socialized as men and women; dominant and subordinate groups and majority and minority populations.
- There may be biological influences, which is not in the scope of this book but can be researched.
- There are gender differences in ways of communicating.
- When we are single, we may not see ourselves as a person who would control or allow someone to control us, but close relationships may trigger these behaviors because we are emotionally involved and spend a significant amount of time with our significant other.
- We often act differently when we are with colleagues and friends or in different settings than when we are with family members.
- Though males are given more societal permission to control, there are female controllers as well.
- There are always individual differences when describing human behaviors, but exceptions do not negate observable, pervasive patterns.

A comparison of recipients of control and controllers.

Recipients of control who take a subordinate role:	Controllers who take a dominant role:
• Have <u>less power</u> or give away power in what should be an equal relationship	• Have <u>more power</u> or take more power in what should be an equal relationship
• Have an egalitarian way of thinking. People are viewed as equal, often working and playing cooperatively	• Have a one-up, one-down, hierarchical way of thinking and frequently work and play competitively
• Accept a *one-down* power position and accommodate and enable the control. They often feel and act powerless until they understand power and become empowered	• Take a *one-up* power position. They usually act powerful and superior
• When aware of the concept of power, view power as unlimited. Empowering others does not reduce personal power, but enhances personal power	• View power as limited. Empowering others diminishes personal power

• Have *open* minds that are accepting of new information but can be too open and internalize unjust criticisms	• Often have *closed* minds that resist giving up control, accepting differences of opinions, or learning more about dynamics in personal relationships
• Are aware of their *feeling* self and do not rely exclusively on their thinking self	• Rely on their *thinking* self rather than acknowledging and expressing feelings
• Are *emotionally open* and willing to share feelings	• Are *emotionally closed* and less willing to share feelings
• Direct anger inwardly toward the self	• Express their anger outwardly at others, as a way of controlling
• Attribute fault to *internal causes* and blame themselves for not being able to improve the relationship. Often believe that "there is something wrong with *me*."	• Attribute fault to *external causes* and blame their partner for relationship problems. Often believe that "there is something wrong with the *other* person."

• Have more knowledge about dominants, regarding what is pleasing and displeasing to prevent being emotionally and mentally abused	• Have less knowledge about subordinates, often implying that subordinates are inferior and not worthy of concern
• May *look weak* on the outside, but usually have inner strength, which has developed from being in emotional pain	• May *look strong* on the outside, but often lack inner strength
• Often have more power than they realize in personal relationships	• Often have less power than they think in personal relationships
• Experience emotional pain for long periods of time	• May experience shock and acute emotional pain when a spouse leaves because they have not heard prior conversations regarding problems in the relationship
• Are *likely to change* behaviors because of their open mind and being motivated to move beyond their emotional pain	• Are *unlikely to change* controlling behaviors because of their closed minds. Controlling behaviors have been effective in getting needs met so are likely to continue

Common characteristics of <u>recipients of control</u>

Looking at the differences in characteristics between people who are controlled and controllers provides an understanding of how control dynamics continue within relationships and groups of people. When viewing the characteristics of those who function in a subordinate role and are recipients of control, they actually have less power or give away their power in what should be an equal relationship. They often take a subordinate, one-down position and enable the controlling behaviors. Controlled persons are hesitant to learn and talk about power because typically, they have not thought about power, have not incorporated power into their way of living, but have experienced power being used against them. When equality is embraced, power is viewed as unlimited and not diminished when it is used for empowering others. Rather, the power increases.

In their personal relationships, most recipients of control view people as equal. People work and play cooperatively together. Needing to be one-up is not a consideration, priority, or motivation. When socialized into a cooperative way of thinking, the competitive style of thinking doesn't make rational or relationship sense. Recipients of control usually experience good communication with other people, but have difficulty communicating in their marriage because power differences, gender differences in communication and emotions are involved.

Recipients of control often have *open* minds and readily learn empowering strategies. Part of their motivation is a desire to move beyond being angry, confused, and frustrated, which are predictable feelings when being controlled. They are more emotionally open, and as a result run the risk of internalizing controllers' abusive and untrue criticisms. If the controllers' words are heard frequently over time, they may actually *become* the inadequate person that they are labeled. Being emotionally open, they also internalize the guilt that is projected toward them, which is a method control-lers use to get their way. And often, persons who are controlled are too trusting, naively believing that controllers have more knowl-edge, that what they say is truth, and that controllers have their best interests in mind.

People who are experiencing someone controlling them are usually aware of their feelings, are also more willing to share feel-ings, and are often accused of being *too emotional* by controllers. They learn that sharing feelings is emotionally unsafe with control-lers who may use the information in a distorted way to be superior. Recipients of control often come to recognize that their need for emotional connection will not be met by a controlling person. This need is met with their children, where they are loved and needed, and with friends, parents, or colleagues who are emotionally safe and may be experiencing similar relationship dynamics. Sharing with each other is validating and supportive and is a different expe-rience than communicating with a controlling partner. Women and minority groups, like any oppressed group of people, often gather together to share their experiences of being controlled in efforts to gain a better understanding of their experiences. Connecting with others, individually, or within a group is validating. Controllers are often critical of their partners meeting with friends, accusing them of commiserating and feeling sorry for themselves. Controllers may also experience insecurity and resentment when their spouse and children share with *others*, rather than them, not realizing that they create an environment that discourages communication of feelings and experiences.

Persons who experience emotional and mental abuse often di-rect their anger inwardly, which may be a major factor in depres-sion. Anger is internalized because the expression of anger is dis-couraged by the dominants. Emotionally stuffing the anger poses the risk of losing control of internal anger when "pushed to the edge," and then subordinates are called over-reactive, crazy, or other disrespectful names. Another outcome of repressing anger is vulnerability to physical illness.Recipients of control think and feel that they are at fault for relationship problems, which is what they often hear from their controller. They blame themselves for not being able to please the controller and try to be the kind of person that the controller wants, but they are not always clear on what that is, because the expectations change. Usually they believe that there is something *internally* wrong with them, rather than something *externally* wrong. It is part of the empowerment process to recognize that the major cause of dysfunction is not totally within oneself, but is the controlling behaviors of a controlling mate, parent, colleague, or an oppressive social system.

Controlled persons often make excuses and *protect* their controller with remarks such as, "She/he had a bad day," or, "She lost her temper, but that's just like her mother and she can't help it." Less powerful people feel that they don't deserve to set limits and hesitate to confront or leave a relationship that is emotionally abusive. The belief of controlled persons, which is instilled by continued demeaning statements, is that *they* are the most dysfunctional in a controlling relationship. However, they are likely to be *healthier* emotionally than the controller unless the control has been so abusive that it has caused total resignation and hopelessness.

To survive and to avoid punishment, controlled, less powerful people have extensive knowledge about dominants regarding what is pleasing and displeasing, dislikes, likes, and moods. They learn which topics to avoid discussing and what behaviors, attitudes and services please dominant persons. Subordinate people often know more about their controllers than they know about themselves.

Controlled persons are often silent and do not disagree or confront their controllers when controllers speak *for* them, describe them, or make decisions for them because they fear possible repercussions. Nor are they likely to offer feedback or criticize the controller out of fear of conflict or reprimands.

When people are emotionally and mentally abused, they may look weak and dependent on the outside. However, because of their struggles and emotional pain, which can be on-going for long periods of time, they develop internal emotional strength and clarity in their thinking. When in crisis, they discover their inner strength and power, especially when they are protecting their children. Looking back at their decision to leave an abusive marriage and the necessary steps involved, people marvel at their courage, strength, and power, especially when they were protecting their children. We often do not know our capabilities and personal strengths until they are tested.

Controlled persons are open to making changes because they are motivated to move beyond their emotional pain. Having open minds, they are willing to learn strategies to decrease the amount of enabling behaviors, set limits, and create a life, based on their own values. Just thinking about a life that is not directed by a controller is motivating.

Other behaviors of recipients of control

✓ Blocks or becomes numb to inner feelings;
✓ Tries to be heard and taken seriously, but is often unsuccessful;
✓ Works extended hours or participates in other activities that delay going home;
✓ May become less sexually interested because 1). They are verbally attacked with unfair and abusive criticisms or sarcastic remarks—often couched in humor—about their not wanting to be sexual; 2). There is a lack of emotional

intimacy within the relationship; 3). There is stored-up anger toward the controller; 4). They do not feel respected or loved in the relationship; or 5). They do not trust their partner.

Reflecting:

What are my thoughts about power?

How do I enable the controlling behaviors?

What behaviors are life-diminishing and need changing?

My current challenge:

Common feelings of recipients of control

For less powerful persons, *feelings* are expressed far more than *thoughts*. They may be:

- Feelings of low self-esteem
- Feeling like a servant and martyr, like "I have to do it all."
- Feeling resentful, exhausted, discontented, and empty inside
- Feeling trapped or stuck
- Feeling the loss of parts of self, including talents, interests and personal goals.

- Feeling dislike for the controller and wanting to escape
- Feeling that "My primary relationship is the only place I cannot get along."
- Concluding, "There is something wrong with me."

Reflecting:

The feelings I most often experience are . . . .

How do I take a subordinate role in relationships?

What behaviors are life-diminishing and need changing?

My current challenge:

Physical symptoms of recipients of control

- ✓ Headaches
- ✓ Fatigue
- ✓ Insomnia
- ✓ Chronic pain such as fibromyalgia
- ✓ Chest pains
- ✓ Backaches
- ✓ Digestive disorders
- ✓ Auto-immune disorders
- ✓ Allergic responses and skin disorders

✓ Anxiety and panic disorders
✓ Physical exhaustion
✓ Depression is a natural outcome of being controlled. _O_ppression is often the cause of _D_epression. There is always the question about whether antidepressants will help a controlled person. If medication removes negative emotions, we may lose the motivation to change enabling behaviors, confront controlling behaviors or leave an emotionally abusive relationship.

Reflecting:

Am I experiencing physical symptoms that are related to the stress of being controlled?

How can I take better care of myself?

My current challenge:

Experiences of recipients of control

- Ted felt discounted and minimized:

    If I got close to her dysfunction, I got sucked up just like it would be with a huge vacuum cleaner. I would spin around in the confusion for a long time and then somehow escape, look back, and wonder what happened. I felt discounted and minimized, but it took me a long time to figure this out. When I questioned her behaviors, she said that my feelings and opinions were exaggerated and ridiculous. I felt that I was in the relationship for what I could do, and not for who I was as a person. The money I earned was insignificant to what she earned and she ridiculed me often about that. I often wondered why she stayed with me, if I was that bad. I was not treated poorly in my work relationships. In fact, it was the reverse and I would sometimes grow tired of so many people wanting me to help them with information or problem-solving. I always heard that it takes work to keep a marriage going. Well, it takes even more work if it is only one person in the marriage doing the work. And for sure, any amount of work isn't going to work if it's a one-person effort in a two-person relationship.

- Carrie shares her experience of feeling powerless:

I didn't understand anything about control and power in relationships, even though it was happening to me every day. Because of my lack of awareness, I couldn't even describe my experiences. So I can't say I felt powerless because the word was just not in my vocabulary. What I did feel was that something was very wrong and that I felt trapped without options. Now I know that this is being powerless. I was also powerless in not being able to change the relationship so that it had at least some emotional intimacy, which to me is what makes a marriage relationship different from other relationships.

I began to understand my own powerlessness and learned ways to keep my power, rather than giving it away. When I confronted, I did not cry or have angry outbursts. Before, when I lost control of my feelings, I was told I was over-reacting, out-of-control and that I was the problem. The other thing that bothered me was it felt like he was competing with the kids for my attention, but this didn't make any sense to me. When he'd complain about the attention I gave to our children, I had to start setting limits, which was emotionally scary, but he has started doing less complaining about the time I spend with the children.

- Shari shares her experience regarding her self-esteem:

I felt okay about my roles as a mother, in my work, and in friendships. The only place I did not feel okay was in my marriage. I knew I was not living up to all of his expectations, so I thought that there was something wrong with me. I couldn't get out of the negative feelings of being inferior and guilty. As I lost self-confidence and self-esteem, I tried even harder to live up to his expectations and cater to his needs. Sometimes that required getting a lot of things done in a short period of time without any mistakes. I always wanted his approval, but it never happened. It took me a long time to realize that controllers do not give their approval, regardless of what you do, how much you do, or how well you do it. I really had to start trusting what I was seeing and hearing, without distorting it in ways that protected or made excuses for him. Now, after a lot of learning and healing, my self-esteem is back to where it was before I met him. Having children made the frustrations and pain in my marriage worthwhile. I am so very grateful for them.

- Mel shares his feelings of emotional pain:

I was confused because I could not sort out what was really happening. Mostly I felt anger and frustration and that I could never do anything right according to my wife. I kept very busy which I now realize was my coping strategy. I could always find many things that needed to be done so my busyness kept me away from interacting with her.

In the evenings, she would announce when *she* wanted to go to bed and we were all supposed to immediately do the same. Sexuality was an issue. We both work and if we could have related as a team as far as the household chores in the evening, I think it would have made a big difference as far as being sexual. But the usual scene was that she was on the couch watching TV and I was trying to get the household chores done, so I could have a few minutes to relax. In the meantime, as I watched her sit in front of the TV, I grew resentful. So by the time I got to bed, I was angry because there was no teamwork in doing household tasks and I was tired. Because of my resentful feelings, I had less interest in being sexual. Sometimes I would start an argument to avoid sex, or get busy with a project and come into bed late, hoping she would not wake up. When she was nice, I was always suspicious that she wanted something from me and sex seemed to be on the top of her list. I was accused of being weird and not wanting a relationship. Not wanting a relationship, in her language meant not wanting to be sexual.

I learned that I did not have to be a servant or a father or a child in my adult relationship and I had been all three. I was respected at my work and I realized that I should be respected in my marriage as well. I also realized that I needed to take better care of myself and get out of the pain and confusion, so I couldn't keep letting her convince me that I was inferior and incompetent. I started to realize that I was okay and that there wasn't something innately wrong with me. Since I had the courage to leave, I no longer experience emotional pain and unhappiness. When I left, I felt relieved. Now I have to let go of my anger and forgive her when I'm ready.

- Jan shares about being over-extended:

I was very busy taking care of our children; the house, yard, and bills; the accountant and payroll clerk for his business; and studying at night with the kids. Most of the time, I accepted my busy life. I was grateful that I had good health and slept well so that these things were possible. But I had little time to take care of myself.

At some point in time, I asked him for help, but it never happened. I was told that I was making a mountain out of a mole hill because with the household conveniences, it should take only a couple of hours a week to keep the house clean. So of course, the fact that it did take longer than two hours was my fault and I believed what he told me for a long time.

Life was so busy that I didn't think very much about my relationship, but when I did, it felt like pinching a black and blue mark on my arm—still there, still hurts. I focused on keeping all the balls in the air so there wouldn't be any major flare ups. I tried to keep the peace which meant I was compliant, didn't rock the boat and wasn't always honest. I said yes a lot when I really wanted to say no. If I had thoughts, opinions, or feelings, I kept them to myself or discussed them with a friend. I knew all of his expectations, but I wasn't always able to meet them, and if I did, there would be other expectations that would come up.

With the help of therapy, I started understanding what control does to a person. I started moving out of the victim position. I realized I had been enabling and have been codependent as well. Now I understand how I let him make me feel guilty. I have a lot of recovering to do but with each step I take, I feel better.

■ Shari shares her experiences of feeling frustrated:

> I felt a lot of frustration because nothing ever changed. Whenever he needed me, I was supposed to be there but when I needed him, he was nowhere to be found. Every day I started out with a good attitude, but there was usually some kind of hassle. I think I loved him too much and tried too hard. I grew discouraged about the relationship but my love was always there. In the early years of our marriage, I was always willing to go the extra mile, despite the fact that my efforts received no notice or credit. My frustrations and anger disappeared when he was on a golf trip. It was like a hurricane had just taken an exit from my life and I felt free. I loved his absence and dreaded his return because then all of the hassles and tension came back.

■ Cindy shares her experiences of feeling angry and resentful:

> I remember the day when I said to myself, 'I cannot stay healthy with this much anger inside of me. I have to do something.' So I stepped back from him and his expectations, detached, and started putting energy into my own life. I had to get clear on the difference between enabling and caring for others in healthy ways. As I started to confront the controlling behaviors, the conflicts increased, and so did the distance between us. I didn't like the escalated conflict, but I started to welcome the distance between us. He is often like two different people. He can go to church and be cruel on the same day. What he says one day does not match with what he is doing the next day. But this no longer frustrates me because now we just co-exist.
>
> I joined Al-Anon with a friend and am learning to let go of my anger and resentments. I am no longer discontented

and empty. My life is full of people whom I choose to be with, who are healthy and have good energies and who are creative and carry on conversations about the blessings of life. I don't have to be in emotional pain because of a controlling partner.

- Cindy explains how she always felt inferior:

I felt inferior, but only when I was with him. Then I figured out that he was making everything my problem. I started working on not getting hooked into his negative comments or unrealistic expectations. I always thought change was possible. But I was getting less hopeful and knew that whatever I was experiencing now would be what I would experience in five or ten years. And I didn't want to live the rest of my life like the way I had been living. It got to the point where he had nothing that I wanted or needed. My well-being depended on getting away from him. And when I left, he kept telling me how much he loved me. There was no indication of his love through all of those years.

- Ted, sharing his experience of how he felt trapped:

I was so focused on her that I lost me. This wasn't all her fault because I let it happen. Every day she criticized me and was negative about almost everything. I felt trapped. It was a long time before I realized that I did have options and one of them was to leave. But I worried about my children and if they would understand. Then there was my family. I wondered about what my mom and dad and sisters would say, even though they had experienced her control. I thought that they would think that I should be able to handle it or fix what was wrong and stay in the relationship. There was a long period of time when I thought I should stay, and in the next minute I thought I should leave. There came a time when it was no longer a question of *if* I was going to leave the marriage. It had now become a question of *when* I was going to leave. And the answer to that was when my last child graduated.

▪ Susan shares how she compromised herself:

I didn't like who I was when I was around him, which was sullen, silent, and filled with frustration and anger. I kept many parts of myself hidden from him, such as my ideas, thoughts, and spiritual self because I knew I would be ridiculed. When I think about it, these are parts of me that are the most important to who I really am. I learned to never talk about feelings and never complain because he thought that my life was wonderful just being with him.

He was always angry regardless of what I tried, so I started to ask myself, 'Why try?' His anger came out in sarcasm and constant criticism. I would never know what he would attack me for. And one day when he was scolding, I was on the floor and curled up in the fetal position to protect myself from his emotional and mental abuse. I vowed that I would never let him hurt me and that he would never see me cry again. I was emotionally shattered, despite the fact that he never physically harmed me. From the day that I hit my emotional bottom, the fear of losing my mind or losing myself prompted me to make some difficult and crucial decisions in my life. But it took an emotional crisis for me to say, 'No more.'

▪ Beth shares her thoughts about wanting to escape her relationship:

I had thoughts of escaping the relationship since the

day after we were married because I felt something was not right. I knew I would have to be able to financially take care of myself before I could leave, so I worked hard to get promotions, and it felt good to be valued at work. I dreamed of a day when I could escape from my controller. I grew more confident and knew that I would be able to take care of myself and my family.

Denial helped me cope, and so did keeping busy. I would have felt more loss of my true self, but my children were a large part of my life. That's where the caring happened, the working together and laughing. The controller was outside of the emotional circle, never sharing any loving and caring expressions. Though I am a feeling person, I had to start using my head. Instead of letting my emotions drive me, I had to start thinking clearly and being more decisive. I had to reject what was coming from him that was inappropriate, untrue, or manipulative.

- Cindy shares her experiences:

    I had no quarrels with anyone and had no other relationship problems other than in my marriage. With growing awareness I started seeing the controlling behaviors that created problems. It became clearer that I couldn't stop the relationship from continuing to deteriorate. I realized that the problems and the emotional distance in our marriage were not all my fault. I began realizing how he was creating the hassles and then blaming me. I finally started to think my own thoughts, feel my own feelings, have my own opinions, and make choices that were more in line with my values.

- Greg talks about his faults:

    I thought that our problems were my fault and she told me

that often. I asked her to go to marriage counseling and she said, 'We don't need marriage counseling. Just look in the mirror and you'll see the problem.' When I said I was leaving, she wanted to go to marriage counseling, so we started going. But she would think that the therapist was picking on her and change therapists because she didn't like what they would suggest. After seeing four counselors, I knew that there would never be any changes. I finally concluded that everything cannot always be my fault. I stopped listening to her blaming and let it go in one ear and out the other. This isn't my idea of a good relationship, but I guess I'm not ready to leave. I tell my friends that my relationship is routine, like going to the bathroom. I just do it. Most of the time I don't notice what I'm doing but once in a while, it is difficult, uncomfortable and sometimes even painful.

- Sue shares how she felt that there was something wrong with her:

Not just once did I think this—I thought this for several years! That is what my controller said in sarcastic ways so frequently that I think I was brainwashed. I just kept buying into his statements. I thought I had to have a good enough reason to leave like if he would have an affair or if he would physically abuse me. Sometimes I felt like I was right in the middle of a country western song! Then I started to think that I could survive if I needed to make a change, despite being told I would never make it. The most important thing for me was to understand the ways of control and develop a language for my experience. Part of this understanding was figuring out his one-up, one-down way of thinking and talking.

- Joe talks about his wife:

  I actually used to be scared of her because she could go on a rampage like no one would believe. But if she was confronted, she turned helpless. On the outside, she was like a raw onion, hard and poignant. But if you cook an onion, it loses its power and the taste is a lot less strong than the taste of a raw onion. This was just like her and I don't mean to compare her to an onion but in many ways, they are alike.

- Ellen talks about being vulnerable:

  At the time, I didn't think of myself as being vulnerable. I don't really remember if I thought of myself at all because I was so focused on just staying alive in my relationship. But now looking back, I can see my vulnerability which led me right into working too much, drinking too much, and thinking about what a good relationship could be. It took a family crisis for me to finally decide to leave. I realized that I just couldn't continue to live like I had been living. Rather than go down with the ship, I decided to jump off and swim to shore where I would be safe. The emotional damage that I experienced healed over time. Looking back I was mentally programmed to believe that I was inferior, worthless, incompetent, unworthy, and dumb. How he treated me was abusive. I now realize that he taught me how to be single because he was never a true emotional partner. Since my relationship began, I was really emotionally single but had the restrictions of marriage. The only time I was lonely and vulnerable in my life was the years I was in an empty marriage and wanting an emotional connection. After I left my marriage, I never felt lonely again, and at first, this surprised me.

Common characteristics of controlling persons

Reviewing the chart of differences between recipients of control and controllers, controlling persons actually *have* more power or *take more power* in what should be an equal relationship. By taking a superior, one-up, competitive position, an asymmetrical relationship is created. Work and play are often competitive. Success is achieved when the power position is secured and maintained. Power is viewed as limited so controllers often think that if others have power, there is less power for oneself or for their group. When socialized into a competitive way of thinking, it is difficult to understand the opposite style of thinking and communicating which is non-competitive and egalitarian. At times, controllers think they are being controlled by those they are controlling because they are experiencing *reactive* controlling behaviors of the control recipients, such as rebelling and behaving in other ways to upset the controller. When we control others, the control will usually be returned in some form, at some point in time, according to the universal law, "What goes around comes around."

Persons who control others often have relatively *closed* minds and are emotionally closed as well. They often believe that relationship information is unimportant and don't acknowledge that they have things to learn about relating with family members. They often blame others, refuse to take responsibility for relationship difficulties and seldom acknowledge any weak areas within themselves. Closed minds do not hear, distort what is heard, or reject what is heard as false or unimportant. Controllers often create their own reality, which is saturated with denial, self-protective attitudes, and ways of thinking. Information which is challenging to the controller is rejected. Controllers often stay in denial about their own unacceptable behaviors, which for them are viewed as normal and not abusive. They expect that the people they control will have this same view. With closed minds, the distorted reality keeps mentally circulating, having no way of correcting itself with new, more accurate information. As a result, attitude and behavior changes are unlikely to happen. In organizations, there are some managers that are highly controlling, often driven by their egos and a desire to be dominant over and above any legitimate power they have as administrators. Their control manifests itself by being critical, micromanaging others to the point of being punitive, and holding others more accountable than themselves.

Typically, controllers have been socialized to believe that being emotional is being weak, going to pieces, falling apart, coming unglued, or losing it. Because of this, feelings are often ridiculed and minimized. Controlling persons often respond to questions about their feelings with a statement about what they are *thinking*. Their communication is frequently non-emotional, often about sports, the stock market, or tools and procedures that are work related. Because they are less open with their feelings, they can be mistakenly viewed as not caring. Controlling persons, behind the facade of being emotionless do have emotions and many are very caring. Their emotions include feeling rejected, insecure, confused, and hurt, as well as feeling love and concern for others that may be held within and rarely expressed.

Expressing anger aggressively is how controllers often get people to respond to their requests. If anger works, there is no motivation to discover other ways of dealing with issues. Although aggressive anger expressions create damage in relationships, dysfunctional displays of anger may become a habit that is difficult to break. Not only do controllers direct their anger outwards but carry a great amount of internal anger from childhood experiences, irrational beliefs, or hanging on to old emotional hurts.

Controllers *externalize* the causes for relationship difficulties. They believe that both causes and the cures are external to the self.

Controllers also excuse their inappropriate behaviors by using outside factors, such as drinking too much, having a stressful day, or having to work with incompetent people. They are known to say, "I lost my temper, because of what *you* said." Their conclusion that there is something wrong with the other person plays out in many areas of their life, including negative opinions of doctors, therapists, teachers, and even their children. Externalizing fault removes the responsibility to participate in making changes. Controllers are usually more dysfunctional than the person or people they are controlling because of their pattern of blaming others, their strong, locked-in denial system, their emotional self-protection, and their failure to take responsibility for their abusive controlling behaviors.

Controllers have less knowledge about the experience of subordinates than the subordinates have of them. Understanding subordinates carries no interest because controllers view them as inferior and not worthy of concern. Dominants fail to ask for input from subordinates, which results in a poor understanding of less powerful persons' experiences, thoughts, and feelings. However, they often speak *for* other less powerful persons, believing they know and understand their reality and what is good for them. Controllers are like an army of one, surrounding and engulfing who they are controlling and dictating how their spouses, children, and groups of people *should* think, feel, behave, and live.

Typically, controllers look strong on the outside but have less inner strength than most subordinates. Emotional pain develops inner strength, but by staying in denial and blaming others, controllers can side-step their pain for a considerable length of time. In addition, they are not usually motivated to self-reflect nor do they have an interest in developing emotionally.

Controlling persons have power but may not feel powerful. They may think that they are expected to make the decisions and be a major source of the family income, but do not receive the recognition or appreciation they deserve. They are often shocked when a spouse announces that he or she is leaving. They usually have not heard the previous conversations and confrontations or ignore the indicators that the relationship is at risk. Because of denial, intervention in earlier stages of marital dysfunction is seen as unnecessary to the controller and as a result, the relationship continues to deteriorate.

Controllers are unlikely to change controlling behaviors because controlling behaviors have been effective in getting needs and desires met. Their closed minds are often unwilling to learn strategies to decrease their controlling behaviors, which would positively affect their relationships. Change is often viewed as losing certain benefits. Therefore, there is a considerable amount of resistance.

Other common behaviors of controllers

- Inflated ego behaviors
- Dishonest with self and others in order to win or be superior
- Minimal listening, negotiating, and communicating with family members
- Creates problems, but insists that others create the hassles
- Difficulty understanding why people are reactive to their behaviors which they often view as helpful rather than controlling
- Selective memory blocks out when they are emotionally and mentally abusive
- Uses a do-it-my-way approach

Reflecting:

What behaviors are life-diminishing and need changing?

My current challenge:

Thoughts common to controllers

For controllers, *thoughts* are expressed far more than *feelings*:

- Controllers have low self-esteem, which they do not acknowledge.
- Examples of controllers' thoughts are:
  - "I am powerful; I am not dependent on my relationship,"
  - "I do it all and get nothing in return,"
  - "I'm justified in the positions I take,"
  - "I'm right and have a right to control,"
  - "There are no problems in my relationship,"
  - "Expressing feelings is a weakness,"
  - "There is something wrong with *you.*"

Reflecting:

What thoughts are life-diminishing and need changing?

My current challenge:

Physical symptoms of controllers

- ✓ Headaches
- ✓ Elevated blood pressure
- ✓ Chest pains, neck pain, backaches
- ✓ Numbness and loss of balance
- ✓ High risk for addictive behaviors
- ✓ Digestive disorders
- ✓ Unexplainable physical symptoms that hinder routine performance
- ✓ Heart disease

Reflecting:

Am I experiencing physical symptoms that may be linked to my controlling behaviors?

My current challenge:

Experiences of controllers

- Ted talks about low self-esteem:

  I came to realize that my primary focus and main priority was money and the power that money gave me. Money was my self-esteem fix so it was pretty important. When my wife told me she was pregnant, I was upset. I said that I did not want a third child. She told me that she felt that the reason I did not want another child is that I could not put the child on my financial statement. That was a wake-up call for me. I started looking at myself. I had to admit that money was just one of my problems. When my wife spent time with the children, I would be jealous, moody, and resentful, but it took me a long time to get honest with myself and change my behaviors.

- Arvid tells how he tried to hide his insecurity:

  Every day I put on a show that the relationship didn't mean anything to me, but that's not what I felt inside. I didn't like sharing my emotions, especially the ones that would make me look weak or scared. But I really was weak and scared, and I think that's why I tried to control my wife and kids. When I learned how to let go of fear, I started giving up my control, which was very hard for me.

- Bret shares his angry and resentful thoughts:

  I really had a problem with her kids when I was married the second time. I wasn't nice to them at all because I thought they were more important than I was to her. She would always defend them and acted like they couldn't do anything wrong. Now I realize that she wouldn't have had to defend them if I wasn't attacking them and putting them down so much. I know that I wouldn't like her treating my kids like I treated hers. But I couldn't help myself. I kept on doing it over and over again. Now my wife and her two children have left. I think she left because of the way I treated her kids. I don't know because she never told me. Now the house is perfectly clean. The extra bedrooms are empty and the laundry is just my own. I am at a total loss.

- Katie talks about her husband:

    I guess I did control. I just thought that my husband should take care of me. He would call and say he was working overtime so he didn't come home right away after work. I would find his pay-checks to see if he was really working overtime like he said. And I'd check his cell phone to see who he was calling or if anyone was calling him. I don't trust him, but he's never done anything that made we wonder what he was doing. The other thing that makes me angry is when he bugs me about finding a job. The last two jobs I had were awful and people were always picking on me. I felt that I couldn't do anything right. I know I was late a few times but everyone does that. It's like my dad always said, 'Life isn't fair.' My husband just doesn't understand how hard life is for me.

- Damon worries about how he fits in:

    I don't know why I just can't be happy when my family does well. I resent my wife when she is successful, and I am moody around her. My two children have exceeded my accomplishments, and I hate to admit it, but I don't know where I fit anymore. Everyone is telling me how great they are, and I feel like a 'nobody.' I still haven't told them that I'm proud of them because if I am honest with myself, their success has created some real self-doubt in me.

- Darin shares his experience:

  I always thought that everyone else was the problem. And I kept getting farther away from my wife and family, but I didn't know how to fix it. I thought I was doing what I was supposed to be doing because I was working and we had a nice home. But there was a lot of tension. I see now where I controlled, but I didn't really get honest with myself until I started a Twelve Step program. Then I realized that I controlled everything and everyone that I could control. My sponsor had to work hard for a long time to help me get my head on straight. Making amends was really hard to do. I feel closer to my family than before, but I know I have to stay alert so I don't go back to my old ways.

- Joey talks about his criticizing:

  Okay, I criticized her and it probably wasn't right. But she makes it sound like I am abusing her or something. I've never laid a hand on her. But she has turned really cold and uncaring. Sometimes she doesn't even have supper made when I come home and I get upset. She gets home at 4:30 so should be able to put together something to eat. She always takes care of the kids, but they always come first, and I am sick of it. She'd do anything for them, but if I ask her for one little thing, it's a big deal. And I let her do anything that she wants to do. I don't know what is wrong with her—seems like she just doesn't want to be around me. I hope she gets over her moods.

- Joey talks about being like his dad:

  I didn't treat my wife any worse than my dad treated my mother. Sure, I am sarcastic sometimes but I'm just teasing and she never thinks anything is funny. I think I married somebody like my mom, cause my mom was mad at dad a lot of the time because he was either working, playing soft-ball, or at the bar. My wife is a lot like her and is angry a lot of the time, but doesn't get upset with the kids very much – just with me.

- Jamie shares her experience of being a controller:

When my husband said that he was leaving me, it was a big shock. I didn't think there was any problem. I criticized him a lot and though I knew it was wrong, I kept doing it. He is a good person. I don't' know why I kept badgering him. He said that he had tried many times to talk to me about the criticisms, but nothing ever changed, and if it did, it was only for a couple of days. I must not have heard what he was saying or didn't think he was really serious. So when he said he just couldn't take it anymore, had rented an apartment, and was moving out, I was scared and hurt. I begged him to stay and not leave, but he said he didn't trust me to stop the control. I was almost sure he had someone else that meant more to him than I did. Now he is living with his sister who has never liked me.

- Dave talks about his controlling:

I was a big controller but I really wasn't very happy. I thought that my wife was stubborn when she wouldn't go along with what I wanted. I really thought there was some-thing wrong with her because she wanted so much attention. My buddies say that I'm changing and call me hen-pecked, a coward, and that I'm starting to think just like a woman. Well, I am thinking that their relationships aren't very good either.

- Shane talks about his marriage:

She always wanted more from me than I could give or that I knew how to give her, mostly in terms of what she said was closeness. I thought I was close. I'm home every night. When she started being upset every day, I didn't know what to do, so I started working more. At work, I know what I am doing and the more I work the more I get paid. But now she is complaining that I am gone too much. I can't win!

- Ed shares his experience:

I always wondered if she was meeting someone. I questioned her about what she did and where she went. She told me to follow her for a week, and then I would know. She said that I would get bored because she did the same thing every day: work, come home, or do some errands for the family and then come home. The other thing that she did that bothered me was that she was always upbeat and could always figure things out. I remember telling her in a critical way that she could fall into a pile of trash and come out smelling good. She took it wrong and thanked me for the compliment. I wish I was more like her. She has lots of good friends, and I resent them. I told her once to go marry her friends.

- Sheldon shares his experience:

She always complains when I work late or when I have to spend some time doing errands. I'm supposed to always be home if I'm not working. But when I get home there is no conversation. She greets the dog with a 'Hi!' and a pat on the head, but with me there is barely a 'Hello.' So then I wonder why I needed to get home because it is like I don't exist when I get there.

Chapter 7

Communication

The most basic and powerful way to connect to another person is to listen. Just listen. Perhaps the most important thing we ever give each other is our attention.—Rachel Naomi Remen, physician, author

Few of us took educational classes on how to communicate, despite the fact that we communicate almost every day in many situations and settings. When we are speaking, our communication is not only with our words, but how the words are spoken and our body language. Good communication requires commitment, time, full attention, and continuing practice. Communication break-downs are caused by communication errors, including not listening; taking a superior, one-up position; blaming; interrupting; taking over the conversation; and not being honest.

Effective communication involves speaking on different levels. Each level has a certain style and purpose:

Levels of communication

1. **Social:** Social communication is important for connecting with others, and is friendly, polite, and respectful. There is little disclosure of feelings, personal ideas, or goals. It includes greetings such as "Good morning!" and "Have a great day!"

2. **Information sharing:** This level of communication involves sharing facts and information, such as providing directions and discussing the plans regarding children's schedules, the grocery list, or other non-emotional topics.

3. **Sharing feelings:** This level of communication requires being aware of one's feelings and being willing to share emotions, which creates a deeper relationship than we have with general acquaintances. We learn from experience to share with trustworthy people in our lives so that our thoughts and feelings are welcomed and respected and there is no minimizing, teasing, or judging.

4. **Emotional risk-taking:** Deeper self-disclosure occurs at this level. We may feel vulnerable because we are taking a risk when we discuss our feelings about important relationship issues, which may create conflict. On this level, we may also share personal information, feelings that may not be readily accepted by others, internal emotional struggles, or personal decisions. Though this type of communication usually takes place with people we trust, there are times when we make disclosures with emotionally unsafe people and are ridiculed, or the information is used against us.

5. **Nonverbal communication:** This communication is expressed through facial expressions and body positions and movements. Body language can communicate many feelings including anger, boredom, disagreement, love, caring,

empathy, and joy. Nonverbal communication also happens when people are on the same wave-length and can intuitively sense what the other person is feeling and thinking.

We usually speak on the level we have been spoken to and also have a sense of what type of communication is comfortable to the other person. We do not share our deepest feelings in response to a social greeting, such as "Hi, how are you?" The exception is if the person is very close to us. We have our deeper conversations in private settings with a trusted person. Likewise, if someone is talking about their feelings on level three because they trust us, it is inappropriate to respond with a social statement or factual information, as is communicated in levels one and two.

When women talk to their women friends, they communicate on all levels and often on level three. This level creates bonding and this is one of the reasons why women place a high value on their friendships. Men often have friendships that do not involve sharing deep feelings and because of this, they often have a poor understanding of women's friendships. Women will say that the only reason they are able to stay in an emotionless marriage is with the help of their friends, because with their friends, there is mutual sharing of feelings, which results in bonding together, along with emotional support.

Our socialization influences our communication. Most men's comfort zone is levels one and two, whereas many women communicate on all levels. Men often communicate on all levels during courtship, but slowly return to levels one and two: social communication and information sharing. This poses a problem because it is levels three and four where emotional bonding takes place, which is important to women who have been socialized to value affiliation. Social interactions and sharing information (Levels 1 and 2) are important ways of communicating, but do not create and sustain relationships that are of special importance to us. Levels one and two are ways we communicate to colleagues, supervisors, sales persons, and customers.

For people who are uncomfortable or not interested in talking about feelings, there are ways of ending communications on level three and four. Diverting to a different topic, or using trite phrases such as, "Well, it will be better tomorrow," or, "You are always too emotional" are ways of shutting down the communication and forcing movement toward more comfortable, unemotional topics such as sports or the weather. Closing off communication is a way of controlling another person by the way we communicate.

The levels of communication also help to explain one of the reasons for different levels of sexual interest. Emotional bonding occurs on levels three and four, which is not the type of communication that most males prefer. Without emotional intimacy, most women experience sexual activity as only physical, without emotional meaning, and their interest in being sexual declines. An insightful cartoonist observed this dynamic and drew a husband and wife holding up signs. The husband's sign read, "No sex, no emotional relationship" and the wife's sign read, "No emotional relationship, no sex." This coincides with the common belief that men have sexual affairs and women have emotional affairs. And, as with any description of human behavior, there are exceptions.

■ Claire talks about communication in her relationship:

> I feel closer to people when the conversations involve sharing ideas or feelings. However, my marriage was on communication levels one and two, which left me feeling disconnected from him. When I was talking about feelings, he would pull me up to level two by discounting my feelings. The levels that he likes are the way I talk to a waitress or sales clerk and there is no real connection in these

relationships. Since levels three and four were non-existent in our communication as husband and wife, I increasingly felt like I was living with a person I should know, but really didn't know.

However, when I shared with him that I was leaving the relationship, this totally reversed. He wanted to talk feelings and I was not interested in communicating on a deep level. In the past, I wanted to share feelings and he refused to listen or talk, but now *he* wanted to share feelings. I was tired of my painful feelings and wanted to move on. So I purposefully used *his* tactics to keep us communicating on levels one and two. When he started talking about his feelings, I changed the topic or made a comment to end the conversation, like, 'I know you'll be okay.' I wanted to stay away from feelings, and I didn't want him thinking that there was any chance that I was coming back and being in a relationship with him. So I just kept avoiding any emotional conversations because I know myself well enough that if he would have been nice to me and taken some responsibility for the problems, I probably would have caved in and returned to the dysfunctional relationship.

Women learn to be cautious when sharing their feelings and experiences not only with men, but also with women. They learn that there are women who are receiving benefits from being in relationships with controllers and these women often support, defend, and make excuses for the controlling behaviors. They take offense at information about dominants using power to control in emotionally abusive ways.

There are males who want close relationships like women. They want to share their deep feelings in their relationships and are moving beyond the stereotypical male directive that sharing feelings is a sign of weakness. However, they may be ridiculed by other men when they are interested in sharing emotions and their deeper thoughts. A place where men share feelings and are accepted is in Twelve Step recovery meetings. For many men, this is the first experience of seeing other males self-disclose, share deep feelings, and be emotionally supported by other people. In this safe environment, men's lives are transformed as they open up and share what they have long harbored within themselves.

Reflecting:

Do I communicate on all four levels?

What is my experience when I share deeper feelings?

How do I feel when someone communicates on levels three or four?

My current communication challenge:

Communication requires good listening

Many people think that communicating is about speaking. Listening is believed to be less important, and many of us are poor listeners. Good listeners respect the speaker and focus their attention so that they can really hear the other person. There is no interrupting, criticism, judgments, evaluations, or body language that conveys disagreement or disinterest. Out of respect, we listen and wait until it is our turn to speak.

What most people want is to have a caring person to simply listen to them. They want to process thoughts and feelings with people who will not judge or preach to them. Most responsible adults want to make their own decisions, rather than being told what to do and will ask for advice when they want feedback or someone's expertise. They would like their thoughts, likes, dislikes, frustrations, opinions and feelings to be acceptable communication topics, especially when communicating with a significant person.

- Jake talks about his father never really listening:

> When I talk to him, he usually starts to give me advice and takes over the conversation, so most of the time I just stop talking. He never really listens to me so our conversations are mostly about him. As long as we talk about sports or fishing or things like that, it goes okay. But I can do that with anyone. I would like a deeper conversation with my dad, but I don't think that will ever happen.

Learning better listening skills can have valuable rewards in personal relationships. The following are helpful questions regarding listening.

Are we listening respectfully?

1. Am I totally attentive?
2. Do I let other people know that I am interested in what they are saying?
3. Do I show interest nonverbally through eye contact?
4. Do I ask questions to draw out the other person and learn

more about what was meant?

5. Do I refrain from doing other things while listening?
6. Do I let the other person completely finish and not take over the conversation?
7. Is my body language disrespectfully communicating that I disagree or am disinterested?
8. Do I allow my mind to drift away from what the speaker is saying?
9. Do I refrain from mind reading?
10. Do I really try to understand what the other person means from their viewpoint?

- Chad talks about communication.

  I know I need to listen more attentively even though I may not like what I am hearing. I am so used to interrupting, discounting, pointing out errors, or figuring out what I am going to say before my wife is finished, or I'll get defensive about something and my anger comes out. I know why she isn't talking to me about important things, but it's hard to fix old habits.

- Mary shares her experience of her partner's feelings:

  I always thought I wanted my partner to share feelings, but when he would actually share what he was feeling, especially his sad and insecure feelings, I was very uncomfortable. I listened, but I thought he was really falling apart. I just wanted to take away his pain and I didn't know how. I need to get used to him sharing his deeper emotions. When I am emotional, I know that I'll be fine. I should know that he is going to be okay and just listen to him and ask him how I can be supportive because I don't always know.

Reflecting:

How do I feel when I am not heard?

How do I rate my listening skills?

How can I improve my listening?

My listening challenge:

Communication problems due to power structures and socialization

We may be very effective communicators, but when power structures are unequal, our communication skills are disabled. For dominant people who think in terms of one-up and one-down, speaking is often considered to be the one-up position. When a controller takes a superior position, there is judging, criticizing, minimizing, ridiculing, and offering what are believed to be the right solutions. These controlling behaviors sabotage meaningful conversation. Problem-solving is quite impossible. Partners end up in frustration and often start to remain silent about an increasing number of topics, such as raising children, in-laws, politics, religion, sexuality, and the emotional hurts that are happening in the relationship. These topics are sure to create communication conflict and have no resolution so they are avoided. The outcome is having fewer topics to talk about, which makes a relationship increasingly distant.

When power structures are unequal, men have more difficulty

understanding women's ways of communicating, and women become even more confused about how men communicate. Controlling men expect themselves to be one-up in communications and actions, and women want to be close and emotionally intimate. Men are often not interested in listening to feelings and dislike when women go "on-and-on" about what they may view as trivial problems.

We are not inferior communicators, but men and women are speaking, to some extent, in two different languages, from two different viewpoints and power positions; and with different goals. We are also discouraged from speaking in the opposite style. When women use a competitive and more powerful style of speaking, they are likely to be viewed as being aggressive. When men use a cooperative style, women are often drawn to them, whereas some men will view them as weak and non-decisive.

Our adult responsibility is to learn effective ways to communicate that will bring people together, rather than communicating in ways that are alienating, disrespectful, self-serving, and create unnecessary tension and stress. This requires equal power structures. It will help if we understand gender differences in communication and recognize that when our relationships are egalitarian and the goal is affiliation, we are more likely to be honest with each other and share our inner feelings. Children, like adults, will share and be more honest when there is emotional safety.

Reflecting:

My current communication challenge:

When I communicate with my controller, what happens?

When I am not being heard, what do I do?

My current challenge:

Empowering communication strategies for recipients of control

Communication strategy 1: discovering an emotional language

When we develop an emotional language and use our own voice, we can articulate our experiences, which is self-empowering. Often, it is difficult for us to find the right words to describe what we are feeling. We know something is wrong in our relationships, that we are too stressed or that we have emotions that we can't accurately capture with language. The feelings are undifferentiated and roam around in our minds. When we discover a word to describe the feeling, we can then "pin it down" and make it real to us. Naming the feeling clarifies it. It is no longer eluding us. This may happen through a flash of insight, or we may hear a word and know that it is the exact word that explains our situation. When we name the feeling, we can then work with the feeling. It is ours. We can take charge and make choices as to what we are going to do with the feeling. We may say, "Oh, that's what's happening. I get it. Now I can deal with it."

The words involved in discovering our voice are unique to each one of us but here are some examples:

- Control: I am being controlled.
- Getting hooked: I go along with manipulative behaviors.
- Feeling stuck: I feel like I am a hostage.
- Anger and hurt: I feel angry and hurt when I am being controlled.
- Discounted: When I speak, my listener dismisses or minimizes me.
- Vulnerable: I feel emotionally scared.
- Risk: I'm taking a risk and am not sure what will happen.
- Self-doubt: I am unsure and lack confidence.
- Defensiveness: My partner or I become angry and sarcastic.
- Manipulation: I feel hooked into doing something that I don't want to do.
- Overwhelmed: I have too much to do and too many people depending on me.
- Feeling empty: I feel numb, like a void.
- Feeling used: My partner takes for granted what I *do*, and I do not feel loved for who I am.
- Feeling resentful: I just did something that I did not want to do because I felt pressured.

When we grow in awareness about our feelings, we can put a name on what is happening when we are being controlled with behaviors such as minimizing, manipulating, one-upping, or using guilt to get compliance. By developing our language and discovering and using our own voice, we are more able to identify the controlling behavior and directly state what we are thinking and feeling. We can speak with clarity when we set limits and state that we are no longer willing to be a recipient of emotional and mental control.

Reflecting:

My current challenge:

Communication strategy 2: being assertive

If we are passive, we are not respectful of ourselves. When we are aggressive, we are not respectful of others. Assertiveness is being honest and respectful to both ourselves and others. When we experience controlling behaviors directed toward us, we can make statements clearly, firmly, and directly, such as "No!" or, "What you just said is verbally abusive to me," or, "Please stop manipulating me with guilt." It may be a challenge for us to actually communicate these simple statements without taking them back, apologizing for saying them, or feeling guilty because our controller chooses to have hurt feelings when faced with the truth.

The basics of being assertive:

- Communicate in a neutral, middle power position rather than a superior, one-up, aggressive position; or an inferior, one-down, passive position.
- Set a time and place to speak to the controller.

- Rehearse in your mind or write down what needs to be said. You can also think about possible responses by the controller and mentally prepare assertive responses in return.
- Start sentences with "I," rather than "You," to avoid blaming statements.
- Speak with truthfulness, firmness, respectfulness, kindness, and in normal voices tones.
- Listen as well as speak.
- Be specific about the behavior that is offensive to you by speaking directly, rather than expecting the person to "get the drift."
- Use short sentences when confronting.
- Resist the temptation to end the conversation because of emotional discomfort.
- Stick to the specifics of the current situation, rather than bringing up past hurts.
- Repeat the original statement if the other person becomes defensive, starts discounting what is being said, or changes the topic.
- Go slowly and pay attention to what is happening in the communication process.
- Take a time-out if there is the possibility of an eruption of anger.
- Practice calming inner self-talk.
- Being assertive also means affirming others. Thank your controller for listening and for her/his time.

Communication is a process. When there are communication errors the process breaks down. It is like driving a car. When the wheels fall off, or the brakes don't work, or the engine breaks down, the car is unable to take us to our destination. We automatically stop and repair the car. It is the same with communication. We cannot continue to communicate with a process that is broken down and expect good results. We have to stop and reflect on what needs to be repaired. Did we start attacking each other? Is someone shutting down? Is someone becoming angry? Is our partner not listening? These errors have to be corrected before we continue to share feelings, ideas, or negotiate problems in the relationship.

Reflecting:

What is the most difficult part of being assertive?

My current challenge:

Communication strategy 3: self-advocacy

When communication is abusive, we can tell the controller that we are no longer willing to put up with verbal or mental abuse. At the end of a sentence, we need to drop the level of our voice, which conveys that there is nothing more to talk about. Self-advocacy is using our words and asking for what we need. It is learning to say no when we need to say no, or we can say, "Not now, but I could do it later," or, "I have plans, so I can't do that."

Standing up and advocating for ourselves is likely to be viewed by a controller as being aggressive, selfish, and unappreciative. If we suspect that these accusations will be made, we can be prepared for such statements. We can resolve to not internalize the statements as truth. We can decide whether or not to confront the statements.

Some statements are so off-base, false, and manipulative, that they are not worthy of being heard.

- *About silence:* there is a type of silence that is created because the controller is taken off-guard and has no response, because he/she is faced with the truth. When this silence happens, do not break the silence in order to make it more comfortable for the controller. This is a learned skill in how not to be a rescuer. Silence can be quite uncomfortable but let it take its course.

Reflecting:

My current challenge:

Communication strategy 4: avoiding power struggles

Power struggles occur when there is an unwillingness to negotiate and compromise due to a strong desire to win. Because we don't want to lose or be one-down, we tenaciously hold our position and a power struggle is created. Many power struggles escalate into a shouting match and the only outcomes are anger and emotional exhaustion.

If a power struggle is diagrammed, it is a pattern of one person taking a one-up position and the other person responding with another one-up statement. This pattern continues as a series of one-upping the other person. Voices escalate and body language becomes more intense. The desire to win brings forth many controlling tactics, such as accusations, blaming, and using words such as "always," "never," or "should." Most sentences are started with "You" and are usually blame statements. In a heated argument or power struggle, the rules of respectful conflict resolution are broken; participants verbally attack each other, and the real issue gets lost in the flurry of anger. If the power struggle becomes too heated, the argument can escalate into physical aggression, or in contrast, one of the participants may cave in and concede because of frustration or exhaustion. A solution or a compromise doesn't happen.

Example of a power struggle:

Person A: "You have spent way too much money on that boat!"

Person B: "I bought the boat because it was on sale for almost half price!"

Person A: "It doesn't matter if you bought the boat on sale. You never talked to me about what you were doing." (*voice becomes louder*)

Person B: "Do I have to talk to you about every little thing? Well, give me a break!" (*body language communicates anger*)

Person A: "Well, I'm responsible for the credit card also, so I should know the charges on our card, especially big items!" (*voice becomes louder*)

Person B: "Why are you making such a big deal about this? Do you just want to fight? You are being impossible!"

Person A: "You are so irresponsible and unfair!"

Person B: "And I can never do anything right according to you!" (*angrily walks out of room*)

As in most power struggles, nothing was resolved, but there were a lot of personal attacks, which feel like arrows coming from someone that we care about. This example addresses a real problem regarding spending, but many arguments that escalate into power struggles happen over things of little importance. In a couple of days we often cannot remember what the argument was about. The stress and anger that is generated is almost always disproportionate to the problem. There may be some underlying relationship issues that are festering and rather than discussing the *real* problem, partners engage in power struggles over minor issues.

Though we may resolve to avoid power struggles, we may find ourselves right in the middle of an argument that is on a crash course. At this point, we need to keep in mind that in the early stages of an argument or power struggle, we can either escalate or de-escalate the argument, which requires self-control.

If anyone has been drinking or using drugs, there is no point in engaging in communication because it is likely to end up in a power struggle. We can also reduce the number of power struggles by deciding whether an issue is important. If it is a minor irritation or incident, it is not worth a power struggle. If it is important, both partners need to commit to talking about it rationally and respectfully and agree to solve the problem.

- Ellen shares her experience:

> I excused myself and stopped talking with him because our tempers were close to getting out-of-hand. Then he told me that I was running away from the problem, and I said, 'Yes I am, because this argument isn't going anywhere.' That was the first time I had the courage to confront his comments, and he was surprised. He looked at me and said nothing. The fight was never mentioned again and the problem didn't go away.

Power-struggle tips:

- If a person tries to hook us into an argument, we can keep our cool and ignore the hook. If we become drawn in, the other person is in control.
- We can refuse to engage in a power struggle in front of children or the first thing in the morning before everyone goes to work or school. We don't want our children to start their school day being upset and we don't want negative feelings to bleed into our whole day.
- We can stay calm and de-escalate, rather than escalate the power struggle in early stages.
- Our heightened emotions can take over our rational mind. If this happens, it is important to remind ourselves that if we can't speak in normal and respectful voice tones, we need to wait with the discussion until we are calmed down.
- Validating the thoughts and feelings of the other person is a way to diffuse defensiveness and anger. "That is a good idea," or, "I think I understand you, so now we need to think of how we can resolve our differences" are statements that reduce the tension and increase the chances for successful brain-storming and resolution.
- If verbal statements become more aggressive, the best strategy is to take a break: "Let's take a time-out and have this discussion after we have both cooled down. How about 7:00 tonight?"

Power struggles simply drain our energy, create stress and negative feelings, and nothing gets resolved. Besides having an emotional hangover, there is usually a period of silence between partners who are each stuck in negative feelings that can last for long periods of time. This is not a good use of our personal energies and is not respectful of ourselves or of the person we claim to love.

When we have a re-occurring conflict, each person can move slightly toward the center in their positions. For example, if one partner tends to spend too much and the other person is extremely frugal, both persons can agree to move toward the middle. The changes need to be clearly defined. We can become skilled in conflict and understand that almost everything is negotiable, except for safety issues.

Reflecting:

How can I reduce the number of power struggles?

How is our relationship affected when we argue?

My current challenge:

Communication strategy 5: planning and rehearsing confrontations

Carefully planning what we want and need to say helps us to keep centered and focused. We can write out and edit our writing until it is exactly what and how we want to communicate. We need to be specific when talking to our controller about the mental or emotional abuse. Making it clear as to what we will no longer tolerate is important. Statements can be made, such as, "I am no longer going to be quiet when your controlling behaviors are affecting the children," or, "I'm no longer going to ask permission to spend money on needed supplies for our family," or, "I am no longer going to be worried about hurting *your* feelings when I confront your verbal abuse," or, if the conversation is escalating, "I am excusing myself from this conversation," or, when frustrated, "I am tired of living like this."

Don't be surprised if your controller acts as if nothing has been heard. Controllers' ways of dealing with confrontation might be to ignore what is said, and think that we will eventually settle down and forget about it. Or, controllers may use their pattern of excusing their behaviors by assigning blame to an external cause. If we are confrontational about a situation that was hurtful, they may tell us that something stressful must have happened during *our* day and that we came home and dumped our anger on them. By focusing on external causes, they excuse themselves from taking personal responsibility. If communication ended at this point, the controller did "win" because he/she managed to end an unpleasant conversation, but we also "won" by standing up for ourselves and confronting, even though there was not a totally successful resolution.

Reflecting:

My current challenge:

Communication strategy 6: staying credible.

Staying credible requires not having angry outbursts or emotionally breaking down and crying. When we lose control of our behaviors, we will be dismissed as out-of-control, and we become "the problem." It doesn't work the same for controllers. When controllers get abusive with their anger, they often claim that someone *made* them lose control and often do not take responsibility for their aggressive behaviors.

Staying credible is talking about specifics and speaking in normal and confident voice tones. In all of our interactions with controllers, whether they are a spouse, mother, father, child, or employer, we want to present ourselves in a confident manner, neither superior, aggressive, and one-up; nor inferior, passive, and one-down. By doing this, we will not be giving our controllers a reason to discredit what we are saying.

Regardless of how credibly we confront an issue, we may be accused of creating a hassle. Controllers twist and distort words, and disagreeing with them is often viewed as creating an unnecessary problem. When a controller is confronted, the person who is confronting may be labeled as mean, unreasonable or other derogatory names.

- Melanie shares her experience:

> When he emotionally stomped on me by putting me down, I ignored it some of the time, but when it was important or very disrespectful, I started to confront his put-downs. I learned that it worked better to confront in a monotone voice and keep the confrontation short and to the point. And I usually didn't wait for a response. I just left quietly, after saying what I needed to say in a kind but firm way. When I did it this way, rather than cry or yell, I wasn't discounted by being called too emotional. In fact, he had no words to say.

We can communicate in ways that put the responsibility where it belongs, rather than assuming we are at fault. For example, rather than saying, "I don't understand you," (suggesting we are at fault), it is better and perhaps more accurate to say, "Could *you explain* that more clearly?" Women usually put the blame on themselves. Women will say, "I hit a deer on the highway," and because of feeling at fault, they feel guilty, whereas men are more likely to say, "A deer hit me on the highway." Saying it this way does not generate guilt and is a more accurate way of describing the situation.

Reflecting:

My current challenge:

Communication strategy 7: standing firm in a neutral position

We can observe the way controllers act in their power positions. The *one-up* position is, "I am so strong and I am right." This is an aggressive position. The *one-down* position is, "I am so weak, and you are wrong if you insist that I do something." The result is that by taking a one-down position, the controller manipulates and puts the other person down by implying their inadequacy and then *resumes the one-up position.* Knowing this, we can hold our position, whether the controller takes a one-up position, or a one-down position. If our request or statement is met with defensiveness or anger, which is a one-up position, or a guilt statement, which is the one-down position, we can repeat the same request or statement in the same, credible manner, using normal voice tones. *Controllers often don't know what to do when someone stands firm in an assertive, equal, middle position, which is neither one-up and superior, nor one-down and inferior.* Often, if we maintain our credibility and understand the one-up, one-down dynamic, we can experience much more success in having our statements heard.

- Jane relates her experience:

> My husband would usually drink beer while he was driving. I often worried about his driving because I never knew how many drinks he had had before we got in the car. He always insisted that he drive and that I was making a big deal out of nothing. But I worried about the kids every time we drove with him. I practiced in my mind what I was going to say. One day, when Tim and I were alone in the car, I said to him, 'Tim, the children and I will not be riding with you if you have been drinking, or have beer in the car.' His response was that I always over-reacted, that one beer wasn't going to hurt anything, that he would drink what he wanted to drink, and that I was basically crazy. He was really defensive. [This is a one-up position]. So I repeated the statement: 'Tim, the children and I will not be riding with you if you have been drinking or have beer in the car.' This time he started doing the 'poor me,' [one-down position] and carried on about how I was always telling him what to do and that I had ridiculous demands. I repeated the statement once again: 'Tim, the children and I will not be riding with you if you have been drinking or have beer in the car.' There was a long pause. I didn't break the silence. I could tell he was very uncomfortable. He got out of the car and went into the house. I really didn't know if he would come back, but he did. He didn't bring his can of beer. From then on, he did not drink when we were with him, but still drank in the car when he was alone and eventually was given his third DUI and entered treatment.

> Reflecting:
>
> My current challenge:

Communication strategy 8: asking questions

We can ask questions such as, "What do you mean?" or, "Could you repeat that, so that you are more clear?" A controller often hesitates to repeat a remark because it was abusive, distorted, exaggerated, or untrue. A typical reaction of controllers, when they are asked to repeat what they just said, is silence. Or, they may become defensive because they feel they are being challenged. We can then restate the question. We are conveying the message that we are no longer willing to be doormats to walk on, dumping grounds for their anger, and are holding the controller accountable for what she/he says.

> Reflecting:
>
> My current challenge:

Communication strategy 9: providing less information and fewer apologies

Providing too much information is a common behavior of less

powerful people. When we provide too many details, it sounds as if we have done something wrong. When asked by a controller, "Where have you been?" we often explain how we used our time, why we needed to go someplace, who we were with, and why it took so long. Keeping communications shorter is more effective because we are not taking a one-down, apologetic position and there will be fewer verbal accusations or sarcastic comments that come back at us in an abusive way. It is also a way to retain our personal power by proactively choosing what we want to share. To a controlling question, we can make short statements, such as "I was doing errands." It doesn't hurt to be a bit mysterious at times, rather than spilling out everything that we did, all the reasons for doing it, and making excuses for doing things that do not require excuses.

As recipients of control, we often think that we are the cause of problems because our controllers have told us that we are the one at fault. Because of accepting the fault, we justify what we do and make apologies when we have done nothing wrong, usually to avoid a conflict and restore some semblance of connection in a relationship. Unless we change this behavior, our self-esteem and self-confidence will continue to be diminished. We don't have to feel as if we have to justify the space we take up on the planet, nor do we have to make excuses and apologize for where we go and whom we are with, or be dishonest about what we are doing when there is no reason to be dishonest.

If our controller interrogates us, or makes sarcastic remarks, we can respond with "yes," "no," or "whatever." To a question such as, "Were you with your friends?" we can respond with a "yes," or "no." To a sarcastic comment such as "I suppose you had a great time without me," we can respond with "yes," or "no," or "whatever," or offer no response. We can convey in kind and short sentences that we are responsible adults who do not need a controller to tell us what to do. Controllers' behaviors are about being superior, but if we refuse to play their mind games, controllers are disarmed.

- Margaret shares her experience:

> I felt that I had to apologize for spending money on the kids, being with my friends, working late, and visiting my parents. When I bought new clothes, I would hide them for a while. When I wore the new clothes and he asked about them, I would say, 'Oh, I've had this outfit for a long time,' or I would say, 'It was such a good sale that it made sense to buy it!' I finally decided to be more honest and not apologize for things that I didn't need to apologize for. He gets angry if I am dishonest or honest, so I might as well be honest.

There are times when the decision is made to provide *no* information. For example, recipients of control may implement a plan of leaving the relationship without communicating such intentions. This decision is made to prevent angry outbursts and the possibility of intensified control. This is another reason why controllers are often shocked when spouses leave. Many controllers accuse their spouses of being mean and unkind for leaving abruptly, never realizing that the leaving was planned so as not to have the controller be upset, angry, or escalate the control.

Reflecting:

My current challenge:

Communication strategy 10: refusing to rescue

We rescue our controller when we make an honest statement, but when our controller acts emotionally hurt or offended, whether the feelings are real or manipulative, we retract what we said even though we had every right to talk about our concerns. This is a form of enabling emotional and mental abuse. When we rescue, we give away our power. When we make a statement, we need to leave it as it is. A visual image of this is setting something on a table and leaving it there, without picking it up. Likewise, we do not take back what we said if it was honest and was presented in a credible way.

Another type of verbal manipulation is when controllers accuse who they control of bad-mouthing or being negative when their abusive behaviors are confronted. However, talking negatively *about a person* [bad-mouthing] is different than *describing negative behaviors*, which we have a right to do when we are being emotionally or mentally controlled.

Reflecting:

How do I rescue my controller by retracting what I say?

My current challenge:

Communication strategy 11: talking less and doing more

Rather than talk, talk, talk, which we have probably realized doesn't work anyway, we can start to *talk less and do more.* Instead of complaining that we never get to do what we want to do because of our controller, we can make plans for ourselves and proceed with our plans. If a controller is angry and obnoxious, we can leave the house with our children, if there are children. We don't have to lay out the details of our plan. If our controller has been drinking excessively at a party, we can find a safe ride home and refuse to accompany him/her to a similar event in the future. We can stop participating in meaningless activities or spending time with dysfunctional people. We do not have to explain our decision, lie, make excuses, or attribute our decision to someone else, which are all ways we avoid saying the word "no."

When we are talking less and doing more, we can stop answering the phone or we can excuse ourselves and hang up the phone rather than listen to badgering abuse and false accusations. We can ignore text messages without an explanation or change our phone number. We can stop asking for permission and do our normal activities without an explanation. *Doing* is being proactive; enabling is being reactive.

We have a right to make choices. If we are hesitant about doing what we want to do, we can ask ourselves, "What is my controller going to do, divorce me?" That probably won't happen because the controller is often more dependent upon the person being controlled than the reverse. Besides being dependent, controllers know that a divorce will mean a financial set-back, which they strongly resist, to the point that many spouses end up thinking that the bottom-line of their relationship and their divorce was about money and possessions. They wonder if love was ever a part of the relationship.

Reflecting:

My current challenge:

Communication strategy 12: taking time to respond

Recipients of control think that they have to respond quickly to a question or a request. However, we can learn to say, "Let me think about it," without feeling guilty. We can give ourselves permission to take our time and be thoughtful in our responses. This is keeping our power. We can put a controller "on notice" about a future meeting by saying, "We have some things to discuss. 7:00 tomorrow night works for me, how about you?" This conveys the message that *both* people's time is valuable, not only the controller's time. By setting a time in the future to meet, the controller may wonder what will be discussed and she/he may be more attentive to what we are saying when we meet.

For our own mental health, we have to be realistic about outcomes. We do better if we don't attach high expectations to outcomes when we confront issues, or when the emotional and mental controller makes promises or actually makes small changes. This is not being pessimistic. Rather, we are being realistic. If we have unrealistic expectations, we set ourselves up to take an emotional fall when things don't turn out the way we would like, or positive changes do not happen or do not sustain. Rather than attaching to outcomes, we are wiser to stay neutral, do whatever we can, take one day at a time, and be open to whatever happens in the process. This is a way of emotionally taking care of ourselves.

Reflecting:

My current challenge:

Communication strategy 13: responding with agreement

This involves making an unpredictable response by agreeing with the controller. For example, a controller may say, "It seems like you don't want to be with me," or "The kids are always more important than me," or, "The house is a mess – it looks like you haven't done anything," or, "You sure spent a lot of money on groceries!" Instead of defending ourselves, making excuses or accepting the guilt, we can say, "You're right." This is not what the controller expects to hear from us because in the past we have been protective of the controller's feelings and assumed that we were at fault. The *key* to this strategy is *replying without sarcasm*, in a normal, quiet, and expressionless voice.

Reflecting:

My current challenge:

Communication strategy 14: responding only to the content in a message

We communicate by sending a spoken message and often an unspoken message. The spoken message is the *content message* that provides some type of information. The *underlying message* is unspoken and is often negative, communicated by body language and voice tones, which may be sarcastic, angry, or shaming. Using the image of a clothesline, the clothesline represents the message and the clothes that are hanging on the line represent the unspoken, hidden message. We can turn a simple statement into a sarcastic, disrespectful message by our voice tone, inflection, and body language.

This can play out in two ways: either the speaker is sending the unspoken message, or we are "hanging clothes" or attaching meanings to the statement that may have been sent to us with no undertones and is simply a content message. The *emotional part* of a message is *more likely to receive our attention* than the content—the information and the facts—of the message. The emotional message often triggers defensiveness and anger. However, we have a choice. We can respond to the *content* of the message rather than respond to the undertones of sarcasm, guilt, or anger that are sent in the message.

- Sandra tells what happened:

  We were driving by a car lot and I saw this beautiful red sports car and commented on what a great car it was. My husband became very moody and I couldn't figure out what I said that made him upset. I asked him and he refused to talk about it. Later, he said that I made him mad because I knew that we can't afford a car like that and that I was implying that he didn't earn enough money. He felt like it was a put-down. I was just making a comment about the car to make conversation and was confused at his reaction.

If Sandra was being honest, this is an example of her husband adding an unspoken message to what was being said and reacting to what he thought she meant. This scenario could have worked the other way. Sandra could have made the statement about the car with underlying voice tones that conveyed to her husband that he was inadequate because he didn't earn a large salary, but in this example, she insisted that she had no ulterior motive and just commented on the car that was for sale.

In the story about Sandy, her husband "hung clothes on the clothesline" and as a result, he became angry. This can be reversed, and the message can be *sent* with a negative unspoken message. The following are examples of emotional undertones communicating an unspoken message:

Spoken Message	Unspoken Message
What have you been doing *all day*?	You haven't done anything worthwhile.
I was *just being honest*.	You are inadequate if you get upset; even if what I said was dishonest.
You're *wearing that*?	There is something wrong with you if you are wearing those clothes.
Did you *talk to your friends* today?	You should not talk to your friends.
The kids are going *where*?	The kids don't have to go anyplace.
I thought you would be *finished*.	You are inadequate because the job isn't completed.
I guess it's okay.	It really isn't okay.
Sure, *I'll do it...... sometime*.	I probably won't do it.
Where are the *light bulbs*?	Get me the light bulbs.

And you point *is*?   You don't have a valid point and if
                                       you do, it isn't important and you
                                       are wasting my time.

If we are a receiver of a lot of unspoken messages, we can choose to respond to *only the spoken message* and ignore the emotional part of the sentence. For example, when asked what we did all day, we can calmly say, "The usual." To the remark, "Are you wearing that?" we can respond with "Yes, I like it." If we are unsure of what the underlying message really is, we can ask directly: "The sarcasm in your voice sounds like anger. Are you angry about something?" If we are the sender, we can speak directly and not send emotional undertones in our communications. When we are the receiver, we want to refrain from mind reading, attaching emotional undertones, and becoming defensive because of what *we* attached to the message.

Reflecting:

My current challenge:

Communication strategy 15: being selective when communicating

Being selective involves making conscious choices about *who we want to share with*, and *what we want to share*. Not all people are emotionally safe. With controllers, our words may be used against us and when we experience this, we will naturally shut down. This is usually an automatic response, but also needs to be a conscious choice in efforts to take better care of ourselves.

We also have to be aware of "messengers" who share with others what we have disclosed. Usually the message gets distorted as it travels from person to person and a lot of harm can be done. We learn that it is unsafe to share any significant information about ourselves or our relationships, when we are with people who eagerly pass on to others what we share. Acting as a messenger is adolescent behavior, but in some adult social circles, this behavior is common despite its destructiveness.

Though some people may be trustworthy when we share information with them on general topics, they may not welcome sharing at a deep level. We can sense when we are communicating feelings or ideas that are uncomfortable or boring for our listener and usually adjust accordingly. With special friends, any topic is acceptable and there is reciprocity in sharing. These are the friendships that are emotionally safe, so we can truly be ourselves, explore ourselves, and grow on an emotional, mental, and spiritual level.

Reflecting:

My current challenge:

Outcomes when controllers are confronted

Having a controller hear us and be willing to change controlling behaviors may not happen, even if we have well-developed communication skills. However, just being able to speak directly to our controller is a major step in our empowering process. Confronting controllers is emotionally risky because we cannot predict the outcome. It helps to fully prepare by rehearsing what we need to say. We can help ourselves by keeping our confrontations short and specific. By preparing ourselves, we can remain in control of ourselves, be calm and confident, and say what we need to say.

It helps to think about possible outcomes when we confront, so that we can prepare ourselves. Some possibilities are:

- We may not be heard. We may be discounted and ridiculed.
- We will actually be heard. Sincere apologies may be offered. There is willingness to change the specific controlling behaviors that were confronted.
- Promises are made to change behaviors, but promises have been broken before.
- The relationship returns to the way it was; some slight positive changes are made, or the relationship is even more strained.
- Our controller may have more respect for us.

We may or may not be successful when we confront our controller. However, our confronting means that we have made internal changes and are no longer giving our power away by enabling, allowing, accommodating, adjusting, complying, protecting, sacrificing preferences and dreams, and pretending that everything is fine when everything is not fine. If we have gathered up courage and confronted an issue, regardless of the outcome, we are successful.

Reflecting:

My current challenge:

To review:

1. Emotional and mental control is interpersonal violence. The control addressed in this book is *emotional and mental control* rather than physical, sexual, or extreme abuse, which needs law enforcement intervention.
2. Through education, intervention, and empowerment, positive changes are possible for individuals and relationships that are struggling with emotional and mental control.
3. We are often unaware of how we control or how we enable the control. In contrast, there are controllers who deliberately inflict emotional harm on others.
4. Controllers and recipients of control have different degrees of responsibility and fault. Controlling behaviors are harmful to others. Enabling behaviors are attempts to pacify the controller and prevent conflict, but result in fueling, rather than reducing controlling behaviors.
5. Being controlled is emotionally devastating. However, it is not helpful to view ourselves as victims. We can learn strategies to empower ourselves and reclaim our life.
6. We have personal power when we can exit a relationship, job, or other toxic situations. Optimally, as young men and women, our future goals will include securing a good education and developing skills or talents that

generate financial resources. We will then have more options for ourselves and our children. We can carry this message to the next generation as a way to stop the high prevalence of emotional and mental abuse.

7. This book describes attitudes, ways of thinking and behavioral patterns that describe persons who use their power to control and of persons who are controlled. There are exceptions to these descriptions because of individual differences, but exceptions do not negate pervasive, observable patterns.

Chapter 8

Empowering Process for Recipients of Control

A "No" uttered from the deepest conviction is better
than a "Yes" merely uttered to please, or worse, to
avoid trouble. —Mohandas Gandhi

Empowering involves growing in awareness and learning new
skills. Even though a partner may not be willing to go to therapy, it
is very important for the controlled spouse to access some type of
support for healing and empowerment. This might involve working with a therapist or participating in group therapy. Twelve Step
groups are very helpful and are available to persons in a relationship
with someone who is controlling, whether or not they are involved
in a substance or activity addiction. Controllers have many alcoholic, "dry drunk" behaviors. Twelve Step groups are free of charge and
one can share and hear others' experiences. There are sponsors who
provide support and advice that is based on the spiritual principles
of the program.

The following is a healing and empowering process that many of
my clients and workshop participants have used when they were experiencing emotional and mental control in their relationships with
spouses, primary relationships, parents, colleagues, or work systems.

The steps provide a structure for the process of raising awareness, gaining insights, and changing behaviors. After we have moved out of denial, the steps are not rigid as to the sequence because we often intuitively know what needs to be our next step in our healing and empowering process.

Empowering step 1: education to raise awareness

We are socialized to view men as dominant and women as subordinate. Although changes are happening in our society, dominants are more influential. Their characteristics, behaviors, and interests are more highly valued, and they are typically enabled by subordinates. This creates an unequal power structure in relationships, causing anger, distance, dishonesty, fear, and mistrust within the relationship. Communication becomes ineffective. Stress and tension progressively erode the relationship. There are also biological differences and gender differences in communication, which influence the behaviors of subordinate and dominant people.

Besides socialization, other reasons for enabling controlling behaviors include childhood physical, sexual, emotional, and mental abuse and neglect; traumatic loss of a significant person or persons; personal insecurity and low self-esteem; codependency and addictions. However, any person, including those who are emotionally and mentally healthy, well educated, have no debilitating addiction, and have positive self-esteem, can fall into the trap of a controlling relationship.

Gathering data

Keeping a record of what is transpiring helps us to stay out of denial and provides information on which to make informed decisions.

Typical data includes the date and times of abusive verbal statements or behaviors of the controller, the outcomes of confronting the controller, and what happens when we refuse to agree, comply, excuse, or enable the controlling behaviors. If we experience no change in the controlling behaviors even though we are confronting and no longer enabling, we can conclude that change is unlikely to happen.

Data will give us a clear picture of the emotional dues that we are paying in our relationship. These dues involve the mental, physical, emotional, and spiritual sacrifices that we are making by being in a relationship with a controller. The dues also involve the stress and unhappiness that we are experiencing, values that we are compromising, and personal goals that we are not achieving. Documenting whatever transpires regarding controlling and enabling behaviors provides reality-based information on which to make decisions that affect our children as well as ourselves.

Reflecting:

What am I currently experiencing within my relationship?

My current challenge:

Empowering step 2: moving out of denial

When we move out of denial, we recognize the reality of emotional and mental abuse and clearly see that controlling behaviors are harmful to a person's mind, emotions, and spirit. We stop doubting our perceptions, stop minimizing the emotional damage, stop telling ourselves that things will get better, and stop making excuses for the controller's behavior.

Perhaps people have told us, or we may believe that we *chose* an emotionally and mentally abusive partner, and this may be true, but it is easy to get into self-blame when we think in this way. If we conclude that we actually *did choose* an abusive partner, we have to figure out the reasons for our choice. However, another explanation as to why we find ourselves in a controlling relationship is that there are so *many* controlling people. Because of the way women are socialized, the chances are high that they will meet a controlling male. Whatever explanation fits us, we have to become more aware of control and how to stop our enabling behaviors, in order to take better care of ourselves.

Controllers can be very friendly and outgoing, especially during the courtship stage. Often controlling behaviors start by being fairly benign and infrequent but intensify as the relationship progresses. The effects of control vary, but if our self-esteem is far lower than when we entered our relationship, we can be assured that we are participating in an unhealthy relationship, which almost always involves power being used to control another person. When we move out of denial, we see reality more clearly. We can call emotional and mental abuse for what it is: interpersonal violence.

Reflecting:

My current challenge:

Empowering step 3: shifting the focus

When we are being controlled, we naturally focus on the controller and the abusive actions that are directed toward us. We spend time dodging the arrows that are coming our way, trying to cope with the control, and usually thinking that everything is our fault. Shifting the focus from the controller's behaviors to our own behaviors requires emotionally stepping back. We are then more able to see the dynamics within the relationship more clearly.

Shifting the focus is recognizing that we need to:
- ✓ Realize that we cannot change the other person, but we can change our own thoughts and behaviors
- ✓ Acknowledge our socialization and false beliefs that encourage enabling behaviors
- ✓ Learn to invest our energies into increasing our awareness and changing behaviors
- ✓ Clearly recognize how we internalize controllers' criticisms and enable controlling behaviors
- ✓ Learn strategies to deal with a controlling person

Stepping back and focusing on ourselves is empowering. There may be no change in the controller's behaviors, but because we are more centered, we realize with certainty that we are not crazy, that there is not something innately wrong with us, and we are not the one who is always at fault, as the controller claims. When we shift our focus from the controller to ourselves, we can begin to take better care of ourselves, which is necessary whether we decide to stay with the controller, are indecisive about the relationship, or decide to leave the controller.

Reflecting:

What is the most difficult part of shifting the focus?

My current challenge:

Empowering step 4: recovering from addictions

Addictions create a problem in one or more areas of our life. The substance or activity has control over us, rather than our being in control over the substance or activity. The insanity of addiction involves repeating behaviors that are destroying us. Addictions, similar to what happens when we are controlled in relationships, result in feeling powerless. Addictions need to be addressed before any meaningful changes can be made within ourselves and within our relationships. When we are addicted, we lose our credibility and personal power. Not only are we compromising ourselves and walking on a dead-end path, but our controller can assign all of the relationship problems to our excessive behaviors or our addiction. This does not always play out the same if a controller is in the throes of addiction. A controller may view an addiction as either having little to do with relationship problems or he/she may claim that the relationship is the main cause of the addiction.

> Reflecting:
>
> My current challenge:

Empowering step 5: healing childhood wounds

When we have experienced childhood abuse and family of origin dysfunction, perhaps the best choice to make is starting individual therapy where we will be supported and guided through our healing process. However, therapy is not always accessible or affordable, but there are many helpful books written about recovering from family of origin dysfunction.

If our family of origin was dysfunctional, and we were disrespectfully treated, we may want to keep in mind that parents make wrong choices and may fail us in many ways, but our parents are likely to have carried emotional wounds from their childhoods. Many parents do not read books or go to classes to learn parenting skills, so parents often raise their children in the same way they were parented. If we were emotionally abused as children, we may couple with a mate who is controlling, similar to a parent or parents who were controlling. Or, we may be in the same situation as a parent who lived in a controlling relationship, struggled emotionally, and enabled the control.

Healing our childhood pain involves working through the feelings that we had as children and still may be carrying within. Journaling about the painful experiences in our childhood is a way to start this process. We many want to use the format of how it was, what happened, and how it is now. This will help us get in touch with experiences that had a negative effect on us. As adults, we may feel as powerless as we felt as children and continue the pattern of complying and enabling. We can also journal about the safe and supportive people that were there for us, our childhood interests, special friends, and other positive experiences.

As children, we adapted to family dysfunction by using survival strategies, which we created unknowingly, as was described in a previous part of this book. As adults, our childhood strategies are usually ineffective:

- ✓ Being *dishonest* is not effective in avoiding conflicts, in the long-term. Controllers will create conflicts whether we are dishonest or honest.
- ✓ Being *compliant* will result in accepting, enabling, and accommodating controlling behaviors.
- ✓ Being *over-responsible* is thinking that it is our responsibility to change relationships or stop someone from engaging in addictive activities. We feel inadequate when we are not successful.
- ✓ Our *denial* protects us from unpleasantness but also keeps us from reality.
- ✓ *Over-functioning* is often a response to a mate who is under-functioning and leads to high levels of anger, stress, and eventual burn-out.
- ✓ Being *overly dependent* on others may lead to continued unhappiness, and we become at-risk for addictions, depression, and anxiety.
- ✓ *Not trusting ourselves* leads to personal insecurity.
- ✓ *Self-sabotaging* keeps us from achieving what we are able to achieve.
- ✓ *Trying to be perfect* leads to procrastination, self-reprimands, and guilt.

✓ Being *silent, withdrawn, and isolated* in attempts to be invisible, ushers in depression, low self-esteem, and passivity.

✓ Trying to always *be nice* will result in passive and compliant behaviors, rather than standing up for ourselves and setting limits on what is acceptable and not acceptable.

✓ *Using or abusing chemicals* will add another controller to our life. We repeat behaviors that are destroying us, which is the "insanity" of addiction.

Reflecting:

How are my survival strategies affecting my life?

My current challenge:

Healing our childhood wounds also involves grieving the traumatic losses in our lives. We may have lost a parent, due to death, divorce, or mental illness. We may have experienced unexpected tragedy, such as losing a sibling or best friend to an accident or suicide. Grieving is an emotional process with the stages of denial, anger, bargaining, depression, and acceptance. All of the emotional stages and feelings are natural to us, but if we ignore or suppress our feelings or are involved in an addiction, the healing process of grieving is hindered or arrested. Many people have to grieve the loss of their childhoods because they never experienced playful days with no worries because of dysfunctional family dynamics.

Reflecting:

What emotional pain from childhood is affecting my current thoughts and behaviors?

My current challenge:

Empowering step 6: deleting false and irrational beliefs

Almost all of us received information from our culture and family of origin that was false and irrational. Healing involves unlearning whatever we learned that was not true. When we have the feeling of being inadequate and inferior, it is based on an irrational thought. Guilt also stems from an irrational or false notion unless we have harmed someone, destroyed property, or neglected our adult responsibilities. When feelings are based on irrational or false information, we can identify the thought, challenge it, and discard what is false and life-diminishing.

Faulty and irrational beliefs include:

- ✓ I am inadequate.
- ✓ Other people are better and have more value than I have.
- ✓ I am weak.
- ✓ No one likes me.
- ✓ I am stupid.
- ✓ I should be loved by everyone.
- ✓ Bad things always happen to me but not others.

✓ I cannot make mistakes. Mistakes are bad and show how incompetent I really am.
✓ I am who I am and cannot change.
✓ I should take care of others and do it selflessly.
✓ My value as a person is measured by my accomplishments and financial status.
✓ Change and differences are bad.
✓ I should be able to do things perfectly.
✓ When I fail in one area of my life, I am a total failure.
✓ Other people make my life miserable.
✓ Other people are incompetent.
✓ There is something wrong with me.

These negative beliefs adversely influence our feelings, behaviors, and life experiences. Irrational beliefs need to be deleted and discarded from our minds because they are life-diminishing.

Reflecting: An important part of our empowering process is letting go, relinquishing, erasing, removing, and discarding that which is false, negative, and detrimental.

What beliefs do I have that are false and need to be discarded?

What emotions are created by my negative thinking?

My current plan:

Empowering step 7: recovering from codependency

As recipients of control, we are likely to be codependent. We do almost anything to be accepted and loved. We wrap ourselves around a person in efforts to fix, control, be taken care of, or have a reason for existing. If we are male, we are often codependent on our work. If we are female we are often codependent on our partners. We put our energy into pleasing others, especially our partner, to gain self-worth. We focus and invest energy in our relationship and if it is a dysfunctional relationship, we make sacrifices, in attempts to make the relationship work. We are focused on our partner and are concerned about what our partner is doing and not doing, saying or not saying, and the behaviors that are hurtful to us. We are codependent, not because we are unintelligent or inadequate, but because of how we were socialized and what we learned in our families of origin.

Reviewing the chart of the characteristics of recipients of control who take a subservient role gives us a glimpse of why and how we are codependent. We are socialized into these roles from early childhood. There are certain behaviors that are unhealthy, and there are also qualities that we embrace, such as nurturing and empathizing with others. However, when these positive qualities are taken to an extreme, we become dysfunctional. And when our nurturing behaviors are undervalued and unappreciated, we are likely to become angry and resentful.

If we take a subordinate role, we are likely to be followers. Rather than choosing, we are usually chosen. Our primary relationships are very important to us and consume large amounts of mental and emotional energy. We take more than our share of responsibility to make a relationship work. We are the ones who are reading books on relationships, discussing our relationship with close friends, and wringing our hands because our primary relationship isn't improving in ways that we would like. When efforts fail, we feel like a "nothing" and have less confidence about ourselves and our relationships. It is common for us to think that we have no options until we learn that confronting, detaching, or leaving a relationship is actually possible.

We are guilt takers, accepting the guilt and often acting out of obligation rather than choice. Our guilt is mostly irrational because it is rooted in false notions. As we underestimate our abilities, we overestimate the abilities of our controllers. We internalize criticism and seldom question the validity of the criticism. Our low self-esteem makes us feel undeserving, so we are hesitant to ask for help.

We will often allow our partners to invade our personal boundaries, usurp our personal energy, and steal our freedom and joy. Many of us enjoy working behind the scenes where we are less visible and prefer taking a supportive role to others. We take less space than controllers as evidenced by the way we sit, often curled up with our arms around ourselves. Sometimes this is the way we comfort ourselves from the stress of being controlled and living with a dysfunctional partner. There are times when we withhold feelings and information from our controller to prevent conflict. We are often less emotionally dependent on the controller than she/he is on us, although we may not be aware of this. Controlling marriage partners teach us to be emotionally independent because they are often not responsive when emotional support is needed.

When we are codependent, we are likely to compromise ourselves and feel powerless. To heal from our codependency, we have to challenge beliefs such as:

- I am nothing without a relationship.
- If I can be exactly what my controller wants me to be, he/she will love me.
- If I lose this relationship, no one will love me.

- I have to be really nice and should never be angry.
- Poor treatment is all I deserve.
- I should not be upset about being emotionally abused because it is not physical.
- I do not deserve to have my own feelings, thoughts, or opinions.

As we grow in awareness, recover, and start reclaiming our power, we will be able to reverse these beliefs to:

- I am being emotionally and mentally abused. I can call it what it is.
- I can be who I am and like who I am.
- If I lose this relationship, I will survive, coupled or single.
- I don't always have to be "nice" and can share angry feelings appropriately.
- I deserve respectful treatment in all of my relationships.
- I have a right to have my own feelings, thoughts, and opinions.
- I do not have to be in a relationship to have self-esteem and personal value.

- Jan shares her experience of feeling dependent:

> I always viewed myself as the dependent one in the relationship. I tried to always be grateful that he chose such an inadequate person as me to be his wife. I didn't start the relationship believing this, but gradually, because of his negative remarks, this was my conclusion. I came to realize that I was no longer *emotionally* dependent, but was *financially* dependent on him because we had children. Finally I knew that the only positive changes that I could make were within

myself. This prompted me to return to college, finish my degree, detach from his negativity and go about my own life. When I started moving forward, I felt a lot better and my self-esteem and self-confidence came back. Because I was putting energies into my own goals, I was not focusing on him. I often wondered if my distancing was a relief for him. There was no more pressure on him to emotionally or conversationally participate in our relationship.

In our recovery from codependency we realize that we can use our own principles and standards for living and realize that being partnered doesn't make us more valuable than when we are not in a relationship. We are interested in relationships only if there is mutual participation, respect, good communication, and healthy love.

Reflecting:

What beliefs or thoughts do I need to delete?

My current challenge:

Empowering step 8: communicating with a controller

In an asymmetrical, unequal power relationship where control is active, communicating is a disappointing experience. As recipients of emotional and mental abuse, we can stop blaming ourselves and stop thinking that there is something wrong with us for not being able to make communication work. Even if we have excellent communication skills and carefully articulate our thoughts, we may not be heard; we may be discounted, or we may be accused of creating hassles. However, by *speaking the words we need to speak*, we take back our power.

The following is a summary of the communication strategies in Chapter 7. You may want to review this chapter for the full explanation of the strategies:

➤ Strategy 1: Discovering an emotional language helps us to clearly express our feelings and experiences.
➤ Strategy 2: Being assertive is speaking honestly, with confidence and respect.
➤ Strategy 3: Self-advocacy means confronting controlling behaviors and setting limits on what we will not tolerate.
➤ Strategy 4: Avoiding power struggles is a way to conserve our personal energies.
➤ Strategy 5: Planning and rehearsing confrontations helps us to speak with confidence.
➤ Strategy 6: Staying credible means not breaking down in tears or having angry outbursts.
➤ Strategy 7: Standing firm in a neutral position and using repetition is an effective way to confront a controller.
➤ Strategy 8: Asking questions is a way to make a controller more accountable for what is said.
➤ Strategy 9: Providing less information and fewer apologies are ways of keeping our power.
➤ Strategy 10: Refusing to rescue means not retracting a truthful statement that the controller claims is hurtful.
➤ Strategy 11: Talking less and doing more means taking more action and doing less talking.
➤ Strategy 12: Taking time to respond is more effective than reactively responding.

> ➤ Strategy 13: Responding with agreement may be disarming to the controller.
> ➤ Strategy 14: Responding only to the content in a message is a way of making intentional choices about accepting or rejecting what is being communicated to us.
> ➤ Strategy 15: *Being selective when communicating* is consciously choosing what we will share and who is emotionally safe to share our deeper feelings and concerns.

Reflecting:

What communication strategies do I want to implement?

My current challenge:

Empowering step 9: looking at options

When the emotional and mental abuse continues, even though we have used our communication strategies in the best possible way, we may think we have no options. Sometimes we think that we should try longer and harder, despite a history of unsuccessful efforts. During other days, leaving the relationship seems to be the only option. Each of the following options poses a challenge and a risk. Most often, we are emotionally and mentally weaving in and out of more than one of these options when we are experiencing an emotionally and mentally abusive relationship.

❖ Option # 1: remain in the emotional pain

This is not a good option, but it *is* an option and is usually a choice we make by *not* making a choice. Staying in emotional pain is risky because we do not always recognize our own increasing vulnerability and dysfunction. Choosing this option may result in behaviors such as overworking, avoiding going home, getting involved in another relationship, or using alcohol, drugs, or addictive activities to cope with the emotional pain and emptiness of an oppressive and deteriorating relationship. Remaining in emotional pain eventually leads to depression. Not only does depression create emotional darkness and hopelessness, but it also numbs our feelings, including our anger, which is the emotion that is often needed to motivate ourselves to make changes. Option # 1 presents a risk because we may become exhausted from emotional pain or from the activities that we are doing to alleviate the pain and emptiness. We may become entrapped by an addiction, which means we have another controller in our lives. We cannot remain in this option for long periods of time if we are going to take care of ourselves and our children.

❖ Option # 2: emotionally detach from the relationship

Bully prevention programs teach students who experience bullying to *ignore*, *walk away*, or *ask the bully to stop*. In our adult relationships, we can use the same strategies. However, if these techniques do not work with our controller, we need to emotionally detach. Disengagement or detachment is not abandonment of the controlling person. Rather, it is refusing to be manipulated by controlling statements and behaviors or have our moods and daily experiences adversely affected. When we detach, we can create a life that is to some extent separate from the controller but connected to whatever degree is necessary to co-exist and co-parent children.

When we are dealing with a controlling partner, employer, or a family member, and our energies are not creating any positive change, we need to direct our energies into people, places, and projects where our energies make a positive difference. To become clearer on how to invest our personal energies, we can use the Serenity Prayer: *God grant me the serenity to accept the things I cannot change, courage to change the things I can, and wisdom to know the difference.*

By detaching, we no longer allow the controller to create high levels of stress and anxiety in our lives, nor do we enable controlling behaviors. We no longer sacrifice our choices as to how we use our time, what we do, or whom we associate with in order to satisfy the controller. We stop allowing ourselves to be a hostage to whomever or whatever is controlling us. In essence, we "get a life" and create it according to *our* design.

Detachment is:

- Emotionally disconnecting from another's unhealthy behaviors
- Not giving away our personal power
- Not enabling unacceptable behaviors
- Refusing to get hooked into controllers' emotional turmoil and negativity
- Refusing to have moods, thoughts, choices, or plans change because of a controller
- Refusing to internalize unjust criticisms and act out of fear, insecurity, or limitation
- Refusing to believe that taking care of the self and setting personal limits is selfish
- Letting controllers clean up their own messes, such as

relationship problems with children, friends, colleagues, or parents; finances; food; appointments; and laundry

When we detach, we take care of ourselves and honor the life that has been given to us. If we plan to stay in a controlling relationship and stay healthy ourselves, detaching is crucial. Emotionally detaching from a controller is not a total solution but does reduce the stress of getting caught up in the dysfunction. Detaching is difficult because we are accustomed to allowing and enabling the controller's dysfunctional behaviors.

Detaching is based on the fact that enabling dysfunctional behaviors is actually a *disservice* not only to ourselves but to our controller. If we contribute to the success of controlling behaviors, there will be no motivation for a controller to change the behaviors. When we detach and stop enabling, we are using "tough love," which is caring enough to no longer enable behaviors that are harmful to the person we care about, to ourselves, and to our children. Though we may not be able to stop the control, we create a higher probability for behaviors to change because the controlling behaviors are not enabled and supported; therefore, are less successful. If the control does not stop, we know that the behaviors we experience today will be the same behaviors we will experience in one year, five years, or twenty. This is vital information that we need in making decisions about an emotionally abusive relationship.

When we detach, we emotionally step out of the circle of drama and control. In our minds, we stay in our own emotional circle, which usually includes our children, supportive friends, and family. However, if we struggle with codependency, it is very easy to step back into the relationship circle too soon. This communicates to a controller that everything is okay, which is not the message we want to send but is an unspoken message that will be heard. We have to stay out of the drama and control circle long enough for the controller to notice that something is changing. We need to negotiate changes in the relationship *before* re-entering the relationship circle. The mistake we often make is going back into the relationship that was emotionally and mentally abusive *before* any controlling behaviors have changed. Therefore, the relationship dynamics remain the same or deteriorate further.

Whether a spouse or significant other does or does not abuse chemicals, a controller displays many alcoholic behaviors such as blaming others, being aggressively angry, demanding, being dishonest, and living in denial. The Al-Anon program teaches the basic principles of detachment and living a life based on spiritual and mental health principles. Al-Anon groups provide support groups for sharing common experiences and empowering each other. This has literally saved the emotional lives of thousands of recipients of control.

- Chad shares his experience:

> I tried to make my relationship work, but there was no use talking to her or trying to do things together because it was always a hassle. She was so critical and negative of me and also the kids. I started thinking that she didn't really love me but needed someone to control and I was that someone. Divorce was not an option because I didn't want to be a week-end dad. That would have been unbearable. I started going to Al-Anon even though there were only three guys in a group of about twenty-five women. I was surprised that our stories were so much the same, and it didn't matter if we were men or women. I started detaching to survive, and as I detached, I started to see and think more clearly. Although nothing changed in my marriage, I no longer felt like I was crazy or inferior. This provided a lot of emotional relief.

❖ **Option # 3: leave the relationship**

This is a very difficult choice when there are children. If safety is involved, children need to be removed from danger. If there is constant arguing and yelling and children are cowering in their bedrooms out of fear, the children need to be removed from the abuse and provided with an environment that is physically, mentally and emotionally safe.

Working with a therapist or participating in a support group is helpful when making a divorce decision. Not only do we need to thoughtfully consider the many factors that are involved in our decision but also carefully plan the steps of the leaving process, so that there are fewer traumas for all involved. Some adults are angry at the non-abusing parent for not removing them from the controller's dysfunction when they were children. In contrast, some parents say, "My controller controlled me, but when it started to affect the children, I mustered up the courage and strength to leave."

Empowering step 10: reclaiming personal power

Reclaiming our power involves taking charge of ourselves and our lives and using our personal power effectively, which requires becoming more aware of how we unknowingly give our power away. We may have internalized the negative statements made by our controller and are likely to have been influenced by cultural conditioning. Though we may feel that we are powerless, we can reject this belief. Rather than scolding ourselves for not recognizing the control, or for not recognizing it sooner than we did, we can start understanding how we give our power away. Most of us *have more power* than we think we have. However, our personal power is not going to be given or returned to us, nor are we going to be reminded that we do, in fact, have personal power. We may have to be open to new possibilities and start with the thought, "*Just suppose* I have more power than I think I have." Our personal power needs to be experienced as *real* to us, which will only happen if we take some risks and change our passive and enabling behaviors.

In our minds we can think of a controller throwing a ball to us. This represents the controlling behavior. Typically, we return the ball and the control game begins. But we don't have to return the ball, knowing that it takes two to play a game. We can start reclaiming our power by refusing to participate in the controller's manipulative control tactics. A benchmark in our empowering process is learning how we routinely give our power away, even though we may not know we have it.

We routinely give away our power when:

- We are focused on the controller more than we are focused on ourselves.
- We allow our moods to change because of what another person does or says.
- We let a controller's problem become our problem.
- We adjust our thoughts, values, beliefs, and actions to fit the controller's expectations or directives.
- We get hooked into useless arguments.
- We become trapped into thinking that we have to be "super-nice" to our controller.
- We think that we are always at fault.
- We provide information that may be twisted and used against us.
- We keep listening to the badgering, whether in person or on the phone, instead of excusing ourselves and leaving or hanging up the phone.
- We dignify negative comments and derogatory labels by

listening to them.

- We make excuses for, rescue, take responsibility for, or suffer the consequences resulting from controllers' inappropriate behaviors.
- We apologize for no real reason.
- We silently agree to be a puppet, servant, the "parent" or the "child" in our relationship.
- We ask permission to do the things that we want to do, as if we were children.
- We harbor anger and resentment toward our controller, which puts our emotional and physical health at risk.
- We stay in the victim role, which enables the controlling behaviors and results in emotional, physical, spiritual, or mental collapse.
- We believe that there is something wrong with us.
- We fuel the controlling behaviors by enabling, allowing, accommodating, adjusting, complying, protecting, sacrificing preferences and dreams, and pretending that everything is fine when everything is not fine in order to be loved and prevent conflict.

Knowing the basic rules and methods of controllers is empowering

Below is a sampling of controllers' rules and methods, which are mentioned throughout this book, but summarized here. Knowing some of these rules is empowering because people can be released from feeling at fault, crazy and inferior and may be able to see through and possibly dismantle the web of control maneuvers.

Dominant controllers:

- ✓ Keep the rules and methods of control undefined, which is a way of maintaining control. If the rules were actually stated, the unfairness would be easily recognized because controllers' methods are blatantly self-serving.
- ✓ Change the rules whenever necessary to maintain control, receive benefits, or award or protect favored persons.
- ✓ Use a one-up, one-down competitive way of thinking and communicating to gain superiority.
- ✓ Keep subordinates feeling powerless and thinking that they are at fault, to maintain power.
- ✓ Call abusive sarcasm "humor" and ridicule those who don't think the sarcasm is humorous. If controllers think something is humorous, they think it should be humorous to everyone.
- ✓ Have the illusion of knowing it all, but actually operate without feedback from subordinates who withhold information because of possible repercussions.
- ✓ Often unknowingly support the subordinates because the subordinates may learn to "play the system," which means they will get whatever they can from the controller.
- ✓ Have rigid and closed mental structures that are not open to new or challenging information.
- ✓ Have thought processes that are not always logical because motivations are self-serving.
- ✓ View subordiantes as wrong, invaluable, and replaceable.
- ✓ Claim that the dominant/subordinate societal structure is the way it has always been and therefore is the right way.
- ✓ Stay in denial so there is no early intervention that would prevent major relationship crises.
- ✓ Have a selective memory, forgetting their abusive acts and inappropriate behaviors to protect the self.

✓ Focus on what is wrong rather than on what is right and do not communicate positive values or beliefs or share creative ideas on how to improve situations or relationships.

✓ Shift responsibility to others to excuse their lack of knowledge, mistakes, or abusive actions.

✓ There is incongruity between spoken intentions and actual behaviors. Words often do not match their actions.

✓ Are adept at twisting the meaning of words. When subordinates are compliant, dominants view it as *cooperation*. "Stubborn" is the label dominants apply to someone who does not cave in to the dominant's expectations. What is not beneficial to the controller is labeled, "wrong." Confronting controllers or questioning their behavior is often viewed as creating a hassle or not being a team player.

✓ Often become defensive and attack conflicting views, which is reactive behavior.

✓ Are threatened by truth, others' higher intelligence or skill level, progressive thinking, creativity, and change.

✓ Will orchestrate budget cuts in a way that forces subordinates to do the sacrificing rather than the dominants. Dominants will reduce subordinates' salaries and benefits but not their own.

✓ Think that more is better. Quantity is better than quality, which leads to greed, overconsumption, overwork, overcharging, and over-accumulating, which are efforts to portray being a success and are also attempts to feel secure.

✓ Require accountability from subordinates but not from themselves.

✓ Are often fearful of whatever is not measureable or monetary, such as spiritual values, emotions, intuition, the energies between people, and alternative ways of healing and restoring health.

✓ Use dichotomous, either/or thinking, and view stereotypes as true, which simplifies and decreases the mental work of seeing reality and the "whole picture."

✓ Discount visionaries but are not above taking their ideas and claiming them as their own.

✓ Will point out one error in a project and discount the whole endeavor but may then take the project and present it as if it was their creation.

✓ Believe that winning is all-important even if honesty and integrity are sacrificed.

✓ Increase the expectations when people start meeting the original goals.

✓ Withhold affirmations and apologies.

✓ Make agreements behind the scenes for self-serving purposes, which are not documented so they cannot be traced.

✓ Have different standards of behavior. If subordinates go ballistic at work, they are often described as out-of-control and are likely to be ordered to seek professional help or are reprimanded or terminated. If dominants exhibit the same behavior, the dominants' behavior is often viewed as the result of having a bad day, or being stressed out because of the difficulty of their job, and they are excused. They may be advised to take a few days off to relieve the stress of the job.

✓ Want subordinates to be smart but not too smart.

✓ Often think that it is beneath them to greet subordinates with a pleasant, "Good morning!"

Even though we may not be able to create positive changes, knowing many of the rules of control is beneficial because we can then a) Dispel the notion that we are not thinking straight or are inferior, b) See the dysfunction for what it is and c) Reclaim our self-confidence and esteem. Many subordinate people have deciphered the rules and have learned how to work around them. *Knowing* is empowering. Perhaps we will find ways to impact on the self-serving and controlling ways of the dominants. In the meantime, we can be aware of how the cards are stacked and who stacks the cards.

Asking ourselves important questions

If we are being controlled, we can ask ourselves these questions:

- *Who* is wrong with me? rather than *What* is wrong with me?
- Are my enabling behaviors working to prevent conflict?
- Who is really creating the problems in the relationship?
- What am I getting out of this relationship? Yes, we should be getting *something* out of our relationship besides stress, confusion, and conflict.

These questions move us closer to reality. Even if our relationship dynamics do not change, it is very empowering to know in our hearts and minds that we are not solely responsible for our relationship problems. These questions often result in an "aha" experience that propels us into a different way of thinking that is more reality based.

Reclaiming our power involves understanding our experiences. For a certain period of time, we usually have ain't-it-awful conversations with ourselves and with special friends or family members. We struggle with our anger and feel stuck and without options. Sharing our relationship difficulties with trusted persons often validates that we are not crazy, inferior, or wrong in the way we think and feel. By processing with others, we start moving out of the ain't-it-awful stage and realize that *staying inert, confused, believing in our inadequacy and doing nothing is what controllers want.* We also realize *that most of what the controller told us about ourselves is untrue.*

Our rational minds will support us

People who are being emotional or mentally controlled are usually *feeling* people. It is healthy to be in touch with feelings, but sometimes our feelings will lead us down a path of denial, depression and hopelessness, rather than a path of recognizing the dysfunction and starting to take positive actions that will lead to greater well-being for ourselves and for our children. Focusing with our minds is necessary when we learn new behaviors such as setting limits, confronting unacceptable behaviors, making the decision to end a relationship, or planning the steps of actually leaving. Relying more on our mental abilities rather than allowing ourselves to be ruled by our emotions will result in thinking clearly as we address practical matters and make important decisions.

Our rational minds will help us to:

- ✓ Reclaim our power
- ✓ Become more proactive rather than reactive
- ✓ Know how to respond to various controlling behaviors
- ✓ Make good choices
- ✓ Help us set limits on behaviors that are unacceptable
- ✓ Do what we need to do to become financially sustainable, so that we have the option to leave if necessary
- ✓ Redesign our lives

Our feelings will understand if we give them a rest for a while because they are very overworked when we are in a relationship with a controller. And our minds won't get upset if they are used constantly to think through situations and make decisions that are healthy for ourselves and our children.

Positive self-talk helps us to reclaim our power

We all engage in self-talk, which are the passing thoughts that go through our mind. We can consciously create thoughts that will be empowering, rather than scolding or diminishing. Our self-talk can also calm us down, which we need to do so that we make the best possible decisions.

- I can stop giving my power away.
- Nothing can hurt or diminish me unless I allow it.
- I have a right to design my life according to my beliefs and values.
- I have a right and a responsibility to take care of myself.
- I have a right to detach from dysfunction.
- I can put my energies into relationships with people that nurture me and whom I nurture in return.
- I need to reclaim my power so I can be the best possible person and parent, and make good decisions that are in the best interest of my own life and the life of my children.

Reflecting:

My current challenge:

Empowering step 11: knowing personal rights in relationships

As recipients of control, we probably need to be reminded that *we have basic rights* in relationships. Controllers often trample on the rights of others and often claim that they are helping others who cannot manage their lives by themselves. The following list is a sampling of basic rights in relationships.

We have a right to:

- Be treated with respect and courtesy
- Be taken seriously
- Share in decision making
- Be treated as an equal
- Talk things out
- Be free from pressure
- Have our feelings and experiences acknowledged as real and valid
- Receive clear and informative answers to questions
- Live free from unjust criticism, judgments, accusations, and blame
- Feel safe from emotional and physical threat
- Be respectfully asked rather than ordered
- Say no to any request
- Change our mind
- Have our own opinion and make our own decisions about our life
- Communicate openly
- Be treated with honesty and fairness
- Have privacy
- Choose what we do with our body
- Express our feelings and emotions
- Have friendships and activities of interest

- Believe in ourselves and feel good about who we are

Knowing our rights is empowering and having our rights respected is even more empowering and draws us closer to our partner. However, when controllers trample on any of these rights, we have a legitimate reason to confront them in a firm and credible manner.

Reflecting:

What rights do I need to start defending?

My current challenge:

Empowering step 12: becoming more honest

The key reason for being dishonest with a controller is to avoid anger, snarly remarks, and conflict. Though our dishonesty may prevent some troubling conflicts, dishonesty is contrary to spiritual principles. Becoming more honest requires courage. It is saying no when we need to say no, even when it is difficult and may precipitate the controller's anger. Being honest is being congruent with what we are saying and what we are feeling or doing. Though honesty may be difficult, we feel better because we are not betraying ourselves by feeling one way and saying we feel another.

If we are afraid of hurting our controller's feelings by being honest, we need to remind ourselves that controllers are big people, and big people can take care of themselves. We do not have to enable the control, keep their secrets, or tread lightly so that we don't step on their egos and insecurities. If controllers choose to let honest statements hurt them, it is their choice. If they are upset, they can talk directly to us, share with a friend, or start therapy. What is more likely to happen is that they will distract themselves by overworking, gambling, drinking; or watching television, using the Internet, or playing video games excessively, all of which can be totally self-stimulating and self-absorbing. These activities ask nothing of a controller in terms of conversation, honesty, and cooperation, unlike a primary relationship.

It is helpful to ask ourselves why we are staying in an emotionally abusive relationship. When we are honest with ourselves, we may conclude that we are staying in the relationship for reasons other than love. Examples of other reasons are financial security, because we think our children are better off living with both parents, or because we do not want to be a single parent carrying all of the responsibility by ourselves. In honest moments, we may conclude that the love and respect has been destroyed by the controlling behaviors and the relationship is no longer significant to us. When honesty becomes a principle that we live by, we may no longer be able to pose as a happy couple at social functions. Being honest dispels any illusions about why we are staying in a toxic relationship. This brings a clarity that is congruent with what we are actually feeling. We probably won't share our conclusion with our controller because it would do more harm than good. But in our minds and hearts we are no longer deceiving ourselves or living in denial. We clearly understand *why* we are staying in an emotionally and mentally abusive relationship. Though this clarification may seem insignificant, it is emotionally empowering. Because we are being honest with ourselves, we realize that we are making a personal choice and it may no longer be a forced choice.

Reflecting:

I am dishonest with my controller because …

I am becoming more honest by …

My current challenge:

Empowering step 13: protecting personal boundaries

Personal boundaries are the psychological, emotional, and behavioral limits that we set for ourselves. We have a right to communicate what we will do and what we will not do.

We have healthy boundaries when we:

- Learn to avoid getting hooked into controlling behaviors, negative verbalizations, or unrealistic expectations
- Communicate feelings and thoughts with clarity and protect them when they are minimized or ridiculed
- Deflect the guilt that is projected on us by controllers
- Refuse to enable by paying attention, excusing, or rewarding dysfunctional behaviors
- Know that we are not responsible for another person's attitudes, emotions, moods, or behaviors
- Know that we are not our controller's property
- Believe that we have a right to our thoughts and feelings and are separate and unique human beings

Controllers engulf us and as a result, we lose our real selves. They attempt to orchestrate our lives and attempt to take a superior power position over us. By protecting our boundaries, we take charge of our life and refuse to have our emotional, mental, physical and spiritual space invaded.

Reflecting:

My current challenge:

Empowering step 14: being proactive

We have been *reacting* to controlling behaviors for a long time by internalizing controllers' criticisms and doing the dance of enabling, allowing, accommodating, adjusting, complying, protecting, sacrificing preferences and dreams, and pretending that everything is fine when everything is not fine. When we are *proactive,* we plan ahead, take responsibility, and implement a plan in efforts to prevent problems before they arise. Being proactive is being confident in using our personal power to clearly articulate our thoughts and feelings.

Controllers are not always aware of the changes subordinates make because many of them are internal, such as becoming healthier in the way we think, learning self-advocacy skills, improving self-esteem, growing stronger and investing more energy in empowering ourselves. We may return to school, join a support group, or work with a therapist. Many controllers do not notice that the relationship is different until they are inconvenienced or realize they are losing control over their partner. The control may escalate, or they may not say anything because this would be acknowledging that a relationship is important to them.

A pro-active strategy is "pushing the envelope" with our controller to see if we can be who we really are, do what we want, and have the freedom to learn and grow *while we are in the relationship.* No, we shouldn't have to get our controller's permission to learn, grow, and actualize ourselves, but often, this is how it feels. By stretching beyond what we think our controllers will tolerate, we may realize that we have more personal power than we think. By being proactive and stretching their controller's or their own boundaries, many recipients of control start college or finish their degrees, re-train for a different job, work creatively and receive a promotion, change careers, attend weekly support groups, and go on retreats, conferences, and trips. Many of these activities are motivated by the subordinates' desire to be financially and emotionally self-sustaining if the relationship ends. Controllers may knowingly or unknowingly help fund these activities. By pushing the limits, we challenge the controller who may go along with our changes or may escalate the control and be angry, moody, and sarcastic. Our controller's responses, whether positive, neutral or negative, indicate whether or not we can develop our full potential and be accepted for who we really are in the relationship.

Empowering step 15: forgiving

When we are able to forgive, we heal mentally, emotionally, spiritually, and physically. If there is a health problem, many people believe that there is a forgiveness problem. If we hold resentments toward another, we are bound to that person as if by heavy chains.

These people still have power over us. Before we are able to forgive, we have to work through our feelings of hurt, resentment, and anger.

Forgiving frees us from negative feelings, which is necessary for our own healing. It may be a long process before we are able to truly forgive and say, "I bless you; I bless me." We know that we have truly forgiven when we have no negative emotional reaction upon encountering our controller, or, that when we have passing thoughts about that person, there is not a stir of anger or resentment. It is like meeting a stranger whom we are able to greet pleasantly. If we can reach this point, we experience "blessed indifference" toward the person and are emotionally released.

Empowering step 16: empowering ourselves

We can continue our empowerment journey by continuing to learn skills and implement effective life strategies. Personal growth means intentionally providing ourselves with knowledge, respect, caring, love, and emotional support. We can learn to value our feelings, thoughts, ideas, and beliefs.

Increasingly, we can trust our inner truth to guide us in making positive choices for ourselves and for our children. We empower ourselves when we become good friends to ourselves and are healing from past hurts. It is important to spend time with our children, close family members, and supportive friends. If we have people who help us laugh, we want to be with them often. If our children are being playful, we want to join in their many ways of expressing their joy.

We can continue empowering ourselves by:

- Discarding negative beliefs about ourselves;
- Loving ourselves and treating ourselves fairly;

- Seeing clearly and acknowledging, rather than denying what we see;

- Reclaiming our feelings, learning from them, and learning to trust our inner truth;

- Valuing self-nurturing at the mental, emotional, physical, and spiritual levels of our being;

- Continuing to grow in self-esteem, recognizing our value, and believing in ourselves;

- Knowing that when we have to dig deep within ourselves, we will find inner strength. If we don't have the strength to do what we need to do for ourselves, we can gather up our courage and strength and do what needs to be done for our children.

- Focusing more on what we do have, rather than what we don't have;

- Investing our energies in ourselves, our children, people, and activities where our energies make a positive difference and are welcomed.

Our empowerment helps us to live our lives without someone directing our every move. Empowering ourselves will usher in a new sense of freedom because we can be who we are and become what we are meant to become. We will know that we are healing and empowering ourselves when we experience more freedom from our own negative self-talk and we can love ourselves as we love our best friends.

Though many controllers and recipients of control think that if a relationship ends, the next step is to find a new relationship. This belief is highly supported by our culture and our own personal codependency. There are, however, other options, depending on situations that are unique to each of us. Whatever our choice, we need time to heal, learn from past mistakes, and continue to empower ourselves.

Reflecting:

How can I continue to empower myself?

My current challenge:

At a control workshop, participants created the following:

I will never again tolerate a controlling person who:

- Thinks I am crazy, inferior, or stupid and does not treat me as an equal
- Is verbally abusive but denies it
- Is sarcastic and calls it humor
- Has a big ego and constantly talks about him/herself
- Shifts the blame to others to justify or excuse their abusive behavior
- Does not take responsibility for his/her hurtful words
- Totally ignores me and my feelings
- Expects me to "just forget it" after emotionally hurting me
- Refuses to talk and resolve the problems
- Lies, name-calls, and acts superior
- Expects me to be a servant

Every step we take to empower ourselves takes *courage*:

I pray for the courage ...

To accept myself and move beyond my self-imposed
limitations
To walk through my fears
To say no when it's important to say no
To participate in my own healing and choose life
To believe in myself
To make amends when I have harmed others
To stand up for rightness and goodness
To say yes to life
To reach out to others in healthy ways
To trust my inner truth and my growth process
To arrive at my own conclusions
To advocate for the change of inequities and injustices
To receive from others as well as being generous in giving to
others
To be different when the world demands conformity
And most of all, to have the courage to love in an oftentimes
unloving and unkind world—to love myself, others, and Spirit-
God with all of my heart, mind, and soul.

Chapter 9

Relationship Issues and Decisions

> If we don't change, we don't grow. If we don't grow, we are not really living. Growth demands a temporary surrender of security.—Gail Sheehy

Underlying issues of intimacy

Participants in a relationship have different ideas about emotional intimacy in primary and emotionally close relationships. The *independent* person is more often male and socialized to value independence. The unspoken message is, "Give me space, otherwise I feel trapped and smothered. But don't go away. I want you here, but we don't need a lot of interaction." The *connector* person wants emotional intimacy, which involves communicating feelings and non-sexual physical touch. The unspoken message is, "Talk to me and share your feelings with me. I don't feel we have a relationship if we don't emotionally connect." The independent person appears to have more power because he/she seems to focus less on the relationship than the connector does.

We emotionally step forward and sometimes we step back, depending on what is transpiring within the relationship. This back and forth movement may go on for the duration of the relationship and involves using personal power to influence the behavior of a partner. A common scenario is that the connector emotionally pursues the independent person. But this dynamic may reverse. If the person who wants more closeness grows tired of trying to orchestrate more emotional intimacy and is routinely rejected, he/she may decide to stop asking and emotionally step back. When this happens, the roles may reverse and the independent person moves closer. This exchange of roles may result in the connector resuming the movement toward the other partner and the independent person resuming the position of wanting more space. Or, an exchange of roles may be permanent with the independent person wanting more connection, but the partner who previously wanted more emotional connection is no longer interested, because they have given up the struggle for closeness and has emotionally "checked out."

Relationship dynamics regarding sexuality is often a source of misunderstandings, tension and conflicts in many relationships. When a partner chooses not to be sexual as often as the other partner would like, or at a particular time, it can be perceived as controlling by withholding, punishing, or being manipulative. Sometimes this perception is correct. The other reality is that refusing to be sexual may simply be a personal choice. From another point of view, the less sexually interested partner may think that the other partner has excessively high sexual expectations, which produces a feeling of being controlled. Sexuality is a topic that is not readily discussed openly and directly in many relationships. Controllers are known to make sarcastic remarks to the partner who is less sexually interested to instill guilt or to imply that the partner is inadequate or abnormal. However, the controller's sarcasm and anger can drive the partner further away, so this type of behavior often results in getting the exact opposite of what one wants.

Power positions shift when relationships are ending

Power positions may change when a relationship is ending. The person leaving may become the more powerful person. There is usually a difference in how emotional pain is experienced in an imbalanced relationship. A controller, during the marriage, appears to have no emotional pain, whereas the recipient of control may have been struggling emotionally because of being controlled for years. However, when the controlled person decides to leave, the controller may experience the same kind of pain, but it comes all at once—"totally blitzed" as controllers say, with feelings of shock, disbelief, sadness, and remorse. This happens for several reasons:

1. Controllers may not have heard all of the confronting communications of distress up to the time their partner made the decision to leave.
2. Controllers seldom realize how dependent they are on the spouse for many reasons including personal services and meeting society's expectations of being coupled.
3. Controllers do not see themselves as the reason for a partner leaving and often express external reasons to explain leaving, such as, "Friends have told you to leave," or, "You are going through a mid-life crisis," or, "You must be having an affair." The reality is more likely to be that the controlled person has been struggling emotionally and is making the decision to leave a relationship that is toxic rather than remain at risk emotionally, physically, mentally, or spiritually.
4. Controllers have a tendency to stay in denial, thinking that there is nothing wrong within the relationship. In their unawareness, controllers often say, "I thought he/she would never really leave."
5. The spouse who is leaving may have withheld the plans to

leave the relationship in attempts to avoid the controller's anger or escalated control.

6. Controllers usually do not realize that control creates a time-bomb ticking away within the relationship and a crisis is almost inevitable.

The person who is leaving may now have the relationship power. The controller may say, "Write down what I need to do. I'll do it." The controller may promise to listen better, be more caring, and offer apologies. There may be tears along with emotional pleas to the partner who is leaving to remain in the relationship. The controller may want to talk, promise to participate in the relationship, and spend more time with the children. He/she may suggest going to counseling which has met with refusal in the past. Some controllers will call a counselor to find out how many sessions will be needed to get their partner back, wanting a quick solution to the relationship problems, which is unlikely to happen because the problems in the relationship have been long standing, and the relationship has become increasingly dysfunctional. It may be the first time that the controller admits to needing or truly caring about their spouse.

Not all controllers turn the power positions around. Some escalate their controlling behaviors and start to make more demands on the partner who has decided to leave, such as insisting that the person take a psychiatric evaluation. Some controllers believe that since there was no physical abuse, there is no reason for a partner to leave and will follow and badger the partner who has left, make numerous phone calls, and put pressure on the partner to come back. They may make false accusations about breaking up the family for no reason and refuse to acknowledge that the break-up was created by their own emotionally and mentally controlling behaviors. Many controllers warn that there will be financial problems for the exiting partner so he/she will have no choice but to come back. Controllers may also go to family members with slanted or false information. What the controller does not realize is that his/her many different ways of controlling and the intensification of the control actually confirm that the reasons for leaving the relationship are legitimate. When there is escalated control, controlled subordinates feel as if they are literally being pushed to the attorney's door, and there can be no turning back.

There is often a reversal in mindsets. The controller's mind now may be more open because of the crisis, which often brings reality to the forefront. The mind of the recipient of control, usually more open, is now more closed when the controller wants to talk about the relationship and how to fix it. There have been countless times when the spouse who is leaving wanted to talk about the relationship but was rejected. Now his/her energies are directed toward leaving. She/he is not interested in communicating with the controller because communication might result in going back into confusion; there may be more conflict, or there may be persuasion and pressure to return to the toxic relationship. There might be promises to change behaviors, but there is no way to tell the difference between sincerity and manipulation and whether the behaviors will change for a few days or will be sustained. There might be loving words and loving gestures, but all of the attention from the controller feels like too much, and too late. Leaving has taken a lot of thought and energy and because controlled persons are routinely blamed for the relationship problems, they often say, "Blame me, blame yourself, or blame whomever you want to. I just can't do this one more day!" As far as discussing the relationship, the person leaving feels that there is nothing more to say.

The controlled person, who has been in emotional pain for a long time, is carrying out a plan that has been carefully thought out, sometimes over months or years. The decision to leave is not just a whim, or a split-second decision, as the controller often thinks. The difficulty that a controller has in convincing the exiting partner to return to a toxic relationship is made even more difficult if the spouse has physically separated from the controller and is experiencing *living without control*, which is a new experience that provides relief and emotional freedom.

A controller may decide that they deserve more than what their partners were giving them, and may initiate the divorce, as a way to be superior and in control of the situation. To emotionally protect themselves, some controllers decide that the break-up needed to happen and it's time to move on. Often, looking from the outside, it appears that life for a controller *does* move on, without any emotional difficulties. When it is clear to a controller that their relationship is indeed ending or ended, they often start investing energies in a new relationship. Becoming involved with another person is a way of avoiding grief but does not allow for time to reflect upon and change the behaviors that contributed to the break-up of the previous relationship. Controllers who think that the break-up was the fault of a partner have no reason to truly look at the causes of the divorce and learn from the mistakes of the past.

Controllers often exhibit respectful, non-controlling courting behaviors that are effective when pursuing a relationship. However, as the relationship proceeds, the dysfunction is likely to surface and the same controlling pattern and problems will occur in a new relationship. That the controller is in a new relationship may be emotionally upsetting to the spouse who left the relationship. In contrast, the controller's new relationship may feel like divine intervention if there were continual arguments about finances and personal items which delayed the divorce proceedings, or if there was resistance to the divorce in hopes that the relationship could be salvaged. If the controller is involved in a new relationship, there is greater motivation to bring the divorce to closure, and negotiations may be less difficult.

Reflecting:

What reaction do I anticipate if I decide to leave the relationship?

What reaction will I have if my spouse leaves?

My current challenge:

To leave or not to leave a controlling relationship

Before an actual decision to divorce is made, a considerable amount of time is spent thinking about leaving and going back and forth with thoughts of "to leave or not to leave." I once heard a speaker whose theme was "the hardest part of mountain climbing is deciding whether to continue the climb or go back down the mountain." Despite months of training, adverse conditions might happen that puts mountain climbers in jeopardy. The weather may become harsh; some equipment may be damaged causing a greater risk; the team members may be physically and emotionally tired; or the team cohesiveness is breaking down, resulting in the members not supporting one another. The climbers wonder if they should take the risk and keep climbing or go back down the mountain. They try to determine whether a decision to turn back is based on fear or the reality of the situation. This requires analyzing all of the options and possible outcomes, and making the decision. The speaker then related her theme— "the hardest part of mountain climbing is deciding whether to continue the climb or go back down the mountain," to the difficult decisions in life, including continuing or ending the uphill climb of a dysfunctional relationship or work situation that is emotionally destructive and is unlikely to change.

It is no disgrace to stop our mountain climb if it becomes clear that we cannot continue because of adverse conditions that are unlikely to change and perhaps escalate in severity. Controllers negatively affect their children as well as their partners. Sometimes recipients of control feel that they are powerless to defend themselves against the controlling behavior or to leave a controller. But they often gather up incredible energy, courage and strength and go to any lengths to protect and provide physical and emotional safety for their children.

Considerations when making decisions about a controlling relationship

The following are typical thoughts of emotionally and mentally controlled persons when they are contemplating *staying* or *leaving* a toxic relationship:

- Thinking that staying in relationship is in the best interests of children and that the reasons for leaving do not justify the upset to children and other family members.
- Thinking that leaving is necessary because children are living in fear and conflicts feel like there is a possibility of physical abuse.
- Being fearful that the controlling behaviors may escalate if divorce is discussed or the decision is made.
- Thinking that one does not want to be a single parent.
- Thinking that co-parenting will be just as difficult, if not more difficult than staying in the marriage.
- Feeling guilty about leaving and feeling sorry for the controller.

- Having religious reasons such as believing that marriage vows should be honored forever.
- Thinking that there will be financial stress. Though child-support processes are in place, the controller might not continue working or work for cash to avoid child-support. This may not be a concern before a divorce happens and we may trust an ex-spouse to meet his/her child support responsibility. However, ex-spouses actions are not always predictable when they are angered by the divorce, by the fact that time with their children has been reduced, and by financial stress. It is not uncommon for controllers to accuse custodial parents of using child-support checks for personal items rather than for the needs of their children.
- Thinking that the stress of a partner having an affair but refusing to end the outside relationship is too much to handle.
- Thinking that it isn't fair to have to upset the whole family when it is an outside affair that is causing the divorce and the spouse has decided to leave the marriage.
- Thinking that the relationship isn't that bad because there is no physical abuse.
- Knowing that attorney fees will be difficult if not impossible to pay.
- Fearing that the controller's threats to harm himself/herself if the relationship ends, may actually happen.
- Feeling overwhelmed by the separation or divorce process involving attorneys and court.
- Receiving what is thought to be the best kind of love the controller can give, even though it doesn't feel like love and hoping that the loving person in the courting days will come back.
- Dreading being alone.
- Holding personal beliefs such as, "This is what I deserve."

- Feeling that there will be no one to love again.
- Thinking, "I am a failure if this relationship fails."
- Clinging to the hope that the relationship will change.
- Worrying about what people will think or say, especially parents.
- Worrying about losing couple-friends and if they will "take sides."
- Afraid of making decisions because of feeling inadequate.
- Struggling with low self-esteem and insecurity.
- Lacking emotional support of family and/or friends.
- Thinking that leaving isn't possible because of being too depressed.

Women have been socialized to think in terms of their group, rather than being a unit of one and independent of others. As a result, women wonder how a decision to divorce will be received by their children and other people, including parents, friends, clergy, and colleagues. In addition, women are not used to making decisions that might be controversial. These two factors influence women, as they go through the long and difficult process of making a decision about a controlling relationship.

There are other individual needs, preferences, and issues unique to the person's situation when deciding to leave or not to leave. When taking a risk, there is no way to predict what will happen. This causes fear and uncertainty until the day comes when a recipient of control thinks, "Regardless of what happens, it will be better than living like this," and realizes that he/she has no obligation to remain in a relationship with a toxic, dysfunctional partner.

A bottom-line realization in the back and forth thought process is that we are more responsible for our children than for another adult, regardless of what a controller says. Adults have the power and ability to take care of themselves and can seek out professional help if needed. In contrast, children need a healthy caretaker. We are given the sacred gift of life and have a responsibility to take care of it. We may also have been given the sacred gift of children and are responsible for taking care of them in the best way possible.

The process of leaving

People in emotionally and mentally controlling relationships are the only ones who know what is really going on within the relationship. What happens in a relationship can be totally different from the image of the relationship that is presented to others. The initial decision to leave a relationship is only the first step. We re-evaluate a divorce decision with *each step* of the process: attorney meetings, negotiating custody arrangements, splitting the finances and household goods, and going to the courthouse on the day that the divorce is finalized.

Leaving a relationship involves disconnection on many levels, including the emotional, mental, and legal. Some family relationships or couple friendships might become strained or end. Ideally, there are people who understand and are supportive. However, it is not unusual for the divorce journey to be taken alone. It is very helpful to work with a therapist who can provide strategies that will help the leaving process go smoother and offer support if the control intensifies, or if there are thoughts about returning to the dysfunctional relationship because of pressure from the controlling spouse. Therapy can also be very helpful if a couple will be co-parenting and need to determine specific procedures and guidelines so that decisions and actions are in their children's best interest.

If we decide to leave or have left a relationship, we may have second thoughts. However, it usually doesn't work to return for the wrong reasons, such as feeling insecure, guilty because of believing the controller's guilt manipulations, or giving in to the relentless demands of the controller. There are times when both partners come to understand that they cannot return to the relationship as it was in the past because it was too unhealthy. Unless the controller agrees to reduce or eliminate controlling behaviors and the changes are sustained, the control issues will resurface. The person who decided to leave will be faced with the same situation that prompted the initial thoughts and plans to leave, and will feel that he/she is back to square one.

With unchanging, controlling relationships, a decision to leave may be a positive decision. It is healthy to decide to save our lives by stopping a treacherous mountain climb that carries too many risks to our lives and the lives of our children. The recipients of control are usually supported by friends and family when they leave a controlling relationship. Prior to the divorce, friends often stay quite neutral out of respect for personal boundaries. However, it is very common that after a divorce decision is actually made, friends will rally with support, often making remarks such as, "We were wondering just how long you would put up with her/him!" These friends provide emotional support and child-care, and may even offer their homes until other arrangements are made. They at times provide financial help, and are there to help when the moving vans arrive if that is part of the leaving plan.

Male controllers are less likely to have a close, supportive network because their friendships are often not emotionally based. As a result, they frequently face their emotional pain alone and hesitate to reach out to others for help. Some controllers start leaning on children for support and may share the break-up information in a one-sided, self-serving, and self-protecting way.

Usually when the decision is made to leave a relationship, there is a sense of relief because the vacillating thoughts of "to leave or not to leave" come to an end. But even if the relationship was toxic to us, we may experience grieving, which is sometimes unexpected because there was such a strong desire to leave. In some situations, we may leave a person whom we still love but we cannot live with because of the high stress and negative interactions and feelings. When we leave a relationship, we also grieve for our dream of what a relationship, in our minds, could be. We question, wonder, and want to believe that a healthy relationship is indeed possible.

Co-parenting problems

When there are children involved, the post-divorce relationship may be more stressful than the marriage. When living *with* the other parent, we can usually make sure our children are emotionally nurtured, they are heard when they experience difficulties, and their routines are not interrupted. We schedule in time with their friends, help them complete homework, and transport them to lessons. We can tend to their nutrition, exercise, social development, unique needs, and any other concerns we may have as a parent. We usually know what is happening emotionally to our children and to some extent, but certainly not always, we can protect them from emotional abuse. When the marriage is dissolved, we lose some of our personal power to provide consistent care for our children in all areas of development.

Many non-custodial parents are responsible, trustworthy, child-focused, and do what is in the best interest of their children. However, some non-custodial controlling parents are not child-centered, nor do they have good parenting skills. There may be times when the children are brought to places that are not healthy environments for children. We may discover that our children are being taken care of at a friend's house, or that there are times when they are not supervised. Some co-parents behave like a friend or buddy to their children rather than being responsible parents. They may not insist on their children wearing helmets or adhering to regulations regarding car seats and seat belts. They may fail to teach appropriate behavior, routines are not consistent; homework is left unattended in back packs; lessons are not practiced; and children are not held accountable. It is not unusual for a dysfunctional parent to buy children's love by giving expensive toys, activities, or trips. Besides the pain that comes from not being with our children, our stress will be very high if we have concerns about our children's safety and care, and whether decisions are being made in their best interest.

It is not uncommon for children to receive less attention and consideration when a parent enters a new relationship. Not only are children still grieving the break-up of their original family, they may be expected to bond and enjoy being with the new person in their parent's life, even though he/she may be viewed as an intrusion into their relationship with their parent. Children are frequently directed to accept new siblings in a step-family and accept discipline from a step-parent. Adult choices can create very difficult challenges for children who are often expected to make significant adjustments without protest.

There can be many other conflicts that are ongoing. Changing visitation schedules can be an ongoing source of conflict. Some ex-spouses will abandon the family by moving, or by not making contact with the children. Other ex-spouses will try to take over the parenting and be over-involved and controlling. Some controllers bad-mouth the other parent, which is very confusing to children. There may be manipulative statements such as "I wish your (mother, dad) would change his/her mind so we can be a family again." There are times when one parent tries to alienate the children from the other parent to punish the parent who ended the marriage by falsely accusing him/her of breaking up the family. This is confusing to children. They may become angry at the parent who ended the relationship because they have been told that the fault lies with the parent who leaves. If this happens, it is a disheartening experience, and the parent with whom the children are angry is forced to trust that the children will someday be able to weave their way through the manipulating ways of the controller and the children's relationship with the alienated parent will be restored.

- Suzanne shares her experience:

> Before the divorce, he was hardly ever at home and had very little interaction with the kids. When I discovered he was having an affair and it had been going on for several months, I confronted him, but he was not willing to give up the relationship. He didn't want a divorce, but I decided I couldn't deal with him having an outside relationship. After our divorce, he wanted to be with the children all of the time. He told the children that I didn't love them, that I broke up the family, and that he would always be there for them. They started to dislike me because of being told lies that I was mean and didn't care about them. I was devastated. I felt like my heart was cut out of me and I was an empty shell. But I knew I couldn't let my children see what I was going through. I don't know where my strength came from. And eventually, my children saw through the manipulation and dishonesty. We are now emotionally reunited, which is a relief and blessing for me.

Children may gravitate toward the parent who was absent, abusive or appears to be weak and needy. They may feel sorry for the parent who no longer lives with them. The child and parent role may be reversed with the child emotionally caring for the parent. Another problem is that when parents fail to explain some of the causes for the divorce because they want to emotionally protect their children, their children are often confused about why the divorce was necessary. And often, children believe that the divorce is their fault.

Children often become innocent victims, having to make many changes in their lives because of decisions made by their parents. If the children resist visiting their noncustodial parent, the noncustodial parent may accuse the custodial parent of alienating the children. Sometimes parents hear the children's pleas, sadness, fear, and sobs as they leave with the parent they dislike and are separated from the parent they trust in fulfillment of the requirements of the custody agreement. When children are forced to be with a parent who they do not want to be with, they are re-victimized because they are still dealing with the emotional trauma of their parents' divorce. Even if lawyers are involved, the children's best interests are not always seriously considered. Emotional and mental damage is imposed upon children when parental rights negate the rights of the children.

Reflecting:

What are my major concerns about co-parenting?

My current challenge:

Chapter 10

A Challenge Process for Persons Who Control

The best index to a person's character is a) how he treats people who can't do him any good and b) how he treats people who can't fight back. —Abigail Van Buren

People who control others have their own reasons for controlling. If they are men, they have been socialized to be dominant and learn many ways to achieve a superior position by using the one-up and one-down communication strategy. Controlling people are usually a closed system, not open to new information, and as a result, do not grow emotionally. This is similar to being in an addictive process. We grow older, but our emotional and interpersonal skill development is the same as when the addiction began. Controllers' behaviors persist because the behaviors are successful and therefore there is no motivation to learn new skills.

Many controllers do not recognize their behaviors as being interpersonally violent. However, this lack of awareness does not remove their responsibility, just as ignorance cannot be used as an excuse for breaking the law. Controllers do a lot of announcing of what they are against but seldom share what they really stand for, despite the fact that they have many positive values and beliefs. What is important for controllers to learn is that *they are better people than their behaviors indicate.*

Controlling people want outcomes and want the outcomes to happen quickly. In the past, they have solved problems by taking a one-up position, directing others, and making the decisions. This approach is efficient in terms of time, but is often inconsiderate of others. Controlling persons often need to learn that changing behaviors is a *process*, rather than an instant outcome. A relationship that has been deteriorating for a long time will not be restored easily or in a short period of time.

Controllers are usually not willing to seek help, whether reading a book, taking a class, or going to therapy. Some of this resistance comes from the fact that they actually do not think that they are part of the relationship problem because they externalize fault. Controllers usually do not opt for learning about relationships, so early intervention seldom happens, and their relationships become increasingly fragmented. Some controllers come into therapy so that they can help "fix" the controlled spouse whom they have determined to be the source of the problem. If they *do* enter therapy alone, they are not always honest and when talking to their spouse, distort what is said by the therapist to their own advantage.

The first challenge to a controller is to be open to learning about healthy relationships which involve cooperation, respect, and equality. Behavior changes need to be internally motivated and require a restructuring of thoughts, attitudes, and behaviors, rather than superficial and temporary changes. In therapy, workshops, and retreats, I work with many controllers and facilitate their breaking through denial and resistance and modifying their control. Education is usually the first step because education is not judging or shaming. Most of the controllers I work with are men, and they appreciate and respect my direct approach and complain that their partners talk indirectly to them. What they usually don't realize is that people who are controlled do not speak to them directly because they know that there is likely to be criticism or conflict.

For controllers, *being told* what needs to be done is far less acceptable than *being challenged*. Giving up controlling behaviors is almost unfathomable for some controllers and may be equated with becoming a victim and giving up. Controllers often need to be assured that someone understands how emotionally risky this is for them. Change is threatening when it involves giving up power, accepting responsibility for harmful behaviors, making dramatic changes in thoughts, attitudes and behaviors, and accepting the emotional discomfort that is sure to accompany this process. It is a huge leap of faith for controllers to trust that surrendering their control will be beneficial to them.

The following is an empowering process designed for persons who control in their relationships. The steps provide a structure for the process of raising awareness, gaining insights, and changing behaviors. Many controllers have worked these steps and have transformed their own lives as well as their relationships.

Challenge step 1: education to raise awareness

We are socialized to view men as dominant and women as subordinate. Although changes are happening in our society, dominants are more influential. Their characteristics, behaviors, and interests are more highly valued, and they are often enabled by subordinates. Controllers strive to be one-up and superior, which creates an unequal power structure, causing anger, distance, dishonesty, fear, and mistrust in personal relationships. Communication becomes ineffective. Stress and tension progressively erode the relationship. There are also biological differences and gender differences in communication that are influential in the patterns of behaviors for dominant and subordinate people.

Childhood physical, sexual, emotional, and mental abuse or neglect; traumatic loss of a significant person or persons; personal insecurity and low self-esteem; codependency; and addictions are also causes for controlling behaviors. However, any person, including those who are emotionally and mentally healthy, well educated, have no debilitating addiction, and have positive self-esteem, can be controlling in a relationship. Controllers are not always men, but men are given more permission to be dominant and controlling in our society. When we are single, we may not see ourselves as controllers, but close relationships may trigger controlling behaviors because we are usually emotionally and physically involved. We spend a large amount of time with our spouse, which increases the chances of conflict because of different opinions and priorities. We are likely to be less controlling with colleagues and friends, but there are exceptions.

Reflecting:

My current challenge:

Challenge step 2: moving out of denial

Denial distorts reality, keeping us from recognizing relationship problems and involves minimizing the effects of our controlling behaviors. Denial is:

- Believing that our negative attitudes and behaviors are not adversely affecting our lives and the lives of those we claim to love
- Refusing to recognize our abusive verbalizations and behaviors
- Believing that a relationship is not at risk when it is close to ending
- Not seeing a need to make positive choices and changes

In our denial we justify our behavior and blame others for the problems. Moving out of denial involves recognizing our controlling behaviors as abusive to other people. It is difficult to admit that we have emotionally and mentally harmed others. Equally difficult is realizing that we have been sabotaging a relationship that deep in our hearts we want to continue, despite what our behaviors have been announcing. When we move out of denial, we take responsibility for harming others' minds, emotions and spirits. If we are to grow and heal, we need to acknowledge and accept this truth rather than deny or dodge it, run away from it, or mask it with mood altering chemicals or addictive activities.

Reflecting:

My current challenge:

Challenge step 3: shifting the focus

Shifting the focus to our own behavior rather than on our partner is necessary when deciding to make changes in our thoughts, attitudes, and behaviors. Typically we are focused on our partners and believe them to be at fault, uncooperative, stubborn, or too emotional.

Shifting the focus involves recognizing that we need to:

- ✓ Focus on changing thoughts, attitudes, and behaviors that are abusive to others.
- ✓ Reject socialization and false beliefs that sanction and even encourage controlling behaviors.
- ✓ Pay attention so that we realize when our behaviors are controlling.
- ✓ Focus on ourselves in order to learn new skills.

Reflecting:

My current challenge:

Challenge step 4: entering a recovery process for addictions

Addictions create a problem in one or more areas of our life. The substance or activity has control over us rather than our being in control over the substance or activity. We are active in our addiction in order to escape, distract ourselves or feel normal. The insanity of addiction involves repeating behaviors that destroy us, but our denial keeps us from recognizing that we have a problem. Our addiction often becomes our primary love relationship and people become secondary. Addictions are usually time-consuming, which leaves less time for family relationships. If we are involved in any addiction or addictive activity, including alcohol, drugs, pornography, gambling, sex, or video games, we will continue to have problems with ourselves as well as our relationships.

Addictions ask nothing from us, unlike human relationships. We do not have to communicate, negotiate, or deal with our feelings when we are indulging in our addiction. We can entertain ourselves and become totally self-stimulating and self-absorbed. When we are active in our addiction, we do not realize that addictions and addictive activities are cunning, baffling, and powerful. Addictions can destroy relationships, our quality of life, and life itself and need to be addressed before any meaningful changes can be made within us and within our relationships.

Reflecting:

My current challenge:

Challenge step 5: healing childhood wounds

The most effective approach, when we have experienced childhood abuse or neglect, is individual therapy where we will be supported and guided through our healing process. Emotional healing involves working through the painful feelings that we had as children and still may be carrying within. Looking at our experiences as a child often provides us with the causes for our current controlling behaviors. If we had little control over what happened to us as children, we often compensate in adolescence and in adulthood by controlling whatever is available to us to control, which is likely to be the people closest to us. We may want to keep in mind that parents make wrong choices and may fail us in many ways, but our parents also carried emotional wounds from their childhoods, were socialized into their male and female roles, and often parent in the way that they were parented.

We can start by journaling the experiences of our childhood. We may want to use the format of how it was, what happened, and how it is now. This will help us get in touch with negative experiences that had a profound effect on us. We can also journal about people who supported us and were our safe havens. Our childhood interests, special friends, and other positive experiences can be included in our journals.

As children we adapted to family dysfunction by creating survival strategies, which we need to give up as adults, because they are ineffective. In a previous part of this book, there is a description of survival strategies that we may still be using as adults. The following is a review of common survival strategies and the outcomes that we may be currently experiencing:

➤ Being *dishonest* to avoid punishment creates mistrust in our adult relationships.
➤ *Being superior and dominant* ushers in controlling behaviors that are likely to sabotage close relationships.
➤ Our *emotional walls* isolate us from others and hinder our participation in a close relationship.
➤ Our *denial* protects us from unpleasantness but distorts reality.

> ➤ *Procrastinating* diminishes our success and will anger our partners, colleagues, and employers.
> ➤ *Rebelling* results in high-risk behaviors.
> ➤ *Repressing feelings* creates emotional, spiritual, and physical illness.
> ➤ *Being too independent* results in emotional distance in significant relationships.
> ➤ *Becoming ego driven* leads to controlling others for one's own gain.
> ➤ *Creating drama* is exhausting to other people.
> ➤ *Using or abusing* chemicals or being involved in addictive activities adversely affects our lives and the lives of people that we love.
> ➤ *Not giving up our group*, such as spending excessive amounts of time with drinking friends, sabotages family relationships.

Reflecting:

What survival strategies am I currently using and how are they adversely affecting my life?

My plan for change:

My current challenge:

Healing our childhood wounds also involves grieving the traumatic losses in our lives. We may have lost a parent, or a parent was gone for an extended period of time. We may have experienced unexpected tragedy such as losing a sibling or a best friend to an accident or suicide. Grieving is an emotional process with the stages of denial, anger, bargaining, depression, and acceptance. We may want to work with a therapist who will help us work through a grieving process.

Forgiving those who have hurt us is another important part of healing childhood wounds. When we are able to forgive, we heal mentally, emotionally, spiritually and physically. If we hold resentments toward others, these people still have power over us. We need to work through the emotions, including anger and resentments. We also need to look at exactly what happened. We may conclude: "Yes, it happened to me. I was hurt," or, "Yes, it happened, and I was not totally innocent," or, "Yes, it happened and now I realize that I was responsible for creating the harm."

We also have to *let go* of past hurts in our childhoods, in our current relationship, other painful experiences, or our control over someone. We may be emotionally challenged when we have no other option than to let go of someone we love, who may no longer want to be with us and are told that we have run out of second chances.

Reflecting:

What childhood experiences were emotionally harmful to me?

Do I have someone to forgive?

My current challenge:

Challenge step 6: deleting false and irrational beliefs

Almost all of us received information from our culture and family of origin that was false and irrational. We can identify the thought, challenge it, and discard what is false and life-diminishing.

Faulty and irrational thoughts include:

- I am inadequate.
- Other people are better and have more worth than I have.
- I am superior, or should be superior.
- I am weak.
- No one likes me.
- I should be loved by everyone.
- Bad things always happen to me but not others.
- I cannot make mistakes. Mistakes are bad and show how incompetent I really am.
- I am who I am and cannot change.
- I am entitled to others' services and love.
- My value as a person is measured by my accomplishments and financial status.
- Change and differences are bad.
- I should be able to do things perfectly.
- When I fail in one area of my life, I am a total failure.
- Other people make my life miserable.
- Other people are incompetent.
- I am okay, but others are not okay.

These beliefs influence our feelings and behaviors. By holding on to these false notions, we negatively affect our life experiences.

Reflecting:

What irrational beliefs do I have that need to be deleted?

My current challenge:

Challenge step 7: recovering from codependency

Both men and women have been socialized to be codependent. Because we have dysfunctional relationships with ourselves, we have dysfunctional relationships with our partner. We look for someone else to complete us, and it is not a lasting solution. We look outside of ourselves for self-worth and happiness and may be over-involved and codependent on work, money, personal power, and accomplishments. We have all kinds of ways to control others because we are driven by our need to be superior. In our codependency we focus on our partner and are critical about what our partner is doing and not doing, saying or not saying, and how our partner doesn't meet our expectations. There is a hole in our emotional bucket because regardless of how hard our spouse or children try to live up to our expectations, their efforts are never enough.

Reviewing the chart of the characteristics of controllers who take a superior position, which is in a previous chapter, gives us a glimpse of how dominant persons are supported by subordinate people. Some of the dominant qualities will help in getting things done, but these same characteristics often sabotage relationships. We were socialized from early childhood and biological differences influence these roles. We take a leader position; we chose more often than we are chosen, and are confident and secure about our primary relationship. In our striving to be independent, we take less than our share of responsibility to make a relationship work but expect to be supported by others.

We try to influence others to think the way we think and want them to meet our needs and expectations. We are guilt makers, projecting guilt on our partners to get what we want. As we underestimate our partners' abilities, we overestimate our own. Our partners experience us as invading their personal boundaries, usurping their personal energy, and stealing their joy. We prefer to speak rather than listen and have difficulty empathizing when someone is sharing their painful emotions. Our presence is noticeable, by our size and the way we often extend our arms. We try to be fearless and often do work that is dangerous, unpleasant, and physical.

We are likely to be more dependent on our spouses than we acknowledge. Codependency is much like any other addiction and the recovery process is similar. It takes commitment and a willingness to do the emotional work. Our first step is putting the focus on ourselves rather than the partner that we try to control. We have issues that we need to address, including our self-esteem and personal insecurities. Our personal growth will involve surrendering our ego, which has been influencing our behaviors. Like other addictions, we can give up our grandiosity and illusions and make our recovery an ongoing process that becomes an everyday way of living.

- Ed shares his experience:

> Though I resisted every step of the way, there was some place inside of me that knew I needed to make changes because I wasn't really happy. I never viewed myself as codependent, but if it means that we control others, I was so codependent that it was coming out of every pore in my

body. When my wife left, I was pretty lonely. I had a buddy that went to AA and I bought a book on the Twelve Steps and went through it step by step. I think it was the first book I have read since high school. I saw myself all over the pages. I started going to meetings after I knew I couldn't do it myself. When I got to step five and started taking an honest inventory, it was one of the most difficult things I had ever done. I started to see why my wife left. I was controlling my kids and was scared they would get tired of my control as well. So the inventory was really helpful for me. I knew I had to make amends but didn't know how that would change anything. I finally made myself apologize. I didn't get the response I wanted, but at least I feel better for talking about the things I had done that were hurtful. Since the day I knew I had to make some changes, I feel like I am in a totally foreign land. The language is different, like when I learn that surrender and being humble is more important than being strong. I am committed to staying but everything is hard to learn and hard to do. And though it would be easy to return to my old ways of thinking and behaving, I will keep working because I am more peaceful inside.

Reflecting:

What do I need to do to become less codependent?

My current challenge:

Challenge step 8: dealing with five realities

- **Reality #1:** The skills involved in many male occupations and interests are different from the skills needed to participate and sustain close relationships. At work, a competitive approach is often used, whereas relationships require a cooperative, equal-partner way of relating. When controllers have this awareness, they can shift competitive skills to the skills of cooperation and improve their relationships.

  The competitive paradigm has certain requirements:

1. We must be the best, the person who has the most knowledge, the right answers, and is skilled in problem-solving.
2. We must listen for the most important points to assess the problem and fix it. Paychecks depend on this skill.
3. Expressing feelings is a sign of weakness and unwelcomed in the work setting. Self-control is important.
4. Admitting mistakes and ignorance shows weakness.

Opposite skills are required in personal relationships where affiliation and cooperation are necessary:

1. Listening to conversations respectfully, providing solutions only when invited to do so.
2. Functioning as a team with a partner who is viewed and treated as having equal power.
3. Sharing personal thoughts and feelings. Realizing that one does not have to be always right.
4. Solving problems together.
5. Admitting mistakes and making amends.
6. Affirming others.

Controllers are usually amazed at how their relationships change when they become aware of the different expectations in different settings. All it takes is the awareness and shifting skills appropriate to the situation.

- **Reality #2:** The problem and solution are not external to the self. Whereas we would like to believe that we are not part of a relationship problem, the reality is that our controlling behaviors cause harm to others and add stress and tension in relationships. Contrary to what we may believe, it is not the other person's total fault, nor is it the other persons' responsibility to fix what is not working. A relationship problem requires full participation on our part. Looking for outside causes and blaming others is controlling behavior that maintains our superiority, but it is not reality-based thinking. It is like saying we were stopped and given a DUI because a mean cop was picking on us.
- **Reality #3:** Controlling behaviors are similar to an alcoholic's thoughts and behaviors:

  ➢ Restlessness, irritability, and discontent
  ➢ Negative attitudes, disrespectful behaviors, defensiveness, and denial
  ➢ Blaming, judging, and criticizing others
  ➢ Self-pity and defensiveness
  ➢ Manipulative behaviors
  ➢ Anger and guilt is used to control others
  ➢ Grandiosity

If we are controlling others and have many of the characteristics of alcoholic behaviors, we run the risk of ultimately being alone. We may need help in removing ineffective attitudes, thoughts, and behaviors from our lives, which stand in the way of our personal growth and being a healthy partner in a relationship. Twelve Step groups are helpful to many controlling persons, who are quick to say that their lives changed when they started working "Program."

- **Reality #4:** An important question is: "Are my controlling behaviors working?" Controlling behaviors are usually not effective in getting us what we *really* want. Initially, we may think we are winning and getting our own way, but the compliance of others is often rooted in fear, an attempt to prevent conflict, or responding out of irrational guilt rather than free choice and willingness. What will get us what we really want is surrendering our control, viewing our partner as an equal, and becoming the person that our spouse would be interested in being with as a friend and partner.

- **Reality #5:** Our ego creates major problems in relationships. Our egos direct us to be superior and protect ourselves from any type of emotional danger, such as feeling insecure, weak, fearful, vulnerable, wrong, or anything that would cause embarrassment. We can be so ego driven that we invest little positive energy into our relationships. There is so much "me" in a relationship that there is no room for an "us." Giving up our controlling behaviors involves surrendering our ego, which will arrest the process of a relationship's continued deterioration.

Reflecting:

The realities that I need to work on are:

My current challenge:

Challenge step 9: knowing others' rights in relationships

Controllers often do not recognize the rights of other persons because they are socialized to be superior, win, know everything, be right, and take charge.

People have a right to:

- ➤ Be treated with respect and courtesy
- ➤ Share in decision making
- ➤ Be treated as an equal
- ➤ Talk things out
- ➤ Be free from pressure
- ➤ Have their feelings and experiences acknowledged as real and valid
- ➤ Receive clear and informative answers to questions
- ➤ Live free from unjust criticism, judgments, accusations, and blame
- ➤ Feel emotionally safe
- ➤ Be respectfully asked rather than ordered
- ➤ Say no to any request
- ➤ Change their mind

➤ Have different opinions

➤ Communicate openly

➤ Be treated with honesty and fairness

➤ Have privacy

➤ Choose what they do with their body

➤ Express their feelings appropriately

➤ Have good friends and participate in personal interests and activities

➤ Believe in themselves and feel good about who they are

- Mel shares:

    I am working on a lot of things since she told me she wanted a divorce. She has a right to be annoyed when I am not respectful and keep on watching TV when she is talking. She hates it when I poke at her or pinch her butt so I need to stop being so annoying. If I badger her, I usually get my way, but then she gives me the silent treatment. At first I thought she needed to help me change my disrespectful behaviors. When I told her that I am making all of these changes and she should be grateful, she says that in her classroom she doesn't give stickers for appropriate behaviors. Kids get stickers for going above and beyond expectations. So I guess I know exactly where I stand and what I have to do. I'm determined to save our relationship.

Reflecting:

My current challenge:

Challenge step 10: becoming more honest with oneself and others

As children, we were honest until we learned that we could avoid punishment by not telling the truth. If dishonesty worked for us, we probably continued the behavior. We live with our self-created illusions when we are dishonest with ourselves and can become so dysfunctional that we believe our own lies. When the world is viewed as competitive, honesty is often sacrificed in efforts to be superior over others. Becoming more honest with ourselves provides a more accurate view of reality, which is needed if relationship problems are going to be resolved.

It takes a commitment to be honest in all areas of our life. As controllers, we resist being honest with ourselves because it means giving up our superior position and admitting our errors. We would prefer to avoid dealing with our controlling actions that have emotionally harmed others. Talking to someone about our mistakes or writing them down in a personal journal may be the last thing we want to do. It is far easier to talk about what is wrong with *other* people, which has been our past pattern.

Though we may not be aware of it, the people we are controlling often do not provide us with information or are dishonest with us in efforts to prevent conflict. We are viewed as making problems larger than they need to be and being quick to punish and criticcize rather than being part of a solution. Thus, we are often left out of the loop, regarding what is really happening in our families or in work settings.

Reflecting:

In what areas do I need to become more honest?

My current challenge:

Challenge step 11: respecting others' personal boundaries

Personal boundaries are psychological, emotional, and behavioral limits. Healthy relationships have healthy boundaries and it's important to understand the concept of personal boundaries.

We *do not* have a right to:

- Think that we are entitled to possess, diminish, or abusively control other adults or children
- Usurp others' energy by demanding their services
- Dictate what another person should think, feel, or believe
- Touch people who do not want our touch
- Be critical of other people's thoughts, feelings, or plans
- Use others' possessions without permission

- George explains:

    I guess I really did control and try to take over her life. I wanted to know what she was doing, so I'd look at her e-mails and web sites a lot. I checked her cell phone and text messages. I thought she was having an affair because she didn't want to have sex with me, and I knew she had to be getting it from someone. I accused her of not caring, but I acted like my wife had no special place in my life. I thought that would make her try even harder to do what I thought she should be doing. I know that I didn't feel good about myself, so I accused her of the very things that I didn't like about myself. Now I know that some of the things I did were not right. You know, therapy is like going to the dentist. It can get pretty uncomfortable, but you know it's for your own good.

Reflecting:

Do I ignore others' boundaries?

My current challenge:

Challenge step 12: acknowledging and expressing feelings

Many controllers view the expression of feelings as a sign of weakness. Society teaches us to ignore, repress, deny, minimize, and lie about our feelings. The cultural expectations of men are to be non-emotional. As a result, many controllers have an abbreviated understanding of feelings. The most common feeling they have is anger, which is often disguised as sarcasm.

Feelings are messengers that bring important information to us. Maturity does not mean controlling and suppressing our feelings.

Rather, emotional maturity means learning to experience our emotions and express feelings appropriately. If we keep getting passed over for promotions, we may feel frustrated and disappointed. If we have harmed someone with our criticisms or insults, we feel guilty, which alerts us that we need to make amends. If we have achieved a personal success, we feel joy and elation, and people like to see us express these happy feelings. We can express a whole array of feelings such as confusion, rejection, care, love, and gratitude. Contrary to what we may have learned, there is no virtue in being an emotional "straight-line" by keeping our feelings to ourselves and being emotionally closed. Our partners will make attempts to see what is inside us, but eventually they will stop trying.

- Jayson shares his experience:

> I am really uncomfortable when she wants to talk about feelings. It just isn't my thing. On the outside, I try to look strong and independent. But on the inside I am a mess. I put my spouse down a lot, but I think that is because I don't like being dependent on her at all. I sure don't want her to know that without her I don't know what I would do, so I don't understand why I put her down. I have been working with feelings, but it isn't easy. When I opened the door to my feelings, I was flooded and overwhelmed. Slowly, I am getting better at feeling and sharing my emotions.

The feeling of anger often poses a problem for controllers when they are:

- Ignored or rejected
- Treated unfairly, whether it is real or perceived
- Criticized
- Given advice that they do not want to hear

- Met with resistance to requests
- Listening to someone who has different opinions

Anger that we carry from experiences in our childhood is frequently combined with current anger rather than being experienced as separate issues. When we carry childhood anger into a current relationship, we may blow up over little things such as homework left on the kitchen table, a coat left on a chair, or spilled food. Some of our internal anger is rooted in beliefs that may be ego based and totally irrational such as, "I am right," or "I have a right to my partner's attention and support," or "Other people are incompetent."

When we are angry, whether it is generated by irrational beliefs or legitimate anger, there are helpful strategies that can help us work through the anger. The rule of anger releasing is to not harm oneself or any other person. Examples of anger strategies include the following:

- Journaling our angry feelings. We may want to write a letter to someone we feel has harmed us, and make the decision whether or not to send the letter. If we choose to send the letter, it will be received better if our concerns are clearly stated in a rational and reasonable way.
- Non-competitive physical exercise (jogging, hitting a punching bag, and playing racquetball by ourselves are good anger releasing activities)
- Doing all the jobs we dislike doing while processing the anger
- Talking with a therapist or a trusted friend
- Verbalizing the anger in privacy, hitting a pillow or doing something physical that is not harmful to self or others
- Using our anger for motivation to make necessary decisions or changes in our life

- Transforming the anger energy and expressing the angry feelings by drawing pictures or other types of art, listening to music, writing music, poems or prose, or other activities that are of interest
- Directing our anger toward a higher purpose by working for humanitarian causes such as child protection, hunger, sanitary drinking water, homelessness, peace, environmental protection, or working for any cause that we consider worthwhile

If our negative feelings, including anger and resentments are unresolved and not expressed for an extended period of time, we are vulnerable to emotional and physical illness.

Reflecting:

What feeling is the most troublesome to experience and share?

My current challenge:

Challenge step 13: communicating

If power structures are imbalanced, meaningful communication is unlikely to happen and the relationship becomes increasingly at risk. By balancing the power structures, the relationship functions more like a friendship or a team. In addition, as a controller, we need to learn how to listen and also realize that our spouse has different ways of communicating, but those differences do not have less value.

Reviewing the levels of communication in Chapter 7, most controllers prefer to communicate on levels one and two, which are social greetings and sharing information. However, it is the feeling and risk-taking levels [levels three and four] that create bonding in relationships and make a primary relationship different from relationships we have with sales clerks, financial advisors, or colleagues. Anger, often expressed through sarcasm is unfortunately the feeling often expressed in level three communication. A relationship with social and informational conversations and anger as the primary feeling shared on level three does not promote intimacy. Rather, it creates increasing tension, stress and distance.

When we communicate, we always have the choice of being competitive or cooperative in our interactions. Communicating in a competitive way involves taking a superior, one-up position. Aggressive communication, which is angry, sarcastic, and critical, is disrespectful of others. As dominant persons who use our power to control, we need to learn to be assertive, which is communicating with honesty and being respectful of the other person.

As controlling persons, we often depend on our partners to do the communicating. But if we don't reciprocate, our partners will eventually shut down and communication becomes very shallow. This may be more comfortable for us, but does not promote bonding in our primary relationship. What most partners appreciate is processing thoughts and feelings. They do not want to be discounted, given unsolicited advice, or have their decisions made for them. They would like their ideas, likes, dislikes, opinions, and feelings to be acceptable communication topics within the relationship.

Listening is as important as speaking. Good listeners respect the speaker and focus their attention so that they can really hear the other person. There are no interruptions, criticisms, judgments, evaluations, or body language that conveys disagreement or disinterest. Many controllers report positive changes in their relationships when they start to really listen to their partners.

The basics of being assertive:

- Communicate in a neutral, middle power position rather than a superior, one-up, aggressive position, or an inferior, one-down, passive position.
- Start sentences with "I" rather than "You," to avoid blaming statements.
- Be honest, respectful and kind.
- Speak in normal voice tones.
- Listen as well as speak.
- Being assertive also means affirming others. Thank your partner for listening and for her/his time.

Reflecting:

What is the most difficult part of being assertive?

My current challenge:

Challenge step 14: taking responsibility and making amends

Taking responsibility for our controlling actions that are harmful to others is a necessary step in our own healing process. We may have previously thought that it was our mate who needed to apologize because blaming others is how we have excused our inappropriate behaviors. It may come as an unwelcome realization that we are a major part of our relationship stress, tension, and anger.

Our controlling behaviors are emotionally, mentally, and spiritually harmful to our spouse, children, and perhaps many other people. We have offended others by being overly critical, demanding, and sometimes rude and obnoxious. Making amends is necessary to heal relationships that have been damaged by our actions. We also heal *ourselves* when we apologize to people we have hurt. Our resistance to taking ownership of our abusive behaviors and making amends is usually because of our inflated ego and grandiosity, which covers up our personal insecurity and low self-esteem. Our task is to move beyond our resistance and complete the mission.

Our amends need to be sincere rather than a shrug-of-the-shoulders apology. In our culture, it is a sign of respect and more effective when we make direct eye-contact with the person we have harmed. A sincere apology takes responsibility for the harm done to the other person, asks for forgiveness, and communicates a plan for changing behaviors. There also needs to be a commitment to what is being spoken, so that behaviors will be in alignment with the words of apology, will be sustained over time and will not revert back to dysfunctional and controlling actions.

Reflecting:

I take responsibility for ...

I need to make amends to ... for ...

My current challenge:

Challenge step 15: committing to an ongoing growth process

Old habits are difficult to break, as are our ways of thinking that are destructive to ourselves and our relationships. Personal growth involves learning our life lessons so that we don't repeat our relationship mistakes. We can't allow ourselves to go back into our controlling, ego-driven days if we expect to be in relationships that function well. We have started a recovery and growth process and to continue on this journey requires paying attention to our behaviors and relationship interactions. A commitment to our personal growth process, designed by each one of us, is an act of loving ourselves, which we may be doing for the first time in our lives. Rather than controlling others, which creates stress and agitation, we can discover peace of mind, serenity, and gratitude. Our relationships will reflect the same.

We can relax and know that we don't always have to be superior or right. We can learn the importance of self-nurturing on the mental, emotional, physical and spiritual levels of our being. We know we are healing when we have a better opinion of ourselves; we are improving our communication skills which are enhancing the quality of our relationships, and we are routinely focusing on what we have in life rather than what we think is missing.

Our personal growth involves changing our thoughts, feelings, attitudes, and behaviors to be increasingly life-fostering for ourselves and our relationships. It is a life-long process and the results are extremely rewarding.

As we continue to heal, learn and continue our personal growth, we will:

- See reality more clearly and live in less self-created illusion
- Have fewer irrational beliefs
- Have positive self-talk
- Be less driven by our egos
- Be more honest with ourselves and others
- Be aware of our emotions and be able and willing to express them appropriately.
- Have healthy self-esteem and honor ourselves
- Be more compassionate, kind and friendly to ourselves and others
- Be willing to make amends and forgive others
- Be interested in reaching out to others

Reflecting:

What is my plan for healing and growth?

My current challenge:

Chapter 11

Relationship Recovery

Learning to love someone else means working on your relationship with yourself because your ability to love comes from within you. —Laura Ramirez

We can't solve problems by using the same kind of thinking we used when we created them. —Albert Einstein

Almost all relationship commitments are made with good intentions. We have hopes and dreams of having a long and mutually satisfying relationship. We cannot imagine that we might experience unhealthy control dynamics or unresolved issues. Yet, as time goes on and relationship issues arise, marital satisfaction often starts to decline. Participants bring their own dysfunctions, and most of us think that we know how to participate in a relationship despite the fact that few of us had any education on how to communicate effectively, listen respectfully, resolve conflicts, and maintain a healthy and vibrant primary relationship. As the relationship progresses, both persons may become discouraged with their choice of partners, not realizing we are all influenced by our past experiences. When we couple with a person, we become involved in our partner's socialization process, his/her extended families, unhealthy beliefs and survival strategies that were in response to family of origin dysfunction. There are biological differences and there are gender differences in communication which can be frustrating and confusing.

Couples can improve their relationship by reading relationship books and articles, but both people have to be willing to put focused and active efforts into working on the relationship if real changes are going to happen. Relationship counseling has the advantage of a quiet environment to focus and discuss strengths as well as the problems in a relationship. Likewise, in a retreat or a self-help group, there are no distractions regarding work, children, or other activities. When controllers manipulate, are dishonest, make accusations, and blame others, a therapist or a facilitator re-focuses on the issue being discussed. When the recipients of control are passive and compliant, they will be challenged to speak up and participate in a problem-solving process.

The mistake most couples make is that they agree to go to a class, attend a retreat, or enter therapy only when the relationship is so shattered that it is very difficult to change attitudes and behaviors and restore healthy functioning. Controllers often think that their spouses can quickly regenerate the love that has been lost because of their controlling behaviors. If they don't see their spouse returning to their compliant and enabling behaviors, they often accuse her/him of not wanting to work on the relationship, not trying hard enough, or just not caring. Controllers are forced to readjust their thinking when they are told that a relationship that has been deteriorating for a long period of time will not be restored quickly or easily and that it will take focused efforts by both persons.

It is not unusual that by the time a couple starts counseling, the person who has been controlled has already emotionally left the relationship. The controller may think there is no serious problem, and if there is a problem, it is the partner's fault and can easily be repaired. In contrast, the controller might be totally devastated, and the spouse who is leaving is surprised at this reaction because endearing words were never or rarely spoken throughout their relationship. There are situations where the controller tries to convince the leaving spouse to stay in the relationship by making demands or promises or by making statements that instill guilt. When someone puts pressure on us to stay in a toxic relationship it feels like being held hostage. When this happens, a spouse may make the decision to emotionally or physically leave the relationship before the real problem has been identified and there have been attempts by both people to make the necessary changes.

Because controllers often have a difficult time expressing their feelings, mates will complain that the only feeling they hear from their controller is anger. Because controllers are hesitant to share feelings, they can seem to be very uncaring. Many times I have heard women telling their male spouses in therapy sessions, "I don't know if you even love me." The husband's response is, "I'm here, aren't I?" There are husbands who, when their wives are sobbing, act detached and seem unaware of the pain their wives are feeling. Rather than showing empathy or remorse, their body language signals indifference and discomfort at the display of their partners' emotions.

Controllers often do not understand the concept of equality in a relationship. They have been socialized to think in terms of one-up, one-down and have learned many ways to be superior and retain the one-up position. To help controllers connect with what equality means, it is helpful to think of a team.

Question: Have you ever been on a team?
Controller: Yes.

Question: What were the feelings toward your team mates?

Controller: Loyalty, working together, going the extra mile for someone, and trying to play even better if a team mate was injured.

Question: Did you feel connected with your team mates?

Controller: Yes.

Question: That's pretty close to what we want to have in a committed relationship. Relationships are about teamwork, respect, and friendship.

Controller: (nods, communicating agreement)

Many controllers are concrete in their thinking, and "word pictures" can be helpful. For example, a relationship can be described as a growing plant. The seed is planted, but for it to grow, it needs sunshine, nutrients and water, just as relationships need nutrients. If a seed is planted, but there is no nurturing, it should not be a surprise if we come back years later and the plant is dead. Many relationships die simply because they have not been nurtured and are not equally beneficial to each person.

If a relationship is going to be restored to health, both people need to be honest, take responsibility for their part of the problem, and be willing to respond to the challenge of changing dysfunctional behaviors. Controllers learn to surrender the control. Recipients of control learn to reduce the enabling and set limits on what is not acceptable. When entering a reconciliation and healing process, there needs to be a commitment to go to any lengths to restore equality, friendship and improve their communication.

- Common experiences of *both controllers and enablers* in a relationship

❖ May be unaware of controlling or enabling behaviors

❖ Are likely to be in denial, which protects them from unpleasantness by distorting reality

❖ Are at risk for addictive behaviors, such as drinking, using mood-altering drugs, working, sexual, gambling or video games

❖ Often struggle with personal insecurity, low self-esteem, and codependency

❖ Feel unappreciated

❖ Experience anger, distance, dishonesty, fear, and mistrust in the relationship. Communication becomes ineffective. Stress and tension progressively erode the relationship.

❖ Become alienated from the self

As indicated above, there are many emotional dynamics when someone is controlling another in a primary relationship. The controlled person builds up anger because of the many demands, and controllers are angered because their expectations are not met. When anger, sarcasm, criticism and fear are used as ways to control, partners will start to distance themselves. There is dishonesty on the part of the controller in order to maintain a position of superiority, and there is dishonesty on the part of the controlled person in order to prevent conflict. Mistrust is generated because of lies, broken promises, and controlling behaviors. Both people become alienated from themselves because they are usually focused on the other person.

Step 1: balancing the power structure

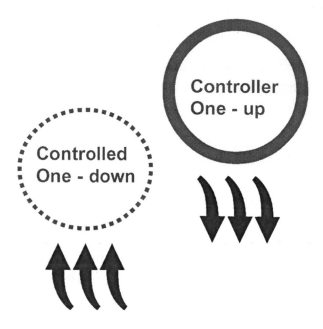

To balance the power structure, changes are made:

1. The recipient of control moves "up" by learning empowerment strategies. The controller moves "down" by reducing or eliminating the controlling behaviors and learning to relate to the partner as an equal.

2. The controlled person needs to learn to become more *closed* to the controller's unjust criticisms and control tactics but at the same time be open to learning how to empower the self. Controllers need to be willing to open up their minds and learn ways of relating that are not emotionally controlling or verbally abusive.

3. Controlled persons learn to balance their feelings with logical

thinking. Controllers, who typically work from their intellect, balance themselves by learning to express their feelings. Controllers feel a risk when giving up control and enablers feel a risk when confronting the control. Eliminating a dominant and subordinate structure is necessary for effective communication to happen.

There is usually resistance to giving up controlling or enabling behaviors because changing ingrained, automatic ways of behaving is not easy. In addition, it may not be an incentive to balance the power if controllers realize that the relationship will become more emotionally intimate which may be uncomfortable. In contrast, enablers hesitate to confront because it might mean even less emotional intimacy with their partner. Giving up controlling or enabling behaviors cannot be a superficial, band-aid "fix" that will be short lived until the relationship crisis subsides. It requires a total paradigm shift which involves changing and at times, totally reversing and revising our ways of thinking. Besides starting to think differently, we have to *activate* our new ways of thinking and new ways of behaving if we are going to achieve a relationship that fosters equality and has equal benefits for both persons.

Characteristics of equality in relationships:

- Honesty with self and others
- Trust and mutual support
- Respect for self and others
- Emotional intimacy
- Behaviors based on willingness rather than obligation or compliance
- Friendship and teamwork
- Healthy levels of self-esteem

- Effective communication involving listening as well as speaking
- Emotional, physical, spiritual health and growth is valued and encouraged by both partners.
- Equality of benefits

Reflecting:

Our current challenge:

Relationship inventory:

1. Is someone in control and the other being controlled?
2. Is someone blaming the other or accepting blame that isn't theirs?
3. Are there certain topics of communication that cause an argument?
4. Is someone not speaking up because they are afraid?
5. Is someone crying often or withdrawing?
6. Is one partner making more concessions than the other?
7. Is someone sacrificing their life interests or values for the other?
8. Is someone not listening or brushing the other person off as insignificant?
9. Is someone apologizing most of the time or is one partner rarely or never apologizing?

10. Are there issues in the relationship that do not get resolved and continually re-occur?
11. Is someone feeling guilty or making another feel guilty?
12. Are both partners interested in creating equality in the relationship?
13. Is someone about to leave the relationship?
14. Is there hope that the relationship dynamics can be changed?

Reflecting:

Our current challenge:

- Gathering data:

It is helpful to document or journal the progress of each step in a process of restoring a relationship, both about oneself, and about the relationship. Gathering data is recording what is happening as we focus on improving our behaviors and assessing the changes in our relationship. Both persons are responsible for data collection. Each step indicates intentions and actions in making necessary changes within ourselves and in our relationship. When we document the growth process, we stay out of denial and determine the progress or lack of progress. If there are no behavior changes on both sides, the controlling and enabling behaviors are likely to remain the same in the future.

Step 2: moving out of denial

Unhealthy denial keeps us from being honest with ourselves. Denial is:

✓ Refusing to acknowledge that we have internal anger, resentment and guilt
✓ Believing that our negative attitudes and behaviors are not adversely affecting our lives and the lives of those we claim to love
✓ Refusing to recognize our abusive verbalizations and behaviors
✓ Defensively protesting when challenged about behaviors
✓ Believing that a relationship is not at-risk when it is close to ending
✓ Not seeing a need to make positive choices and changes

When we are in denial, we do not see how controlling behaviors have strained, stretched, and strangled our relationship. As a result, we do not fix what is broken. This step involves recognizing the truth of emotional and mental abuse, which is harmful to a person's mind, emotions, and spirit and the many ways that controlling behaviors are enabled. At this point, if both people do not move out of their denial and acknowledge the reality of their deteriorated relationship, the relationship will not improve.

Reflecting:

Our current challenge:

Step 3: shifting the focus

Most couples whose relationships are at risk are cross-focused. They are concerned about what the other person is doing and not doing, what the other person is saying or not saying, and about the hurts and hassles that are caused by the other person. If we continue doing what doesn't work, such as focusing on the other person, we will get the same results, which means continuing on the path toward relationship disaster. We may be very hesitant and resistant to shift the focus from what the other person is doing and place the focus on ourselves until we understand why this is necessary.

Shifting the focus is recognizing that we need to:

- ✓ Realize that we cannot change the behaviors of the other person, but we can change our own. If each person concentrates on their own attitudes, beliefs, and behaviors, positive changes can happen. This is true for controllers as well as for those who enable the control.
- ✓ Accept our part of the responsibility in the faltering relationship;
- ✓ Pay attention so that we realize when our behaviors are controlling or enabling;
- ✓ Focus on ourselves so that we can learn new attitudes and skills.

When we shift the focus to ourselves, we can step back and watch how we function and react. We can observe what works and what doesn't work. We can see the part we are playing in the relationship dynamics. Though shifting the focus may sound easy, it is quite difficult because we are not accustomed to paying attention to our own attitudes, thoughts, and behaviors. By shifting the focus, we will start to notice positive differences within ourselves and within our relationships. If neither partner is committed to shifting his/her focus, the relationship will continue to function with the same dysfunctional relationship dynamics.

Reflecting:

Our current challenge:

Step 4: entering a recovery process for addictions

If we are involved in any addiction or addictive activity, including alcohol, food, drugs, gambling, sex, or video games, we spend excessive time stimulating and satisfying ourselves at the expense of our relationships. When gambling is more than a game, we have crossed the line into an addictive process that is likely to create problems in one or more areas of our life. Sexual activity is natural unless we make sexual demands on our partner, use sarcasm when our partner chooses not to be sexual; our thoughts are obsessive and our behaviors are excessive. Many video games involve violence, and our tolerance increases to the point of not only accepting, but being entertained by violent acts. When we need alcohol to routinely escape, fill the emptiness or to feel normal, we are in the throes of an alcohol addiction. Addictions are detrimental to personal relationships and negatively impact our parenting. Our mental and emotional growth process stops and we become more vulnerable to physical health problems.

Addictions affect our thinking and need to be addressed before any meaningful changes can be accomplished within oneself and within relationships. At this point, if a partner is struggling with an addiction problem, and is not willing to start a recovery process, the relationship will continue to disintegrate.

Reflecting:

Our current challenge:

Step 5: healing childhood wounds

Both partners are apt to have emotional wounds from childhood. Counseling, books, and support groups are helpful resources in healing from emotional wounds or losses and giving up unhealthy beliefs, attitudes and behaviors that originated in childhood. We may want to do our individual healing separate from our partner because sharing family of origin or other personal issues with a partner may not be emotionally safe. If conflict in the relationship continues or escalates, a controller can use this information to emotionally abuse in areas where their partner is most vulnerable.

Journaling or sharing our experiences with someone trustworthy is a way of recovering from our painful experiences in childhood. We can identify the survival strategies that we developed in our childhoods and are still using, but which are more than likely creating problems in our current relationship. Once identified, our survival strategies can be modified or surrendered if they are causing problems within ourselves or in our relationships. It is important that we separate anger from childhood experiences from our current relationship anger. Though people frequently drag childhood issues and emotional baggage from past relationships into their current relationships, this behavior is likely to become abusive to partners. Our unresolved emotional pain might be triggered by an innocent statement made by our spouse. Minor problems often turn into major altercations. These types of behaviors are unfair to partners and children.

Reflecting:

Our current challenge:

Step 6: deleting false and irrational beliefs

Almost all of us received information from our family of origins and our culture that is false and irrational. Not only do these false and irrational beliefs affect our own lives, but they spill into our relationships as well. Low self-esteem, insecurity, the need to control others, and enabling controlling behaviors are rooted in false and irrational beliefs. We can challenge the thought and discard what is false and life-diminishing.

Unhealthy relationship beliefs:

- We need to give up interests that our partner does not like.
- There should be no outside relationships.
- Differences in opinions, priorities, and beliefs are bad.
- We need to love each other unconditionally so we can't confront bad behaviors.
- We need to keep problems within the family.
- We should not express thoughts or feelings that would displease our spouse.
- Conflict is bad and should be avoided.
- I need to control my partner.
- I need to accept my partner's abusive behavior.
- I need to meet all of my partner's needs. My partner should meet all of my needs.
- We should be able to read each other's mind if we really love each other.
- We need to give up growing and changing to remain secure.

These beliefs negatively influence our feelings and behaviors. We are not always aware that we have these beliefs, so it usually takes some reflection to see if these beliefs are negatively influencing our life and our relationships.

Reflecting:

Our current challenge:

Step 7: recovering from codependency

As controllers and recipients of control, we are likely to be codependent. Controllers shift responsibility by blaming others. Recipients of control usually take too much relationship responsibility. Being in this cycle creates ongoing conflict, which is seldom resolved. We emotionally and behaviorally spin our wheels and nothing changes. These are some characteristics of codependency:

- We try to control or we enable the control that is directed at us.
- We have difficulty expressing feelings or expressing them appropriately.
- We have difficulty developing and sustaining healthy relationships.
- Our thinking and attitudes are rigid, our feelings are frozen, and our behaviors are ineffective.
- Our good feelings depend on being liked by others, especially our partner.
- Our energy is focused on pleasing our partners.
- We may have too many physical health problems.
- We invade others' personal boundaries or don't protect our own.
- We try hard to satisfy our partner, even if the expectations are unrealistic.
- Our personal interests are put aside and we invest time in our partners' interests.
- Our values are put aside in order to be loved and connected to our spouse or partner.
- We allow ourselves to be motivated by fear and guilt.
- We have a high need for approval.
- We are vulnerable to addictions.

- We are insecure and have low self-esteem.

We started to work on our codependency when we shifted the focus from our partner to ourselves. Our recovery from codependency requires that we stop controlling others, or if we are being controlled, stop sacrificing ourselves to meet the expectations of our controller. At this point if both partners are not willing to address and work on their codependent behaviors, the dysfunctional dynamics will not change.

Reflecting:

My current challenge:

Step 8: taking responsibility for harmful behaviors, making amends, and forgiving

There are different degrees of responsibility for controllers and recipients of control. Controlling behaviors cause harm to others. Enabling behaviors are survival responses to controlling behaviors. They are well-intentioned efforts to cope and prevent conflict but are ineffective in stopping the emotional and mental abusive control.

To heal and restore a relationship requires sharing hurts that have accumulated in the relationship and never been resolved or forgiven. The experiences that keep resurfacing in our minds causing anger, resentments, and distance need to be discussed. Until this emotional work is somewhat completed, we cannot move on and create a new and more functional relationship. When we are sharing how we have been hurt or disappointed in our relationship, we need to be *honest and sincere* when we speak. We also need to truly listen to our partner and share his/her pain. As our partner shares his/her hurts, we may want to correct details, and because of feeling defensive, start discounting and minimizing what our partner is saying. But regardless of what we are feeling, it is not acceptable to interrupt. Our partner deserves respect as he/she expresses past hurts.

Making amends is necessary to heal our relationship that has been damaged by our actions. We also heal *ourselves* when we make amends. A sincere apology takes responsibility for the harm done to the other person, asks for forgiveness, and provides a plan for changing behaviors. There also needs to be a commitment to aligning behaviors with the words of apology, so the changes will be sustained, and will not revert back to dysfunctional and controlling actions. When we are able to forgive, we heal mentally, emotionally, spiritually, and physically. Forgiving requires moving beyond our feelings of hurt, resentments, and anger. It might take a long time before we are able to truly forgive and we may have to forgive several times before we feel that we have really forgiven.

Making amends and forgiving needs to be followed by letting go of the past hurts that have accumulated in the relationship. We probably will not be able to do this until we trust that our partner will not emotionally harm us again. When we are ready, letting go is a total release of the hurts by both partners, so that the relationship can start with a clean slate.

> Reflecting:
>
> Our current challenge:

Step 9: knowing others' rights in relationships

Controllers often do not recognize the rights of other persons and enablers are often unsure as to their rights, so a review of rights is important.

People have a right to:

> ➢ Be treated with respect and courtesy
> ➢ Share in decision making
> ➢ Be treated as an equal
> ➢ Talk things out
> ➢ Be free from pressure
> ➢ Have their feelings and experiences acknowledged as real and valid
> ➢ Receive clear and informative answers to questions
> ➢ Live free from unjust criticism, judgments, accusations and blame
> ➢ Feel emotionally safe
> ➢ Be respectfully asked rather than ordered and say no to any request
> ➢ Have their own opinions and change their mind
> ➢ Communicate openly
> ➢ Be treated with honesty and fairness

> ➤ Have privacy
> ➤ Choose what they do with their body
> ➤ Express their feelings appropriately
> ➤ Have friendships, interests and activities that do not involve a partner
> ➤ Believe in themselves and feel good about who they are

At this point, if both partners are not willing to recognize each other's rights and respect them, there will be no changes in their dysfunctional relationship dynamics.

Reflecting:

Our current challenge:

Step 10: respecting others' boundaries

Personal boundaries are psychological, emotional, and behavioral limits. We have no right to invade others' boundaries, even if they are family members. We also need to be able to protect our personal boundaries. In relationships people are separate human beings and not the property of another to own and control.

We do not have a right to invade boundaries by:

✓ Usurping others' energy by demanding their services.
✓ Dictating what another person should feel or think.

✓ Criticizing unjustly.
✓ Touching people who do not want our touch.
✓ Minimizing or negating other people's thoughts, feelings, plans, or dreams.

We *have a right* to *protect* our boundaries. We are:

✓ Separate and unique human beings.
✓ Not the property of someone and have a right to our thoughts and feelings.
✓ Not the dumping grounds for controllers' unjust criticisms.
✓ Able to choose how we want to respond to another's negative behavior.
✓ Able to confront controlling behaviors, negative verbalizations, or unrealistic expectations.
✓ Able to communicate feelings and thoughts with clarity and defend them when they are minimized or ridiculed.
✓ Refusing to enable or reinforce others' negative behavior by paying attention to it, excusing it, or rewarding it in any way.
✓ Not being affected by another person's negative attitudes, emotions, moods, or behaviors.

Both partners need to have a clear understanding and work within personal boundaries. If either partner is unwilling, the relationship will experience continued stress, tension and conflict.

Reflecting:

How are boundaries being invaded?

Our current challenge:

Step 11: communicating

Couples repeatedly say that the main problem in their marriage is communication. They may communicate well with other people but not in their marriage. Communication problems can have many causes and there are an equal number of solutions. A key reason is that when *power structures are imbalanced*, communication will end up being very frustrating and disappointing. By balancing the power structures, the relationship functions more like a friendship or a team. A second reason for communication problems is that one or both partners are not listening to each other. In addition, there are communication differences between genders, which cause misunderstandings. We have a good understanding of how our own sex communicates, but may become confused or frustrated when talking to a partner of the opposite sex. Our misunderstandings resulting from gender differences are usually not because we are being purposefully uncooperative or unkind. They are a result of how we are socialized. And last, communication is shut down when someone is controlling by being critical, judgmental, and demeaning.

Making efforts to restore a relationship will require developing good communication skills. This involves having respect for one another and the willingness to listen. Hopefully, our efforts in improving our communication will rejuvenate our relationship. However, if our attempts are unsuccessful and there is a decision to divorce, we will need good communication skills when we are working on custody agreements and negotiating finances, property, and household items. More importantly, if we have children, we will be communicating about co-parenting decisions and visitation schedules. Optimally, this will be done in a respectful manner.

- **Basic rules of couple communication:**

  - Totally eliminating profanity and sarcasm
  - Being honest
  - Speaking with normal voice tones even in conflicts
  - Listening respectfully
  - Not interrupting each other

Nothing should come out of our mouths that we wouldn't want our mother, father, or grandparents to hear. The goal is to talk in the way that friends speak and listen to each other, or in the way we converse with and listen attentively to colleagues. It is helpful to start out with light and easy conversational topics and then try issues where there have been disagreements and see how the process goes. Keep the focus on the process of communicating and experiment with what works and doesn't work. Notice when a person takes a one-up position or a one-down position. Talk to each other about how it feels when there is movement from a position of equal power to unequal power, with one person taking a one-up or one-down position. In a relationship where there is equality, the conversation flows more easily.

Listening is important, but we are not always aware of the degree of importance it has in effective communication. Our intention may be to listen, but there may be many distractions that sabotage our listening such as other thoughts, noises, worrying about our own problems, or fear of being criticized. We might think that we know what the other person is going to say, or we might become bored because they are sharing details that aren't very interesting. We can eliminate many of these distractions by staying in the moment, focusing, and knowing that listening is a way to show respect to the speaker.

We can learn how to speak and listen on each level of communication:

- Social
- Information sharing
- Sharing feelings
- Emotional risk-taking
- Nonverbal communication

Notice what you are feeling at each communication level and talk about this with your partner.

We can learn and practice separating the content message from the emotional undertones. The spoken message is the content message that provides information. The underlying message is unspoken and is often negative, communicated by body language and voice tones that are sarcastic, angry, or shaming. The most common unspoken messages imply that the other person is inadequate in some way. Practice sending a message without the hidden, emotional message. Then send a message with a strong emotional message. Note the differences in feelings.

When couples experience a relationship with balanced power structures, which is cooperative rather than competitive, they are usually amazed at how communication becomes far more effective and meaningful. Stress, tension and misunderstandings are sharply reduced, and the relationship is more emotionally bonded, sustained by the equality of partners and a value placed on affiliation. If both people are not actively working on improving the communication, the relationship will not be restored to healthy functioning.

Reflecting:

When do we experience a communication break-down?

Our current challenge:

Step 12: designing a new relationship

We cannot return to the relationship that was in jeopardy. A new relationship involves equal partners taking adult responsibility, cooperating and relating out of respect, caring, and honesty. This requires the controlling and enabling pattern to stop. Designing a new relationship needs to be the work of both partners so that both persons take ownership and make the necessary changes to improve the relationship.

It requires two healthy people to create a healthy relationship. Even though we take giant steps in healing ourselves and our relationship, there will be times when old habits resurface. Personal growth involves staying alert and not becoming complacent. We will have to self-correct when we need to and make amends when we have emotionally diminished or harmed our partner.

❖ Characteristics of a healthy relationship:

- The power structure is reasonably equal. We can feel when our relationship is out of balance. A good relationship is often 60–60, because partners enjoy going the extra mile for the other.
- There are minimal controlling or enabling behaviors.
- There is emotional intimacy, which is not smothering, caretaking, or merging with another.
- There is mutual sharing and concern for the other.
- Each person's true identity is respected and treasured.
- Communication involves speaking clearly as well as listening intently.
- There are equal benefits for both partners.
- Trust, support, and affirmations are provided to the other partner.
- Partners are available to each other when experiencing individual difficulties.
- Partners work together as a team, take time for each other, and have fun together.
- Personal boundaries are respected.
- Participants share on an emotional, mental, and spiritual level.
- There is an understanding that we cannot expect more than we are willing to give in relationships.
- There is mutual appreciation.

Reflecting:

What qualities do we want in our relationship?

Our current challenge:

Healthy relationships require healthy partners, so we each have to be committed to our own healing and personal growth to be the best possible partner to our spouse. Some of us will continue to read books, continue therapy, or attend support groups. Parenting classes are very helpful because there are usually disputes in raising children. We may want to go to a relationship retreat so that we can focus our attention on the quality of our relationship.

If our relationship ends in divorce, it is important that we forgive and re-define our relationship so that we can cooperatively and respectfully be parents and possibly grandparents. Some people are still angry, resentful, and non-communicative with each other for years. This is not in anyone's best interest. We don't want our children listening to our anger and resentments long after the divorce or worrying about how their parents are going to act at social functions such as their graduations and weddings. This will require making our amends, forgiving each other, and being at peace within ourselves and about the relationship that ended.

Equal Relationship

The *basic keys are:*

- Keep the power structure equal and function as a team.
- Be honest, kind, respectful, and polite.
- Nurture mutual love and respect by affirming each other.
- Do whatever it takes to be able to say to each other, **"I'm so grateful that you are in my life!"**

Reflecting:

What am I willing to do to enhance our relationship?

Our current challenge:

Chapter 12

Using Power to Empower Others

The main purpose of life is to live rightly, think rightly, act rightly. — Mohandas Gandhi

Let us strive to build peace, a desire for peace, a willingness to work for peace in the hearts and minds of all people.—John F. Kennedy

To create a world where every person is physically and emotionally safe, has basic human rights, and where no person suffers because of the greed and overconsumption of more powerful persons, will require all people to use their power to empower others. This begins in our individual spheres of influence because we know with certainty, that we have as much responsibility to use our power in healthy ways as do our leaders. When power is used in positive ways, many obstacles can be overcome, many advances can be made, and many lives can be improved. Spiritual leaders have always taught that personal and group power is to be used to empower others. The truly powerful and influential leaders of yesterday and today use their power to negotiate, collaborate, and solve problems to create healthy change and positively affect people's lives.

When we view the lives and achievements of powerful and influential people who empower others, *they use their personal power:*

1. In a moral way, involving right actions toward all people, creatures, and the earth. Because an act is legal does not make it moral. Slavery was at one time legal, but was not moral.
2. In an *ethical* way, which conforms to standards of moral behavior;
3. In an *honest* way, which requires being fair in decisions, adhering to facts, and not being deceitful by saying one thing and doing another;
4. In ways that maintain *integrity*, which means being congruent with oneself, being trustworthy, having life-promoting values, and defending them when facing criticism;
5. In ways that are *responsible*, which involves being accountable for actions, decisions, and the respectful treatment of others;
6. In ways that are *visionary* to see more possibilities, achieve more, and work for the highest good of all;
7. In ways that involve *wisdom*, which requires having inner knowledge, an ability to arrive at high-quality conclusions, and make decisions that are based on correct information and what is beneficial to all people who are viewed as equal and interconnected.

Activating personal power, using these guidelines is what we should be both giving and receiving in all of our daily interactions and in our relationships. We can no longer accept, accommodate, and enable dishonest, un-ethical, irresponsible and self-serving behaviors if we are to heal and evolve as individuals, families, communities, and as a society that interacts with all nations.

The moral, ethical, honest use of power that is embedded in integrity, responsibility, and wisdom is the trademark of a responsible social consciousness. When we have an <u>evolved social consciousness</u>, we:

- Strive for the equality, justice, and dignity of all persons; so that everyone has adequate resources to sustain life;
- Use power in moral, ethical, responsible, and honest ways;
- Work collaboratively toward worthy goals;
- Are passionate, compassionate and take personal responsibility;
- Know that we are all interconnected and that one person's positive contribution enhances the lives of others;
- Believe that the spiritual power of love and kindness is a healing and empowering force;
- Empower others by sharing ideas, knowledge, solutions, support, and encouragement;
- Have a life purpose extending beyond ourselves;
- Courageously stand up for what is right rather than what is popular;
- Are generous with whatever resources we have, including time, talents, and financial resources;
- Are calming, inspiring, and authentic;
- Live our lives by the spiritual principles of truth, wisdom, love, compassion, and gratitude.

If we have personal power, we cannot keep our power hidden and inactive. We can speak up when we are being controlled. We can join with others who have a well developed social consciousness and challenge abusive control and be supportive to those who are emotionally and mentally abused. By taking responsibility for contributing to positive change, we will discover meaning and purpose in our lives, and we will empower ourselves, our children, and future generations.

Our goal is clearly set forth in our country's Declaration of Independence:

> We hold these truths to be self-evident, that all men are created equal, that they are endowed by their Creator with certain inalienable Rights, that among these rights are Life, Liberty and the pursuit of Happiness.

Let us take up the challenge of working together so that every person experiences these rights. This will help to set the stage for peace within ourselves and peace within our world.

References

Miller, J. *Toward a New Psychology of Women.* Beacon Press, 1987

Tannen, D. *You just don't understand: Women and Men in Conversation.* Ballantine Books,1990.

Also By Carol Rogne

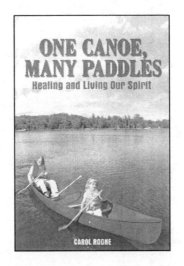

One Canoe, Many Paddles

A crucial step in our healing involves removing what is harmful: false beliefs, resentments, and ways of thinking that are negative, fear-based, and limited. Having removed what is sabotaging our lives, we can then create a life with more positive ways of thinking, behaving and relating, which will move us closer to optimal health on all levels of our being: the mental, emotional, spiritual and physical. *One Canoe, Many Paddles - Healing and Living our Spirit,* describes the personal growth journey from different viewpoints. Life skills are offered that enhance effectiveness, while reducing stress. This book views many spiritual principles, including those of the Twelve Step Program and suggests ways of expressing, celebrating, and livng our spirit with gratitude.

Learn more at: www.outskirtspress.com/onecanoemanypaddles

CPSIA information can be obtained at www.ICGtesting.com
Printed in the USA
237493LV00001B/2/P